The 'Secret' World of
VICKERS
GUIDED WEAPONS

The 'Secret' World of
VICKERS
GUIDED WEAPONS

John Forbat

TEMPUS

Dedication:

To Mary, my ever-loving, patient and indulgent wife.

Frontispiece: Folland aircraft carried out early development work for the Red Dean air-to-air missile, shown here carried by a Gloster Meteor F8. (Derek James)

First published 2006

Tempus Publishing Limited
The Mill, Brimscombe Port,
Stroud, Gloucestershire, GL5 2QG
www.tempus-publishing.com

British Library Cataloguing in Publication Data.
A catalogue record for this book is available from the British Library.

ISBN 0 7524 3769 0

Typesetting and origination by Tempus Publishing Limited
Printed in Great Britain

CONTENTS

ACKNOWLEDGEMENTS

In the process of researching this book and filling out my own recollections, many ex-colleagues and others have made helpful comments and supplied photographs which have served well, to enhance the authenticity and completeness of the Vickers Guided Weapons story. Without being certain of mentioning everybody (and apologising for any I may omit), I would like to thank these helpful friends and colleagues.

Perhaps firstly I should thank Julian Temple, Curator of Aviation at The Brooklands Museum for suggesting I write this history in the first place. Also Museum Director Allan Winn, for his support and the loan of *Fire Across the Desert*, the official story of Woomera and the Anglo–Australian joint project, which provided some of the photographs. I would also like to thank aviation author Bill Gunston for his support and encouragement, including a loan of his own compendious publication of guided weapons worldwide, Mr W. Nicolson (ex-ICI Summerfield Research Station) the Public Records Office and The University of Cambridge library for facilities afforded to assist the research and the curators at RAF Cosford Museum, Bovington Tank Museum, The National Army Museum, The Imperial War Museum, The Science Museum, The Airborne Forces Museum, Doncaster AeroVenture, as well as members of BAE Systems, MBDA, Quinetiq, The Defence Manufacturers Association and several historians mentioned in the References.

Finally, among other colleagues from my time at Vickers, I wish to thank Brigadier John Clemow, who (well into his nineties) has given encouragement and help, also Jim Cole, John Duck, Chuck Fry, Paul DeWinton-Jones, Harry Fryer, John Goodwin, Henry Hunt, Ron Jupp, A.W. Kitchenside, John Lattey, 'Spud' Murphy, Mick Padgeham, Peter Rice, John Stroud, John Whetmore, Richard Williams and any others I may have omitted.

If some of the more detailed diagrams are hard to read, this reflects the archival nature of the originals.

FOREWORD

By Brig. John Clemow, MA (Cantab), FIMA, FIEE, FIMech E
(John Clemow is an acknowledged expert in Guided Weapons technology and development)

This book fulfils an important function in detailing the so far untold story of technological and aviation developments at Vickers, in the relative dawn of Guided Weapons technology – and the management problems involved.

The author, John Forbat, was a Hungarian by birth, and left Hungary in 1936. He went to school in London and lived there throughout most of the Blitz. After the war, he took his degree in Aeronautical engineering and became a graduate apprentice with Vickers Armstrongs. There, he became an enthusiastic early member of the Guided Weapons team, rising to senior designer. His book fills a necessary gap in the history of British aviation developments and in the achievements of Vickers at the site of the Brooklands Motor Racing Track, in Weybridge.

Before the advent of Guided Weapons, weaponry problems can be illustrated by the performance and limitations of the '6 Pounders', which were well known and summarised in such sayings as, 'get him with your shot or he will get you!'. The angry response from Normandy was, 'you couldn't hit the side of a barn at 1,000 yards'. The Armament Design Department was ordered with the highest priority to investigate the reasons why the proof firings of both gun and ammunition were so satisfactory and those obtained under field conditions were appalling, and secondly to recommend the changes that might be made to affect a solution and the timescale. In a matter of weeks rather than months, the problems were solved and the necessary changes made to gun and ammunition.

The designers of the gun had realised that the accuracy depended upon the shell being a very good fit in the gun barrel, and more important was to have a very good fit of shell and shell rifling, bearing in mind that with a high velocity gun the wear would be high. These requirements were easily overlooked in the pressures of war, especially as the gun and ammunition were also used for other less stringent purposes. In fact, it was one factory that had applied to the inspector for a concession to allow a batch of over-machined shells to be accepted. This was approved for this batch only, but in error applied to all factories making this type of shell; a temporary solution was provided by making a neoprene plastic collar to fit snugly over the driving band of the shell. Surprisingly, this worked well. The collars held the shell aligned accurately in the gun barrel, but fragmented and fell harmlessly as the shell left the gun.

The war in Europe ended a few months later and no more complaints were received, so we considered that the local difficulty had been solved. However, it was common knowledge among armaments officers that on average, it took the firing of some 20,000 anti-aircraft shells to bring down each enemy aircraft. Something had to be done to improve the accuracy and the lethality of all kinds of armaments. In the development of complex Guided Weapons, the principle of looking for simple solutions to apparently intractable problems applied as much as it did to the '6 Pounder'.

Brig. John Clemow

With the benefit of post-war tours in Germany investigating the V2 Rocket and the V1 Flying Bomb, then later in the USA, John Clemow's attentions in the Army moved onto the new technologies to create high precision Guided Weapons, and this brought him into the developments of early guidance test vehicles originating from the Royal Aircraft Establishment at Farnborough. The period covered by this book commences during his tenure of various technical posts in the Ministry of Supply, as Guided Weapons were being developed across British aircraft companies. As director of Guided Weapons Projects in the MOS, Brig. Clemow found himself wading into problems encountered with a number of major GW projects, and he physically moved in with several aircraft companies to get the problems rectified and onto programme.

When Sir George Edwards invited him to join Vickers Armstrongs (Aircraft) Ltd as chief engineer, weapons, in 1957, he retired from the Army and joined Vickers. The company had already spent seven years developing ground-to-ground, air-to-ground and air-to-air Guided Weapons for the government, but suffered cancellation of three major GW projects. He took over as the company made the courageous decision to continue on a private venture basis and as an ever more capable technical design team was built under his leadership, embarking on the development of the Vigilant anti-tank missile. Besides completing the development of Vigilant into a successful Infantry and Armoured Corps weapon, the same team developed the Navigation and Attack System for the highly advanced TSR2 tactical strike and reconnaissance bomber for the RAF. The latter project required comprehensive system design and integration, and inventiveness, and the management of contractors engaged a number of technologies ranging from Radar and Inertial Navigation, to automatic Terrain Following and sophisticated weapon aiming, all co-ordinated by central computers. This work became the basis for developing later aircraft such as the currently operational Tornado.

John Forbat

PRELUDE

This fascinating personal account of the behind-the-scenes action at Vickers during the heyday of British aviation and weaponry invention in the 1950s and 1960s, is both authoritative and very, very readable. A researcher's goldmine, this detailed book is crammed with facts, personal anecdotes, previously classified material and comprehensive explanations which, in a very real way, chart the evolution of today's generation of breathtakingly advanced frontline aircraft and their associated weapon systems. All of the hallmarks of modern aviation: accuracy, reliability and technical sophistication, which we take so much for granted nowadays, were then largely unheard of, and today's successful frontline jets are now the product of, what were at the time, seemingly improbable specifications, long hours of detailed analysis, complex trials and sheer inventive genius.

There is, however, a much more human side to the story and this book openly acknowledges the human failings, errors and financial battles – as well as the strong characters, leaders and men of vision – which together combined to dictate the course of events. It is this honest mix of success and failure, trial and error, genius and prevarication, boffins and budgets, which makes this book so appealing. As recently the officer commanding 617 'Dambusters' Sqn and, having so far flown 3,500 hours in fast jets from Tornado GR4s with the RAF to F-117A Stealth Fighters with the USAF, this story of the dynamic linkages between industry and military rings very true to me.

January 2006
Gp Capt Al Monkman DFC MA BA RAF
Permanent Joint Headquarters (UK)
Northwood
Middlesex

Key to using endnote references

Works cited in this publication are listed on page 247. Each entry in the list is numbered and references within the text correspond to this list.

PROLOGUE

This book is intended to provide, as accurately as possible after a fifty-year time interval, a historical account of the Guided Weapons developments by Vickers Armstrongs, (Aircraft) Ltd in Weybridge, Surrey, including some of the political aspects of government contracting. The difficulties in persuading a reluctant Ministry of Aviation and the Treasury to be 'dragged kicking and screaming' into buying the Vigilant anti-tank guided missile are recorded. Developed without government funds, this was, in their language, 'unprecedented'. A British private venture development, Vigilant's trials and tribulations before it was accepted by the Civil Service and the Government, are chronicled in some detail, relying on original government records in the Public Records Office of the National Archive. A list of References is provided, detailing the sources of my information.

Not intended to be a detailed technical treatise, it is written largely from my perspective of (initially) a young trials engineer, who was closely involved in most projects over a ten-year period. Thus, although there was a considerable depth of technical information and discussion needed to paint a representative picture of the developments conducted at Vickers, I have attempted to err on the side of making the story readable and interesting to a technically untrained audience. Though starting at the bottom of the organisation and maturing to senior designer level – short of Management status, I tried to keep myself abreast of the 'big picture', and in this account, factual though sometimes rather technical data is admixed with my own personal anecdotal experiences. I hope that these may help to add life to a tale of technical development at the forefront of engineering of the day, in a large and developing organisation.

The magic of aeroplanes and flying first inspired me as a small boy before the Second World War, when, rarely, a plane dropped advertising leaflets over Kensington Gardens. There we used to fish for 'tiddlers' and watch the old men (some aged at least thirty-five) sail their big model yachts. Sometimes the planes came so low that we could see the pilot's head in the cockpit – and we wondered what it was like to fly. Being lifted up to look through the door of a corrugated skinned Handley Page airliner at Croydon Airport was the next best thing. Then came the war and evacuation.

Newsreels of the Blitz on London and shots of diving Stukas over Poland, then Heinkels and Messerschmitts being shot down by RAF fighters, imprinted themselves on our minds and imaginations. Having found an old wingless biplane in a farm shed outside Melksham in Wiltshire, where we were billeted away from London and family, was a major coup. Safe from prying eyes, a friend and I would climb into the tandem cockpits and waggle the joystick, making engine and machine gun noises till we were hoarse. By the middle of the war, in late 1942, at fourteen I was living back in London and soon got my Fire Guard's armband and steel helmet, for fire watching duty – whenever we could arrange it, this was on the roof of our West Kensington block of flats. The sirens wailed, bombers roared, searchlights stabbed around in the night sky and Ack-Ack guns sent flak among the bombers evading the barrage balloons, and hot shrapnel tinkling down onto the pavements, for us kids to collect as trophies. Air-raid shelters were for grown-ups, who knew the dangers. For us, they were for ping-pong during the day when they were otherwise empty. We were trained to crawl through smoke filled rooms, to extinguish incendiary bombs by squirting water from a hose fed by another fire guard using a stirrup pump in a bucket of water. When bombs fell really close, it was 'you young lad' who was sent on his bike to ride the half mile over streets covered with broken glass, to fetch the fire brigade – which turned out to be on fire itself.

If only we could be old enough for the RAF and fly those beautiful, magnificent Spitfires and shoot Gerries down. I was green with envy, knowing that my older brother's friends were Spitfire pilots and Mosquito train busters. The nearest thing for me was to join the Air Training Corps, where we wore a poor imitation of RAF uniform with high collars instead of shirt and tie, but where we practiced rapid aircraft recognition, learned about the theory of flight, navigation by dead reckoning, practiced Morse-code signalling and of course, lots of 'square bashing'. The major annual event was the two weeks' 'camp' at an RAF station, where we lived in Nissen Huts, slept on 'biscuit' mattresses and lined up with our tin plates for our victuals in the airmen's mess, then washed them up in the trough outside, in steam boiling water, whence it was impossible to retrieve a dropped knife. Then after inspection, we would get runs in the bombing simulator, rifle and machine gun experience and, above all, flying. Never mind that the Short Stirling bomber finished its operational training bombing runs and target shooting over the sea on my first flight – with a mock attack by an American Thunderbolt fighter and took corkscrew evasive action – until I threw up. The 4-hour flight entitled us to a 'flying meal' of fried eggs and bacon, my favourite – almost totally unavailable due to food rationing in 'Civvy Street' – and I was so sick, I could not eat any of it.

But we flew as often as we could and the RAF let us feel we were part of the crew, with a trip to the flight deck wearing our parachute harnesses and helmets with earphones. There were also days out to an airfield, where we could fly in a Tiger Moth trainer and experience the wind and the bumps and even a loop-the-loop, or an Auster side-by-side seater, where we could actually hold the 'stick' and do a little 'dual'. The epitome of this was for the luckier ones, who were able to go on a gliding course. On Hounslow Heath (now Heathrow Airport) barrage balloon winches would pull us across several hundred yards of bumpy grass in a single-seat Dagling glider. There were no two-seat gliders at the school, so we learned by flying solo from the first flight. At sixteen, this was not a bit frightening – just the excitement we craved. When we had become used to handling this almost Wright Flyer level craft up to only about 10ft over the heath, we transferred to the much higher performance Kirby Cadet. Now instead of sitting in the open on a 'keel' with wings and tail attached, we were in an open cockpit without instruments, just a stick and rudder bar, and the plug to release the cable. The instruction was somewhat primitive: 'Just hold the stick about there, off you go' was the gist of it, with perhaps a few shouted instructions from midfield while I flew over the instructor's head. In the Cadet, we could climb to ten stories high, 100ft, and after pulling the plug to release the cable, glide down to a good landing. This was real flying and we were really in Seventh Heaven.

Soon we were also under the virtually 24-hour rain of Doodlebug flying bombs, pitching down as their fuel ran out, to crash and explode on London's houses, causing much destruction and many casualties. I may have seen the first ones while cycling into Kent for camping one weekend. With its throaty pulse-jet roar, it flew quite low right overhead, with Ack-Ack bursting all around it. The usual rain of hot shrapnel had us dodge into a doorway, before picking up more souvenirs. Far from being guided, these V-1 flying bombs landed indiscriminately and we had all too real opportunities to practise the drill; when you hear one approaching, get off your bike, lie in the gutter with hands over the back of your head and wait. If you hear an explosion, some other poor bastard got his chips. The later V-2 missiles that shot up into space before coming down at supersonic speed were equally uncontrolled in where they hit. Unlike with the V-1s, no air-raid sirens announced their impending silent arrival. Once you heard the explosion – always followed by the scream of its falling trajectory – you knew that you were all right this time.

The depth of aviation's penetration into my psyche naturally led to me taking an aeronautical engineering degree, and after passing 'Inter BSc' at school, it was virtually impossible for me to get onto a course in London. Eventually, in the face of floods of ex-servicemen returning from the war, I was offered a course for only two days a week as a temporary measure until a full-time course became available. The Aerodynamics lecturer was emphatic at our commencing lecture; if we had any hopes of passing an Aeronautical degree at the first attempt along with full-time students, 'forget it'. When the year had passed, there was still no full-time place for me, so now having lost any opportunities for aircraft apprenticeships, I had to continue at two days per week and do private study at home on the other days. Out of a dozen or so in the Aeronautical class at Northampton Polytechnic, just two of us made it. In 1950 I was able to look to trying for that aircraft design career, to which I had nailed my flag. It took a few months before I was naturalised from my wartime 'stateless' designation as a pre-war Hungarian immigrant, and it was March 1951 before my 'Secret' clearance came through. That is when Vickers Armstrongs (Aircraft) Ltd accepted me as a Graduate Apprentice.

Arriving for an 8 a.m. start on my first day in my Dad's Morris 8 borrowed for the day, the big car park outside the Design Office was quite empty. It was only when I backed into the first parking space near the main entrance that through the rear window, I saw the name plate growing as it came into view. The name was G.R. Edwards; fortunately I had done enough homework to realise this was our already famous chief designer's parking spot. Quickly, I found another parking space. The first year at Weybridge was spent riveting, fitting, hammering and getting other factory experience with Valettas, Varsities and Viscounts in the factory, at the grand starting salary of £6 9s 8 1/4d for a 48-hour week, while I also got a first-hand view of the Valiant V-bomber prototype being tested. To my great surprise, the wing spars I was assembling closely resembled the design I had calculated and drawn for my recent college course work. Our lecturer must have known more about practical aircraft than we had given him credit for. I also witnessed the immediate aftermath of a test pilot's arrival that would herald an important part of my future work. 'Spud' Murphy arrived for his job interview with chief test pilot Jock Bryce in his RAF Meteor fighter, which he flew like the aerobatic champion he was. Unfortunately, instead of landing at Wisley, he landed at Brooklands where we could all see it – and suffered a brake failure that led to his Meteor being wrapped round a tree at the bottom of somebody's garden. Unhurt, afterwards he pleaded, 'Jock, you have to hire me – I'll be cashiered', and got the job nevertheless, and later, as this book will document, we shared many flights.

My second apprenticeship year started with an interview with the assistant chief designer, H.H. Gardner. A large man with a hawk-like countenance, he looked over his desk and said, 'I am picking people for our Special Projects Section. It is working on Guided Weapons. Would you like me to put you there?' This was not exactly the aircraft design which I had so long craved. Yet, it was clearly something new, with supersonics and all that and still very much within the scope of my degree studies. 'I want to put you into our Trials Section with Barry MacGowan, known as Mac.' This sounded interesting enough and I quickly accepted. Very soon, I entered the Design Office as a very Junior trials engineer. I was into Guided Weapons.

Fifty years later, I am back at the site of those early developments as a volunteer at the Brooklands Museum. On the site of the famous Brooklands Motor Racing Track, which opened in 1907 and which is also the cradle of British Aviation exhibiting the many historic aircraft, engines, racing cars and associated equipment and memorabilia, I am gathering the missiles and related evidence of 'GW' for a third arm of Brooklands Museum.

Chapter 1

THE START OF GW AT VICKERS

The relatively new Special Projects Section I joined in March 1952 later became the Guided Weapons Department, and Henry Gardner then moved up to chief designer, GW. But thinking in Weybridge began immediately after the Second World War, when the company first considered setting up an elaborate organisation for designing and developing Guided Weapons. In a 1960 interview, Sqdn Ldr K.S. Lockie[1] of Vickers reported that this was abandoned due to the insufficient likelihood of the very significant costs being recovered soon enough by sales of weapons to the armed services. Then, in 1949, the government offered Vickers the Sea Slug ship-to-air missile project, but this was declined. By this time, however, Barnes Wallis was following up his successful wartime bomb developments with the early creation of the idea that a TV guided gliding bomb should greatly improve on the accuracy obtainable by free falling bombs. This project became Blue Boar and was later the subject of a contract from the Ministry of Supply.

In the meantime, while the V-bombers were some time from becoming available to the RAF, in response to an invitation by the Government to produce expendable flying bombs for mass attacks, chief designer George Edwards initiated a private venture design – Red Rapier.[2] These would emulate Hitler's mass attacks with the V-1, but instead of relying on scatter shot methods, Red Rapier would cruise at a high subsonic speed at a 50,000ft altitude over a distance of up to 400 nautical miles, guided by a 'TRAMP' Radar beam system. Three jet engines mounted on symmetrically arranged tail fins would drive the large robot aircraft over this range and deliver a 5,000lb bomb load after a 'bunt' that brought the trajectory into the vertical over the target. With a specified accuracy of 100 yards, single 5,000lb bombs or clusters of five 1,000 bombs could have a devastating effect, particularly with waves of up to 100 Red Rapiers attacking together.

By the time this wet behind the ears engineer arrived at Special Projects, Blue Boar trials were well under way and Red Rapier development was advanced to the point of a firm specification under the designation Vickers SP2. Furthermore, a new (originally Folland Aircraft) project was just being acquired under Ministry contract, for an advanced active Radar homing air-to-air missile against bomber targets attacking at near-sonic speeds. This was capable of delivering a 100lb proximity fuzed warhead in all round attack directions, at a range of up to 10,000 yards and heights between 10,000ft and 50,000ft. Delightfully, this was named Red Dean at a time when Dr Hewlett Johnson, well known to be a card-carrying Communist, was the Dean of Canterbury. Since he was popularly referred to in the Press as the Red Dean of Canterbury, we could hardly wait for the missile's name to come off the Secret List.

I reported to Barry MacGowan ('Mac'), section leader of Trials. At the age of twenty-seven, this tall, serious, engineer with bright ginger hair was one of the top team under Henry Gardner and his deputy Eddie Smyth. Having bailed out of a tailless glider in which a well-known test pilot, Robert Kronfeld, was killed, Mac was a member of the Caterpillar Club – and well versed in flight testing. Against my newly increased wage of £8 15s a week – say a little over £400 per year – Mac was reputed to be earning the astronomical sum of £750 per year. He quickly impressed upon me his pride to be working with a company like Vickers, and showed himself to be a meticulous engineer, particularly in the quality of report writing he expected from his staff – nothing less than the standards of the Royal Aircraft Establishment at Farnborough. We had many RAE reports to study, particularly since the RAE tended to do the initial design of most Guided Weapons, up to the point of a contract being awarded to a company like Vickers.

However, the first thing I had to remember before handwriting even the most modest of rough notes or calculations, well before starting to assemble any formal report or memorandum, was to write 'Secret' at the top of the page. Long since unclassified, everything was Secret, except for those fewer matters that were merely 'Confidential', or at the lowest level, 'Restricted'. This became an automatic process in everything we did, as did the locking of all this material into approved security filing cabinets, whose normal drawer locks were complemented by an approved padlock securing a stout steel bar passed down through its drawer handles. Work could not be taken home, all information was on a 'need to know' basis, and Management had to satisfy not only 'the Ministry', but the ubiquitous 'Box 500' Government security office somewhere in MI5. The aura of this environment under which the new area of technology called Guided Weapons was shrouded, added to its technical and professional attractions to make life exciting for a recently qualified engineer at the tender age of twenty three. Happily, all this work has now long been declassified.

However, one of the first stops on my introduction to this newly evolving real world was with J.E. Daboo, a squat, diminutive and brilliant Indian engineer with a Cambridge MA, who was also a graduate of the prestigious College of Aeronautics at Cranfield. In charge of aerodynamics and performance, 'Dab' had the design of Blue Boar well under his belt and was designing the shape and performance of Red Dean and its rocket motor. As I sat down to learn what he was doing, he could succinctly explain the mathematics of missile design parameters and how each interacted with the others, while he simultaneously continued to calculate missile trajectories with his ever hotter slide rule. This habit extended to the largest design and management meetings, during which his work rate on creating missile trajectories never slackened even though he never lost the thread, nor failed to make intelligent points. Thus, I was able to learn the basics of supersonic lift, drag and stability, which were sufficiently new to have had little attention in my BSc (Eng.) course. We would have a long friendship.

Mike Still was in charge of mechanical engineering work and supervised the sub-contractors who provided hydraulic actuators, valves, igniters and a host of related parts, assisted by Reg Barr, Bill Redstone, Peter Rice and others. Much of his time was also occupied by the design of missile recovery systems, with the aim of avoiding the expensive destruction of every air dropped or rocket boosted missile in the trials programme. Ingenious recovery systems were under development, involving everything from parachutes to dive brakes and their combinations, that could land a trials 'round' softly enough on a spike protruding from its nose, for re-use in subsequent trials.

Missile control by autopilots and guidance in the different forms required for each project involved a whole range of electronic designs, as did power supply systems and the radio telemetry required for trials. Electronic engineers abounded in many varieties, ranging from the small, softly spoken, bearded Dr Teddy Hall, in charge of Red Rapier's control and guidance assisted by 'Mac' McDonnell and Ian Hansford among others, to bespectacled control engineer Johnny Johnstone. Away from the main design office, numerous engineers and technicians stared at oscilloscopes and wielded soldering irons at bird's nests of wires on benches in the Brooklands Track's remaining Pits. When not flooded out by excess rains, these were hives of activity by, mainly, ex-Post Office engineers like Colin New, Jack Mullins, Teddy Pierce, Alan Jones, Jack Few, Derek Dix, recent apprentice Don Wells and such, who may not have gone to university, but knew all about oscillators, servo motors and drives, as well as radio transmission with its specialised test equipment. Prolific numbers of Wireless World editions in The Pits were always on hand for tips on electronic circuits. Some of these people must have been over thirty, even approaching forty! In those days before the Transistor, all electronics utilised miniature and sub-miniature thermionic valves, which produced prodigious amounts of heat that had to be dissipated somehow, without baking the whole unit. What is more, they had to work equally well at an altitude of 50,000ft and -60°C as at sea level and +50°C, also withstanding the severe 'g' forces and vibration environments created by jet bombers or rocket motors or both.

Structural design involved yet another set of engineers, with Peter Mobsby and Albert Kitchenside creating the latest honeycomb wing structures, missile body designs to carry rocket motors and their efflux nozzles, fixed and flip-out wing designs, supported by experienced design draughtsmen like 'Tubs' Phil Ashby, Arthur Anderson, Frank Howard and colleagues bending over their boards wielding chisel-pointed soft pencils. 'Mob' had the additional distinction of applying his virile sense of humour through side-splitting cartoons, which regularly made rounds of the office. It was 'Mob' who quite believably drew Dr Hall as a 'ferret peeping out of a bear's arse'. A little more outrageously for our amusement, he related the company 'dolly bird', who regularly turned heads whenever she flounced by wafting her suitably provocative perfume. Mob depicted 'Woking Lil' – a possibly undeserved nick-name – passing outside the window of the management office, with a goggle-eyed manager's erection bursting through the brick wall. Intertwined between the electronic and the mechanical engineers, Roy Baker and Eric Wightman were to the fore in development and the universal interaction with trials. Before computers or even cheap electronic calculators, slide rules still 'ruled'. Yet Roy – who was the first person to acquaint me with the term 'black box' for any electronic system element, years before its time – forecast that the future of industry would be dependent on the ability to store and retrieve large quantities of data.

Where aircraft were to be used for flight testing missiles, otherwise 'standard' RAF planes such as Canberra jet bombers were equipped with complementary control, monitoring and missile launching equipment. This employed many engineers led by Sid Hook, Sid Horwood and more humble design draughtsmen, who stood astride the main aircraft design departments and 'Special Projects'.

Peter Tanner oversaw prototype manufacturing in all its aspects initially in the W103 hangar, ranging from Forman Harry Beauchamp with Johnny Woods, machining, wiring under Sam Hastings, to assembly and with assistance in testing, by engineers from the laboratories in The Pits. That operation was supported by our own Commercial and Purchasing office led by the urbane Alan Moorshead and a more mischievously humorous Bill Murdoch, assisted by the gentle Ozzie Wood and others.

Trials were conducted at RAE-owned ranges on Salisbury Plain, mainly at Larkhill (where Mr Berens, the Range Warden, came to work riding a horse) and Imber, and at Aberporth on Cardigan Bay. Other trials were conducted by the Ministry direct, with aircraft operating from the Armaments & Experimental Establishment (A&EE), Boscombe Down. Vickers also had a permanent trials station in Australia, located at Edinburgh Field near Adelaide, for trials at the desert Woomera Missile Range. This team was set up and headed by Ozzie Wood's brother-in-law, Jack Redpath, assisted by Brian Soan in charge of the trials operations, with general administration headed by Alan Millson. Members of Mac's trials team were allocated to Australia for one-year periods. John Curry was already out there, and Maurice Watson was the next one due to go down under.

Each project's trials programme was undertaken with a series of test vehicles, which in the absence of developed recovery systems were mostly destroyed in the process of the trial. Their performance was therefore only capable of analysis by means of Kinetheodolite film records of flight trajectories and on-board instrument data that were either recoverable after impact, or transmitted to ground stations using Radio Telemetry. One of my first tasks was to configure on-board instruments for measuring accelerations during flight, and to analyse trials results from various media. Recovered instruments and telemetry records would arrive from firings and air drops over Cardigan Bay on a regular basis, and mountains of data had to be extracted. Kinetheodolite film records required frame-by-frame viewing and assessment of missile flight behaviour in real time, telemetry records with typically sixteen channels of data, recorded continuously over 10 seconds of rocket-propelled flight, would enable readings of accelerations, pressures, temperatures, vibrations and gyroscope measured headings, leading to column after column of figures for further analysis. Accelerometer records were frequently made by 'scratch recorders' that had to be recovered from impacted test vehicles. These comprised a stylus moving in response to accelerometer deflections, which scratched a trace onto a clear piece of film previously calibrated with lines, scratched while the instrument was mounted on a centrifuge. We had to make sure that the calibrations were accurate enough to produce useful measurements and have the instrument packages installed in the test 'rounds' before they went to the range.

The volume of analysis that today would be fed directly into a (virtually unheard of) digital computer programmed to print out analysed data, then required manual calculation employing large and noisy calculators. To assist us with this work, there were about ten young girls of the 'Hen Coop'. This apt name would undoubtedly be condemned as politically incorrect today, but these sweet girls, mostly around twenty years of age, who worked with us didn't mind. Originally part of the Wind Tunnel Department when this was Eddie Smyth's responsibility, The Hen Coop girls were led by Kathleen, an efficient and friendly lady more mature than the others – she could have been as old as thirty! Valerie, who had recently married Bob Gladwell in the Aerodynamics Dept., was as much a good looker as any, showing a Hollywood-level panache with a hearty slap across the face of a youthful test pilot who came a little too fresh for her liking. After a flaming red-headed princess of a girl went to Australia to be married, also in her very early twenties, Daphne Boughton, Daphne Morris and Edna were only outshone in attractiveness by the eighteen-year-old blonde Marlene Lees. With great application, industry and noise, they whirled the handles of their typewriter-sized Brunswiga mechanical calculators, and the lucky ones used the near desk-sized Marchant electric calculators. We then plotted graphs and tables of the results and wrote detailed reports for Mac's approval before they were circulated to the appropriate design teams and to management.

For Blue Boar flight trials over Aberporth, Vickers already operated (initially two) Canberra aircraft – the world's first jet bomber (later made under license by the Martin Corporation in America). With unswept wings bearing two Rolls Royce Avon engines, the sleek Canberra B2 carried its bomb load and trials equipment, with pilot, navigator

Fig.1.1 Members of the Trials Team at a typical Christmas Eve party. From left to right: Alan Thurley, Edna, Peter Burry, Ron Jupp, Marlene Lees, Mike Martin, Bert Coleman, Clarice and above, Mike (with the Lea Francis cars in a large garage attached to a small house), Daphne Boughton, another Daphne, John Forbat, John Curry and Henry Hunt above, Kathleen, Valerie and Bob Gladwell. The names on the other faces and some surnames have retreated into the mists of my memory.

and the missile trials engineer, up to a 48,000ft altitude at Mach 0.82 – some 600mph. They were only just entering RAF service, so our pre-production machines were not identical and still represented leading edge aviation – and risk. In the days before airline passenger jet travel was even on the travelling public's horizon, to arrive over Land's End from Wisley in 28 minutes was a big deal. Later, a RAF B29 Washington (American Second World War Superfortress) and two more Canberras were added for Red Dean and Red Rapier trials in England and in Australia.

The Trials Section already in place included Maurice Watson, a couple of years my senior, Reg Mason, recently returned from working at Oak Ridge in Tennessee, and Alan Thurley, whose asthma prevented him from flying. From time to time, Mac or Maurice would arrive in the office carrying flying kit and looking a little dark under the eyes. When after a few weeks he had licked my report writing into shape, one day Mac announced, 'John, I want you to train up for flying with Blue Boar in the Canberra'. He *wanted me* to fly in the Canberra? With racing heart, I could think of *nothing I wanted more*. Besides being kitted out with flying suit, leather helmet with oxygen mask, pressure breathing waistcoat and goggles, I was soon despatched to the School of Aviation Medicine at Farnborough for a medical examination and to experience the ejector seat. The seat was waiting quietly at the foot of a steep ramp resembling the jib of a crane. Reg and I tossed a coin to decide would go first while the other watched – I won and opted not to watch him and risk turning 'chicken'. When I pulled the handle of the face screen over my head, a loud bang gave me a kick up the backside and there I was with my feet dangling into space about 30ft up, feeling rather like a circus clown after a back somersault. Nothing to worry about, and Reg followed. In the event of a live ejection at Mach 0.82, that would be the easy part (assuming that the emergency oxygen supply attached to the seat worked and the cockpit canopy was successfully blown off first).

Firm instructions on making the descent to earth followed:

First of all, unlock the seat harness and get out of the seat as quickly as possible. In the seat, you will fall much too slowly and would certainly freeze to death before reaching the ground. Wait till you are at 10,000ft (estimate this by eye, we don't have barometric releases yet) before you pull the parachute rip chord. Then steer as best you can away from houses and trees and raise your knees, to make a good landing without breaking your legs. Don't forget to release the 'chute as soon as you are down otherwise in any wind, it could drag you for miles.

A little more respectful of high-altitude jet flying in military aircraft, we drove back to Weybridge, ready for our fist trial.

By late twentieth-century standards, visits to other establishments were supported by quaintly cushioned facilities, available even to mere 'Weekly Staff'' levels. For those who did not drive (were there ever such people?) or for long journeys, a chauffeur could be made available. The Vickers Transport Department would supply Austin A40 or to 'Monthly Staff' A90 saloon cars for a trips, saving impecunious engineers from having to show up at the RAE trials ranges or at sub-contractors on their motor bikes, or (as when I became affluent enough) in my chugging 1930 model Austin Seven. Besides the numerous repairs I had to make to this ancient vehicle, my colleagues were much amused by the leaky radiator, which got me to work with the aid of porridge I put into the water, but required a saucepan to collect the drips during the day – poured back before leaving for home. The friendly Transport Manager, E.F.G. Hill, gave willing help, assisted by his wife and secretary Irene, whom he had married 'because' her maiden initials were I.J.K.L. Clearly, he had no other choice! We received rail vouchers for travel to London and beyond – in the case of senior designers and above, for the first-class carriages.

This substantial operation, major sub-contractors and relationships with the Ministry of Supply and the Air Ministry were co-ordinated by Eddie Smyth from his front office next to Henry Gardner's larger sanctum in the big Aircraft Design Building that covered several acres of drawing boards and desks. While Special Projects was part of the one Aircraft Design Office, its serious yet easy going and enthusiastic entity already occupied a somewhat detached presence in its midst.

In a visit on 14 July 1952 to Vickers by assistant director/TD Plans, Mr F. Olaf Thornton, along with a Mr Baker, the RAE project officer F.G. Tarrant and W/C Simpson, GW(Air) of the Air Ministry, insufficient progress with the Blue Boar programme was noted. Internal correspondence retained in the Public Records Office in Kew shows how officials in the Ministry of Supply were at considerable unease concerning the work load Vickers had undertaken with three major projects. Following this visit, a reported interview[3] with George Edwards and Henry Gardner, together with the Ministry's resident technical officer (RTO) on 8 August 1952, with comments by Mr Thornton, is the subject of interesting opinions, quoted in the extracts below:

After a short general discussion the points made in Mr Baker's notes were taken one by one.

Notes on Visit [Items of interest selected by Author]

(1)   The progress on Blue Boar was unsatisfactory and this was attributed to lack of staff...

'In the first place the figure of 44 did not include 20 men in the drawing Office, nor did it include such departments as Aerodynamics, Stress, Weight Control, Wind Tunnel, Mechanical Test etc. These are run as service departments, which provide specialised effort as and when required. Vickers maintained that it would be very uneconomical to create separate Aircraft and Guided Weapon departments for these services.

When comparing Vickers with firms who have a completely self-contained Guided Weapon organisation it should be remembered that the figure of 44 at Vickers is not in any way comparable with figures for self contained Guided Weapons organisations because it does not include any of these service departments nor of course does it include the Experimental Shop which at the time of the report employed 94 men on Blue Boar...

Note. There appears to me to be a fundamental difference between aircraft and electronic design, the former is very broadly designed, built and then flight tested, whereas the latter proceeds on a try and see basis and then tested to see if they work. These then go through innumerable modifications and tests, the modifications being made physically in the Lab by the technician, i.e. they do not go through the process of redesign in the Drawing Office followed by construction in the Experimental Shop, and when the right combination is found in the Lab then the design is formalised...

(3)   Project Engineers. [This refers to Ministry Engineers... Author]
GWRD believe that there should be a PSO level man in technical charge of each project: Blue Boar, Red Rapier and Red Dean.

Vickers are unwilling to take on such a man on Red Rapier while it is a Private Venture and certainly while it remains a Private Venture on the part of Vickers it is not for the MOS to say who Vickers should or should not take on. Smyth deals with the other two projects and because they are in very different states of development (Blue Boar is well advanced while Red Dean is only just beginning) one project engineer is in the opinion of the firm adequate for the two projects...

(5) Distribution of Electronic Strength between the 3 projects.
It has been stated that the electronic section for Red Rapier is extremely well staffed with a good section head while the corresponding section of Blue Boar is bad and for Red Dean does not exist.
This is misunderstanding of the facts, as the real high quality electronic effort is required on the guidance system. The guidance system for Blue Boar is being undertaken by EMI and for Red Dean by GEC and only on Red Rapier is Vickers responsible for the guidance system. To put the Red Rapier guidance team on either of the other projects would, in the opinion of Vickers be a gross misemployment of these men and they would probably lose them as a result...

(10)   General Suitability of Vickers. [3]
It was stated that Vickers were, as far as military aircraft were concerned, essentially a bomber firm and therefore showed greater interest in Blue Boar and Red Rapier than Red Dean, which is essentially a fighter weapon.

Quite apart from the fact that a bomber firm should be particularly suitable for developing methods of attacking bombers, I think that the history of these jobs should be remembered. Blue Boar was being developed by Vickers on contract and Red Rapier as a Private Venture though with MOS knowledge and support, while Red Dean was being developed by Follands. When Follands wished to drop Red Dean, Vickers were approached but said they did not wish to take on the work. The late Chief Executive Guided Weapons then went to the top of the Vickers organisation (Mr Weeks) and exerted very great pressure that they should take it on in the national interest because they were the only firm who were considered really capable of undertaking this very important project (Red Dean) and in whom the Ministry of Supply had every confidence. This was done with the full knowledge of the prior Blue Boar and Red Rapier commitments...

(11)   Estimation.

To attempt to lay down what is little more than an arbitrary programme and then to blame others for failing to carry it out is a travesty of the functions of a Government Department...

(14)   Conclusion.

There is no real clash between Blue Boar, Red Rapier and Red Dean, nor would there be any appreciable acceleration of the other two if Red Rapier were dropped...

In preparation for this visit I arranged a meeting with Mr Tarrant the RAE project officer on Blue Boar, and wing commander Simpson of GW (Air), to ascertain their criticisms of Vickers...

...... My conclusion is that there is no real clash between the Blue Boar, Red Rapier and Red Dean, nor would there be any appreciable acceleration of the other two if Red Rapier were dropped. My recommendations are:

(a)   That a contract for Red Rapier be placed as soon as possible as while this job remains a Private Venture, the MOS are in the weakest possible position to influence the deployment of men on the job.

(b)   That Vickers be asked to draw up their own programme for the next six months for all three weapons and that this be sent to the MOS and that it should form the basis for future action pending any CS(A)/CGWL agreed programme.

Signed off by F. Olaf Thornton AD/TD. Plans, this long note was sent up the line to the director general (DGTD/A) and to the controller, CS (A), who demurred from agreeing some of the points, but, nevertheless, concluded: 'On the other hand I entirely agree with Thornton's recommendations and suggest that you accept them'.

This went to the controller of Guided Weapons and Electronics (CGWL) with his own handwritten note, saying, 'You will be interested to see this file. At present it appears as though we may rest assured'.

The Ministry of Supply was clearly torn between trying to micro-manage these programmes at Vickers, and the subsequent realisation that it was not a Government department's place to tell a contractor how to run his business. The net result was that Vickers could continue all three projects with contract cover from the MOS – until much later, when other factors led to cancellations. Meanwhile, Vickers Guided Weapons Department was set up as a separate entity from the Aircraft division after all, and a new building next to the Vickers Apprentice School was built to house the whole operation. The Pits, the W103 hangar for Environmental Testing and other work, as well as other outlying buildings, remained in operation, but the main Experimental Shop under Peter Tanner, with Harry Beauchamp, Sam Hastings and technicians including John Duck, was relocated in the new GW building, along with Design, Project Management, Trials and the other departments. Eddie Smyth remained in day-to-day charge, reporting to Henry Gardner as director and chief designer. However, reliance of the Aircraft division was considerably reduced, being mainly for wind tunnel work and the nascent PEGASUS computer capability. Flight testing with pilots, navigators

Fig.1.2 Test pilot 'Spud' Murphy in the Canberra at 40,000ft, snapped by me.[103]

Fig.1.3 Navigator Don Bowen.[103]

and aircraft maintenance also remained with the main Flight Test Department at Wisley airfield, employing GW personnel for its own equipment and engineering aircrew from the Trials Section.

By 1954, major expansion was taking place, with the recruitment of senior project managers and numerous supporting engineers to work on the three projects, considerably raising the level of technical and professional capabilities of the GW Department. While this heralded larger and more diverse operations, it was still much smaller than most other GW organisations and remained a closely knit and enthusiastic young team.

Other major UK projects were being pursued at Bristol Aircraft and English Electric, which were respectively engaged on Red Duster (eventually in as Bloodhound) and Red Shoes (eventually in service Thunderbird) ground-to-air missile developments, Fairey Aviation with Blue Sky (eventually in service as Fireflash) air-to-air missile, de Havilland with Blue Jay (eventually in service as Firestreak) air-to-air missile and Armstrong Whitworth with Sea Slug. Problems with some of these projects would later have repercussions in the management of Vickers Guided Weapons at Weybridge.

Fig.1.4 Our B-29 'Washington' Superfortress and an aircrew, before a trial with the 5,000lb Blue Boar test vehicle. From left to right: navigator Don Bowen; trials engineer George Errington; second (test) pilot Eddie McNamara; anonymous; trials engineers Frank Cox, John Whetmore and Pat White; flight engineer Pat Toll; test pilot and Captain 'Spud' Murphy.[33]

Following chapters include numerous extracts, diagrams and photographs from previously Secret reports and correspondence. The reader may rest assured that these documents have long been declassified and that any 'Secret' markings can be safely ignored.

Chapter 2

RED RAPIER EXPENDABLE BOMBER

Before a Guided Weapons Department was mooted at Weybridge, chief designer George Edwards initiated and oversaw the beginnings of a programme of development aimed at filling the RAF's bombing capability gap, as the Cold War was making its early threats. In 1949, the RAF was still flying Lincolns and generally heavy bombers designed during the period of the Second World War. Although specifications for the new concept of unarmed, high subsonic speed V-Bombers flying at 50,000ft altitude had resulted in RAF Operational Requirements (ORs) being issued back in 1946, the resulting Vulcan and Victor bombers specified to carry a 20,000lb bomb load were even then not expected to be ready to enter service until the mid-1950s. To fill the gap, the nearest aircraft performance immediately available was by the USAF's late WW2 B-29 Superfortress, of which the RAF ordered a quantity of eighty-eight.[2] These aircraft could carry a somewhat lesser bomb load at well below sonic speed and up to only 35,000ft. Another shorter timescale OR had been issued in 1948 (the B9/48), with similar performance to the 1946 ORs, but with a lighter bomb load of 15,000lb. This became the Vickers Valiant, with swept back wings carrying four totally buried Rolls Royce Avon jet engines in an aerodynamically clean design overseen by George Edwards. Valiant first flew in 1951 amid much excitement at Weybridge and Wisley, where flight testing commenced as the Experimental Shop build at Foxwarren was quickly followed by manufacturing at Brooklands. This employed large stressed skinned wing sections built on jigs, with new technology hydraulically operated machinery. Nevertheless, the in-service date was clearly several years ahead.

Short Range Expendable Bomber (SREB)

Warnings about the Soviets' apparent intentions of attacking NATO led to invitations to the aircraft industry in late 1950, to fill the immediate European Theatre needs. The SREBs would be launched from multiple catapult-style mobile launchers, to obliterate a target area more effectively than the latter day V-1 Doodlebug. The Air Ministry invited studies[2] from Avro, Bristol, de Havilland and Vickers. Later, Fairey Gloster and

Saunders-Roe Aviation were also invited to submit designs and, after Bristol and Vickers produced designs, specifications began to crystallise. Soon after, OR 1097 (Issue 3, 17 December 1950[4]) was issued to achieve the quickest means of creating a defence/attack system. In an 18 January 1951 note, Vickers offered[2] its private venture, SP2 when in 1951, on coming back into power,[2] Winston Churchill was made aware of the threat's perceived magnitude, he demanded 'super priority' be placed on the project, and eventually, in 1952, after the numerous other designs were distilled, Vickers received indications of anticipated MOS contract funding. This envisaged the construction of twelve ⅓-scale recoverable models of Type 719 for trial in Australia, by dropping from a B29 Washington over Woomera, and development of the full-scale aircraft Type 725.

Except for the guidance and control systems being developed by the recently established Guided Weapons Department, development and construction of the Red Rapier models and full-scale aircraft system, including its rapid ground launch facility, was the responsibility of the original Vickers Aircraft team headed by George Edwards. A leading role was taken be Peter Stannard, an experienced Vickers designer, assisted by Reg Barr, Jim Dacre, Roy Gates and others of the aircraft team under Henry Gardner and Hugh Hemsley, with co-operation from Special Projects/Guided Weapons Department.

At a meeting headed by Dr R. Cockburn of MOS at Weybridge, reported in July 1952, it was agreed[2] that the general economy of the Expendable Bomber was established, and that mass production was practicable. However, Government funding would be required to pursue guidance development. It then took numerous design iterations, competitor comparisons and even more Ministry meetings, design debates and decision hold-ups, before the specification became firm enough to enable MOS to place the order for twelve ⅓-scale prototypes for testing of the aerodynamics and basic performance in air drops from B-29 Washington aircraft at Woomera. This order only came in August 1953, by which time, over more than two years, Vickers had expended considerable effort and monies without receiving Government funds – and dropping trials from a Washington aircraft had commenced at Woomera. Cover for the Guidance System was not received until 30 October 1953, per Contract 6/C/WPNS/464/C.B.10 (d), with a limit of £450,000.

Twelve full-scale trials models were also considered necessary, including a structural test model, the fuselage of which was subjected to tests in 1954. In the context of the technologies to be used being well known and considered to carry low risk, the specification was nevertheless ambitious for the times. The contract including the full-scale Red Rapier for structural testing to the SP2 Specification, is perhaps best summarised by the following items extracted from a Vickers brochure.

Ref. 99235, dated October 1951.[4]

Main dimensions: Length 45.39 ft., Wing Span 32 ft., Wing Area 282 sq. ft. Body Diameter 32in.

Launching: Mobile, compressed air driven catapult accelerates the 12,000lb all up weight missile with initial total thrust of 485,000 lb. at 30.4g to 148 kts. over a distance of 35 ft., at 25° launch climb angle. (Figs 2.5 & 2.6)

Range: 400 nautical miles (737 Km) on 250 gallons of fuel in wing tanks plus 50 gallons in centre fuselage tank.

Bomb Load: 5,000lb single or 5, 1,000lb bombs with lateral impulse for separation.

Power: Three Rolls Royce RB93 (Soar) engines, of 15in diameter producing a total of 5250 lb. (23.4 KN) static thrust.

Altitude at target: 50,000ft (15,690 M) – actually projected at 51,500 with zoom to 55,000ft.

Cruise Speed: 475 knots, Mach 0.83 (875 Km/Hr)

Guidance: Initially by Flux Gate compass, then 'TRAMP' Radar beams system based on a form of Gee-H or Oboe already in use with aircraft navigation.

Accuracy: 50% error probability of 100 yards (91 M)

Terminal phase: Engines stopped, zoom up to lose speed before a 'bunt' manoeuvre into a vertical dive over the target, eventually the wing attachment commanded to release and jettison along with fairings and the engines, with a guide surface tail parachute deployed to limit the dive speed to 800 ft./sec. Continued guidance down to 20,000 ft. (Radar horizon), when the streamlined bomb(s) are released and the aircraft is broken up.

The launching site was required to provide a clear 'avenue' of a 60ft base and 180ft long, to allow climb to a height of 50ft. All the equipment, including stores required, was to be readily mobile, being carried on trailers towed by tractors. The compressed air for the catapult was stored in separate reservoirs, which could be charged continuously. Rapid loading was ensured by an extension of the catapult which permitted preloading. The machine was to be launched at an angle of 25° to the horizontal, and with 30g initial acceleration, reach a speed of 250ft/sec after a run of 35ft. After launch, the flight path elevation decreased as the aircraft accelerated, with locked elevators. The elevators were freed 12 seconds after launch, and actuated by a piston that was controlled by measured dynamic pressure. The aircraft then climbed at a constant indicated airspeed (IAS) to 50,000ft in the first 100 miles of flight. Guidance during this period was by Magnetic Fluxgate Compass, the remainder using the 'TRAMP' system, which interrogates two ground beacons, such as the Eureka highly mobile beacon. The system was capable of guiding a large number of missiles simultaneously and thus meet the requirement of batches of up to 100 missiles being launched against a target. With hindsight, the development programme's anticipated eighteen months' completion was grossly optimistic.

Red Rapier's SP2 design shows the main wing made by seam-welding six steel channel box spars to a preformed steel skin. The only ribs were used as fuel tank ends. The wing tips and ailerons were of light alloy construction, to permit magnetic guidance (the compass being housed in the starboard wing tip).

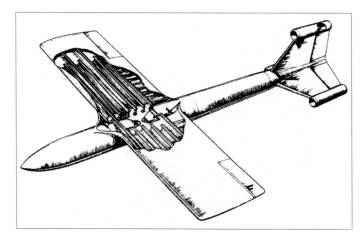

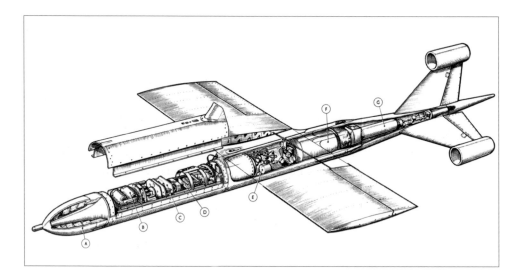

Left: Fig.2.1 This depicts the General Arrangement and some internal details of the SP2. The fuselage[4] (and similarly the tail unit) was constructed of a welded steel tube with frames and crate guides welded in place.

Below: Fig.2.2. This shows a cut-away drawing of the ⅓-scale recoverable model.[4]

Rapid launching sequences were made possible by preloading missiles from an extension of the catapult launcher. The engines would be run up to the cruise design speed, taking over propulsion totally once the missile left the launcher. See Fig.2.5, Diagram of mobile launch ramp with the flying bomb in position. Also see Fig.2.6, Gantry and support structure for the launch ramp.

Trials with ⅓-scale (Type 711) models were a necessary precursor to the building and flight testing of full scale (Type 715) Red Rapiers. These were carried under and released from B29 Washington aircraft, flying over Woomera in Australia.

As shown, the models carrying data recorders were designed for recovery and to be reused after trials, allowing for a full trials programme with only twelve models.

B-29 Washington aircraft were already in RAF service, as a stopgap before availability of either the V-bombers, or of Red Rapier itself. Three of these aircraft were allocated to Vickers Armstrongs, two for Blue Boar trials in Australia (one based at Wisley in England); one (WW353) in Australia was also used for trials with the ⅓-scale models

Fig.2.3 Photograph
of Red Rapier
⅓-scale model (Type
711) carried under
the B-29 Washington
aircraft over
Woomera.[2]

of Red Rapier over Woomera. After numerous modifications including removal of the aircrafts' gun turrets and the installation of the necessary power supplies electronics, and other trials-related equipment, this aircraft was capable of carrying these Type 711 models under the rear bomb bay, for release between 8,000ft to 30,000ft at 180 to 200kts. Trials were designed for measurement of its aerodynamic characteristics and for development of the Mk. II and Mk. III autopilot control systems. The forward bomb bay was reserved for Blue Boar trials.

In the year August 1953 to August 1954, some twelve drops were made from the B-29 Washington at altitudes of around 30,000ft over Woomera, with some of the models being repeatedly recovered, enabling up to five flights of the one model.

The recovery method (similar to that we developed for Blue Boar) and the sequence of its operation following the aerodynamic and other tests for which they were required, were in themselves a major design and development task. The sequence is summarised in Fig.2.4. on the following page:

The missile carrying forward and rearward cameras was typically released at 8,000ft altitude, for testing the recovery system; 9 seconds after release, its Guide Surface Parachute retaining bolt was detonated, deploying at Stage 3, prior to breaking the model into its several sections for recovery by a number of parachutes.

The nose end deployed the main parachute and its ballast weight was blown off, exposing a spike that enabled the section to land softly enough for recovery and re-use. Each section was designed to land at no more than 50ft/sec. The parachutes were designed and made by the GQ Parachute Co. in Woking.

Project Manager Eric Wightman oversaw the trial drops at Woomera, and requested a GSAP camera installation to record the descent. In Weybridge, his engineer, Chuck Fry, made a special mounting, designed to shear away from the Red Rapier model on impact and to be thrown clear by springs.

After some weeks, an irregularly shaped parcel arrived for Chuck, which proved to be a totally flattened GSAP camera. Since the camera was on free loan from the RAE at Farnborough, with a straight face he returned it to RAE stores, who accepted it without comment!

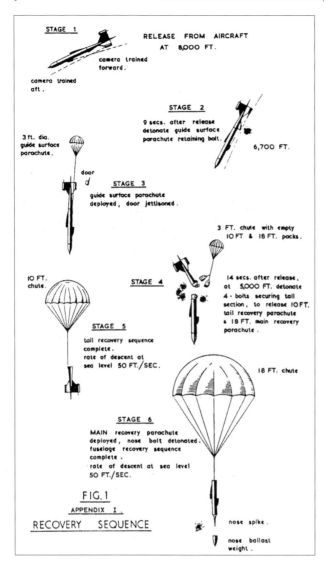

STAGE 1

RELEASE FROM AIRCRAFT
AT 8,000 FT.

camera trained
forward.

camera trained
aft.

STAGE 2

9 secs. after release
detonate guide surface
parachute retaining bolt.

6,700 FT.

3 ft. dia.
guide surface
parachute.

door

STAGE 3

guide surface parachute
deployed, door jettisoned.

3 FT. chute with empty
10 FT & 18 FT. packs.

10 FT.
chute.

STAGE 4

14 secs. after release,
at 5,000 FT. detonate
4 - bolts securing tail
section, to release 10 FT.
tail recovery parachute
& 18 FT. main recovery
parachute.

STAGE 5

tail recovery sequence
complete.
rate of descent at
sea level 50 FT./SEC.

18 FT. chute

STAGE 6

MAIN recovery parachute
deployed, nose bolt detonated.
fuselage recovery sequence
complete.
rate of descent at sea level
50 FT./SEC.

FIG. 1

APPENDIX I.

RECOVERY SEQUENCE

nose spike.

nose ballast
weight.

Left: Fig.2.4. Red Rapier ⅓-scale model recovery sequence.[2]

Below: Fig.2.5 Red Rapier Mobile Catapult Launcher, with missile shown loaded ready for launching and in the release position, before take off.[58]

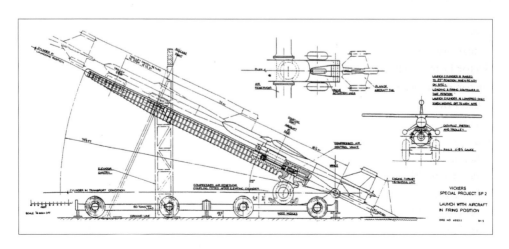

VICKERS
SPECIAL PROJECT SP 2

LAUNCH WITH AIRCRAFT
IN FIRING POSITION

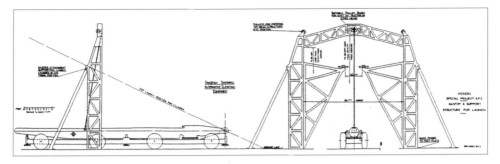

Fig.2.6 Gantry and support structure for Red Rapier Mobile Catapult Launcher.[58]

Following the launching of Red Rapier, the sequence of control commands during the climb, cruise under guidance and the final zoom and bunt manoeuvre into the dive onto the target are shown on a diagram (Fig.2.7), following through stages from launch to strike.

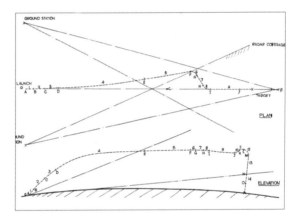

Fig.2.7 Sequence of Control Commands, from launch to strike onto target.[58]

Horizontal manoeuvre for course corrections relative to the Radar coverage is shown in the upper part of the diagram. Vertical plane movements of the initial climb, cruise and the dive onto the target into a vertical trajectory are shown in the lower part of the diagram.

Sectors A to D represent initial unguided flight from launch to flight altitude reaching near horizontal.

Sector D to E represents flight with magnetic guidance.

Sector E represents arrival into Radar cover and switching on Radar equipment, which takes over at F.

Sectors F to J represent approach to the target and manoeuvring under Radar guidance.

Point J is where the missile commences its upward zoom to reduce speed and to gain height.

Sectors J to N represent the bunt into vertical dive and guidance down to the Radar Horizon.

Sector N to O represents the period under gyro stabilised guidance, releasing the bomb at Point O.

Guidance and Control of Red Rapier in these early days of the October 1951 Vickers design report was diagrammatically depicted with the indicated central 'brain' that received guidance inputs from the magnetic compass element and from the Radar guidance element. The 'brain' provided outputs to the gyro-stabilised autopilot, which controlled the pitch, yaw and roll axes via the missile's elevators, rudder and ailerons. The 'brain' also gave the commands for the zoom and bunt manoeuvre for entering the dive over the target, and it provided appropriately timed commands to cut the engines, detach the wings and release the warhead.

The gyroscopes in the autopilot are erected to the vertical, once the missile is flying along a horizontal trajectory at cruising altitude. Turns before Radar guidance are made without banking. Corrections demanded by Radar guidance are made with banked turns, with the gyro-erection system and the dynamic pressure control of elevators turned off. After a correction turn has been followed for a fixed time, magnetic guidance is used during the straight sector toward a final turn onto the correct track, now with gyro-erection and dynamic pressure elevator control turned on again. The further turn at Point H reverts the system to banked turn and then at Point I on the correct track, turns remain flat and the gyros are accurately erected, to ensure correct spatial references during the bunt and final dive manoeuvres.

The block diagram in Fig.2.8 depicts this arrangement, showing the autopilot two gyroscopes mounted on a platform (table) that was mechanically steerable about the

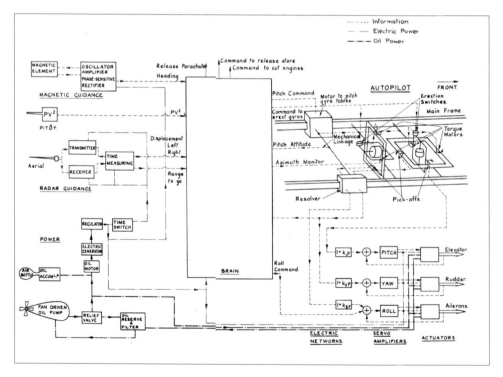

Fig.2.8 Block diagram of the system 'brain' connecting attitude reference to flight controls.[58]

pitch axis. The gyro-erection commands and switches shown were used to initiate and to execute the erection of the gyros and again to free them, during the different phases of manoeuvring under guidance already mentioned. They also came into play for the zoom up and bunt manoeuvre into the vertical dive towards the target. Because of the greater than 90° range of pitching angles from climb and over the bunt manoeuvre, the platform carrying the gyros had to be moved by over 90° to retain its horizontal surface, when the gyros could maintain their proper spatial references without toppling. The mechanical linkage for moving the platform is shown in this block diagram.

In the absence of externally independent spatial references, the accuracy with which the gyros could be erected with respect to the vertical must come into question, since control during the vertical dive was dependent on this accuracy. It appears that the stability and accuracy of horizontal flight and the wings remaining level after reaching cruise altitude must have been assumed to a be good enough spatial reference to which to erect the gyros. Accuracy was assisted by gyro drift effects being minimised during the short duration of the manoeuvre.

Alan Thurley of the Special Projects (GW) Trials Section in Weybridge was involved with much of the guidance planning, the bunt manoeuvre and the following vertical dive trajectory towards the target. Naturally, the number of computations required exceeded what could reasonably be achieved with a slide rule so without today's computers, and the 'Hen Coop' was brought in to help with their mechanical calculators. Computation of such trajectories was, of necessity, complicated, combining the variables related to guidance signals, response of the missile's autopilot and its control elevators, then the aerodynamic effect of the missile's trajectory. The mathematical equations for such work were mostly based on approximations for parameters that were assumed to be roughly constant over short time periods, typically one half second. The accuracy and effectiveness or the equations could not be verified until these equations were put to the test by computing many iterations reaching well into a trajectory.

While the Hen Coop girls could rapidly follow the equations and input them into the calculators, producing rafts of figures for subsequent plotting onto graph paper, they did not understand the equations themselves. Consequently, when things went wrong, the figures they were producing did not mean very much to them. Alan would check the figures from time to time and while the mathematics were clearly still being fine-tuned, he was offered several pages of trajectory results that looked all too strange. On more careful analysis, he found that the missile's elevator angle demanding the manoeuvre – normally in the region of zero, to plus or minus the limiting angles of the control mechanism's 20° – was being computed, unnoticed, without hesitation, interruption or reporting – as 526°, one and a half times round the circle! One big laugh for the engineers and a lot more machine calculations after the equations were further modified.

Originating with the Government's Telecommunications Research Establishment (TRE), later the Radar Research Establishment (RRE) at Defford and Malvern in Worcestershire, the TRAMP guidance system and the airborne electronic equipment was being developed by Dr E.A.G. (Teddy) Hall and his team in Weybridge. At the same time, structural tests of the full-scale Red Rapier fuselage and the assembly for carrying five 1,000lb-bombs were proceeding in the Aircraft Division's Mechanical Test Department, along with the Launching Ramp.

For the full-scale launching trials and flight trials slated for 1955, initially Gosling Rockets or Cordite charges were considered for providing launch acceleration, until the compressed air launcher shown in Fig.2.5 was available.

Functioning of the compressed air launcher was based on German experience with their wartime V-1 launcher, improved by development at the RAE. The engineering details arising from this involved a cylinder of launcher length, slotted along its top surface. A piston whose 'tongue' protruded through the slot carried a wheeled trolley, on which the aircraft was mounted. A launch bracket allows only forward freedom for the missile for release, at the end of the launch sequence. A steel ribbon 1¾in wide by 5ft 16in is secured inside the upper surface of the cylinder at the base (firing) end. This ribbon is fed through the piston over rollers, to lie against the bottom surface of the whole cylinder length. As the piston moves forward under 3,000psi air pressure during launch, the ribbon is fed through the piston's rollers to the top surface of the cylinder, where the air pressure forces the ribbon to seal off the slot and maintain the launching forces behind the piston as it moves forward.

After Red Rapier's three Soar engines' thrust has been confirmed by a thrust gauge, firing is initiated by rearward movement of a Firing Valve, when 3,000psi air pressure is applied to accelerate the piston and the aircraft up the 35ft-long ramp. On reaching the 250ft/sec launch speed at the end of the ramp, the piston's 'prodder' at its front end penetrates a replaceable diaphragm in a water tank at the head of the launcher. The prodder, with its tapered section, is resisted by the water, which can only escape as a spray, until the thickened root of the prodder closes tightly into the diaphragm frame and brings the piston and trolley to a halt. At this point, the compressed air behind the piston is released and deflected downwards, where it cannot impinge on the tail of the aircraft.

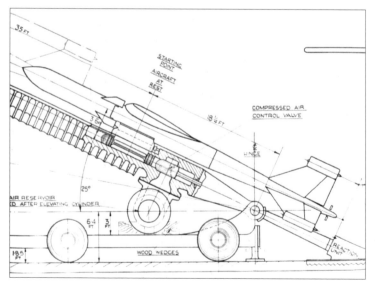

Fig.2.9 Detail from Fig.2.5, showing the piston that carries the missile to launching speed.[58]

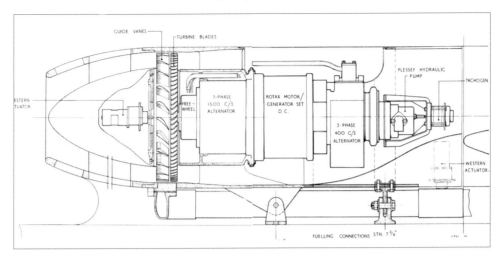

Fig.2.10 Ram Air Turbine for full-scale Red Rapier (replacing earlier tail end 'windmill').[59]

The water is effectively re-circulated for use in the next launch, and the piston and trolley are hauled down to the start position, ready for the next missile to be loaded by a special rapid loader.

As the aircraft leaves the launcher, its own engines' thrust maintains acceleration and powers it throughout the remainder of its flight. While electrical power is shown on these drawings as being provided by a 'windmill' at the tail, later developments used a ram air turbine to provide both electrical and hydraulic power.

The full-scale tests vehicle (Figs 2.11 and 2.12) was designed to accomplish the complete mission including launch, cruise climb, guidance to the target and the final zoom climb and bunt into the vertical bombing dive onto the target. Except for the small marker bomb in place of the 5,000lb warhead and the recovery system with nose spike for its final 'landing', the main difference was that launching power was provided by two Gosling rocket motors that were jettisoned after burnout. Following the twelve recoverable ⅓-scale models dropped from the Washington for basic aerodynamic and autopilot trials, twelve such full-scale test vehicles were designed to be reused. As with operational bunt and dive manoeuvres, following a guidance signal, the engines are stopped and the guide surface parachute is deployed. At 20,000ft, the marker bomb is released and following that, the dummy warhead and the wings are jettisoned. As the main portion of the fuselage nears the ground, the main recovery parachute is released from its stowage in the tail cylinder. A hydraulic shock absorber assists the main recovery spike to decelerate the mass smoothly on striking the ground. The recovery sequence can be initiated by barometric overrides, in the event of the missile dropping below its programmed flight path.

The latter 'chute is also used in operational bombing dives, to limit the descent speed to no more than 800ft/sec. The lower end of the dive over the target is shown in Fig.2.13, omitting the altitude range between 46,000ft and about 25,000ft. In this diagram, the operational 5,000lb warhead is shown, with its stabilising fins. The cluster warhead of five 1,000lb bombs are depicted later in this chapter.[58]

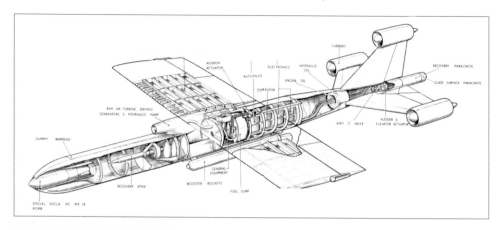

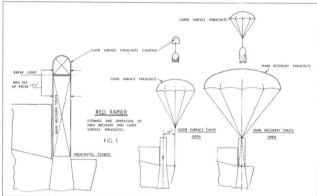

Above: Fig.2.11 Full-scale test vehicle with 500lb marker bomb.[59]

Left: Fig.2.12 Recovery employing small guide surface parachute, which later deploys the main parachute.[59]

The 9ft-diameter guide surface 'chute opened at 50,000ft and 800ft/sec. aircraft speed slowing the aircraft weighing 11,700lb. Its deployment rate being restricted by a device to control its rate of opening, the snatch load was thereby kept down to 13,000lb. Applied throughout the vertical descent under continuing guidance, till the engines were destroyed and wings were jettisoned, speed was kept to the maximum of 800ft/sec. – or Mach 0.85.[60]

For trials, the main 64ft diameter recovery parachute, weighing 70lb including lines, was stowed 'behind' the guide surface 'chute within the tail tube diameter of 12½in occupying 40in in length (Fig.2.12). It was designed to open at 5,000ft altitude when speed had fallen to 250 ft/sec, and to bring the remaining 4,000lb-weight main fuselage down on its hydraulically cushioned spike at 40ft/sec.[60]

TRAMP Radio Guidance of Red Rapier[61]

In the days of thermionic valves and before transistors or, indeed, accurate Inertial Guidance, let alone GPS satellite navigation fixing, the guidance of Red Rapier over 400nm to bomb a target with the desired accuracy requiring 50 per cent of hits to be within 100 yards was no mean ambition. Jamming was also to be avoided to the greatest extent possible, and the Operational Requirement demanded the capability to attack at

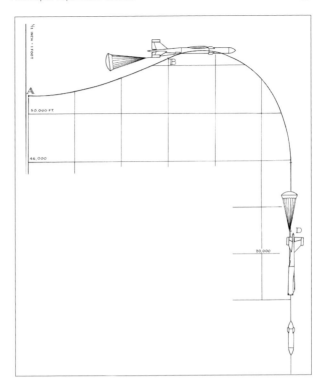

Fig.2.13 The zoom climb and bunt manoeuvre initiation, with engines being cut and guide surface parachute deployed.[58]

least five targets simultaneously in all weather conditions and to control up to 100 such expendable bombers. Determination of 'fall of shot' was another desirable outcome. Attacking industrial targets and troop concentrations, Red Rapier would be subject to attack by ground defences, so as high a handling rate as possible was required. All this had to be achieved at the lowest possible cost, manufacturing between 500 and 5,000 missiles annually.

The January 1952 referenced technical note[61] by Dr E.A.J. (Teddy) Hall followed visits to, and discussions with, the Telecommunications Research Establishment (TRE) at Malvern, Worcs., which later became the Royal Radar Establishment (RRE). In 1951, Radar was still better known as Radio Location and Radio Direction Finding (RDF), and was gradually transmuting into the new term RADio Direction And Range, or RADAR. Vickers attended a meeting at TRE in March 1951, at which films relating RDF's evolution into Radar and Basic Radio Location were shown. More specifically related to the Red Rapier project, films were shown relating to ground-based beam systems, whose paths from multiple ground stations as measured by pulse travel times established intersecting lines on a map carried by aircraft. Such maps were inscribed with the generally hyperbolic patterns of lines, whose intersections defined the aircraft's position. 'Gee' was one such system (as used on our trials Canberras). Other variations of the principle developed for the RAF included 'H' and 'Oboe'. Following that meeting, H.R. Johnson of TRE was motivated to write to Eddie Smyth at Vickers, making clear that the 50 yards positioning accuracy discussed for Red Rapier during guidance by such means was not a certainty, but might be achieved during development.

As described earlier, initial guidance prior to arriving within the range and height coverage of the proposed ground-based Radar guidance systems, Red Rapier followed magnetic guidance depending on a Flux Gate compass mounted in its wing tip, assisted by a gyro-stabilised spatial reference. The choice of Radar system was influenced by the fact that with 'H', the aircraft interrogates two ground station beacon transponders and calculates its position. This requires considerable computing capability within the aircraft. The alternative Oboe employed similar beams and time measurements, employing beacon transponders carried in the aircraft. Here, the aircraft's position was computed at the ground stations – and this would then need to be transmitted to the aircraft. This system requires the ranges from both stations to be available at one place and also adds a need for a centrimetric radio link between the ground stations. This would come with unwanted operational limitations, as well as technical difficulties in transmitting the required manoeuvring demands to the aircraft.

The TRAMP system chosen was a compromise between 'H' and Oboe, typically employing two ground stations relative to which the target's position is precisely known. In this, a train of timing pulses is initiated from the ground and is then finally assembled in the aircraft. Somewhat complicated to illustrate, the time plot Fig.2.14 shows a Marker Pulse 'a', sent from a ground transmitter and received by a responder beacon in the aircraft and then returned as pulse 'b' to the ground. This pulse arrives at a time proportional to twice the distance of the aircraft from the ground station 'r'. On receipt of the 'b' pulse, a 'c' pulse is generated and a pulse 'd' is also generated on the ground, lagging the Marker Pulse 'a', by a time proportional to twice the target range 'R', known from maps. This involves approximations, which are close enough in the circumstances of Red Rapier flying at its constant cruising height. The time difference between arrival of the 'b' pulse at the ground station (to generate 'c') and the generation of the 'd' pulse is proportional to twice the distance of the aircraft from the target range arc. This is called 'residual range'. If the pulses 'c' and 'd' are immediately sent to the aircraft, suitable circuits can calculate its range from the target ΔR_A. Employing two ground stations (with different pulse recurrence frequencies or PRFs), the aircraft can compute its explicit position at the intersection of the two residual range arcs ΔR_A and ΔR_B. Fig.2.15 shows the geometry of this target location in plan.

The radio frequencies to be used were in the 200MHz range with a 4MHz bandwidth, employing Rebecca Mk.4 transmitters and receivers. The guidance electronic circuits dealt with Pulse generation, allowing sixty-four different codes, pulse decoding and the Tapped Delay Line (with eight taps spaced at the pulse spacing determined by the PRF), enabling all pulses to appear at different points simultaneously. The subject of Magnetostriction Delay Lines appears to be relevant to this and was discussed in a report of February 1954.[65] Possibly for greater flexibility and accuracy, this consisted of a mechanical nickel wire in which mechanical stresses are induced, interacting with input coils and transducers. Such a delay line for use in the aircraft needs a length of 10ft, which appeared only to be possible with a curved line, resulting in pulse shapes being affected. The highly technical nature of this subject goes beyond our current scope.

The above diagrams only represent the outlines of the overall electronic design of the system, further detail being recorded in the report describing the workings of the Residual Range Demodulator and other essential parts of the system. These enumerate

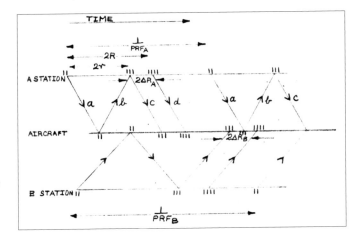

Fig.2.14 TRAMP guidance pulses time chart with PRF's for Ground Stations A and B.[61]

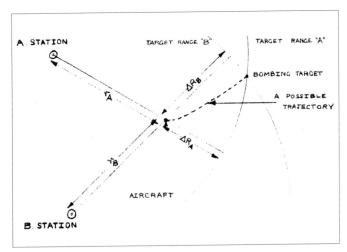

Fig.2.15 TRAMP guidance target triangulation in plan, showing ranges from Ground Stations.[61]

the number of valves required for each function and the total numbers of valves requiring power and heat dissipation.

The accuracy of TRAMP guidance seems to have been considerably dependent on the accurate timing of pulses controlled by the Tapped Delay Line. This was sufficiently critical for special consideration of any effects on it, of vibration and accelerations during the flight regime. Besides that, with active guidance and control over the flight distance and during the dive onto target down to 20,000ft, the expected accuracy of bomb release and direction was expected to be consistent with the desired probability of hitting close to the target. The effects of winds during the free-fall period would add dispersion, possibly doubling the initial 100 yards 50 per cent miss distance requirement (later changed to 250 yards anyway). The cluster of five 1,000lb bombs with its own dispersion method as shown in Fig.2.17 was intended to permit straddling of appropriate targets, which may not require the penetration of a 5,000lb warhead. A Policy Meeting at MOS in April 1953[63] altered the Primary Load to ten VT fuzed Mk.9 500lb bombs and wind tunnel tests were done on cluster bomb elements as late as November 1954. Provision was also to be made for alternative incendiary bomb warheads.

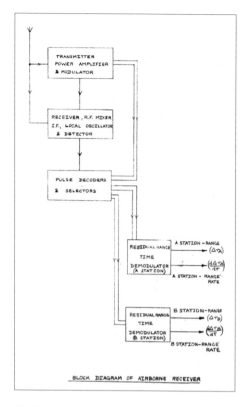

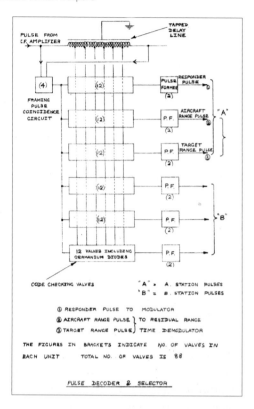

Fig.2.16 a and b Diagrams representing the main system elements and the critical Pulse Decoder & Selector.[61]

Fig.2.17 a and b Cluster dispersal mechanism.[62]

In June 1953, further aerodynamic estimates were made for a High Capacity HE bomb weighing 6,000lb, to compare the drag and thus the effect of 100ft/sec. side winds on accuracy. A 'boat tail' at the end of the bomb reduced drag (and the resulting wind effect) – such that the drag without it was 70 per cent higher. Such detail combining guidance design with warhead design brought necessary refinements to the potential of Red Rapier.

Automatic evasive action against enemy ground fire added a further requirement in the Operational Requirement for Red Rapier's trajectory towards the target. This projected guidance continuing in the presence of a corkscrew-like manoeuvre alternating 1g left and right turns. This was a desirable facility to be provided, so long as it did not adversely affect the overall performance and the cost of what was required to be a cheap and easily manufactured mass-attack weapon system. Armour plating was required to protect the guidance equipment against anti-aircraft fire, and the thickness requested by the MOS led to concern about its 400lb addition to Red Rapier's weight.[64]

Development of the ground station equipment in conjunction with TRE and the airborne transponder system was a major effort in Teddy Hall's department at Vickers, with detailed design brought to an advanced stage. At a meeting on 27 June 1952,[66] the company confirmed its ability to mass produce Red Rapier along design lines thus far established, with the choice of TRAMP guidance (referred to there as 'feed back Oboe'). In Stage A, the completion of two Ground Stations by TRE was shortly due, and airborne equipment by the year's end, for installation in a Vickers Valetta aircraft, for flight trials to establish and confirm the principles of TRAMP. Two further sets of 'breadboard' equipment destined for early full-scale Red Rapiers were to be ready. In Stage B, covering the effort required to build twelve full-scale prototype aircraft for launch by Vickers, three pairs of Ground Station beacons were proposed for contracting out to Mssrs Murphy in collaboration with Vickers and TRE. Furthermore, fifty sets of airborne equipment were being commissioned, based on the two 'breadboard' units flown in the Valetta trials. Besides producing the autopilots required for the trials, Vickers was taking over responsibility for the siting and operation of the Ground Stations, with help and advice from TRE.

All this privately funded work continued to await Ministry of Supply contract cover, eventually promised in early 1953, but only provided in the August. This was after more than 2½ years, during which time the MOS had kept Vickers on a short rein with regard to specification details and collaboration with TRE, the RAE and other parties.

The building of the desired twelve full-scale Red Rapiers (Type 715) and its trials programme was to follow the ⅓-scale tests into 1955, with Woomera considering the preparation of a new 400nm region for Red Rapier on the range. In March 1954, the UK Ministry of Supply office in Melbourne wrote to the Controller of Aircraft in London,[67] questioning the MOS resolve as to proceeding with Red Rapier, in view of Vickers' pressure to 'get on with it' and the considerable investment required by the Australian Department of Supply.

His fears were evidently justified, because on 30 September 1954, the Ministry of Supply cancelled Red Rapier altogether. It took until September 1957 before the total to be paid under the separate £450,000 guidance contract of October 1953 was agreed, truncated to £372,000.

Why, after so much investment and progress, should this all go to waste?

The Government's statement indicated that there was no longer a requirement for a flying bomb. A complete change in Government policy had taken place, replacing the ground-launched flying-bomb concept with manned bombers and stand off weapons

(Blue Steel launched from Vulcan and Victor bombers). This would complement the 'ultimate' deterrent of the ballistic missile with a nuclear warhead. After a national expenditure of nearly £2 million,[2] of which the engine development accounted for over 50 per cent (in the order of £60–80 million at 2004 prices), the project's design and manufacturing teams were disbanded. Fortunately, as Blue Boar was also being cancelled, Red Dean was building up to require more and more people at Vickers.

Chapter 3

BLUE BOAR GUIDED GLIDING BOMB

The gross inaccuracy of bombing during the Second World War was well documented by both sides. Consequently, as early as 1946, the Air Staff issued a requirement regarding the 'Control of Bombs'[6] which led in November 1947 to a development proposal for a controlled Bomb by R. Smelt,[7] of the Royal Aircraft Establishment at Farnborough. RAE was the principal design authority and medium for Guided Weapons, and in March 1949, RAE Tech Note No.GW 35[8] began to illustrate a design for guided bombs under the name of Blue Boar. Concurrently, Barnes Wallis of (among other leading edge designs) Bouncing Bomb, 'Tall Boy' and 'Grandslam' fame, at Vickers Armstrongs, began studies on Blue Boar at Brooklands in Weybridge.[1] Bonser's report after initial studies concluded that guided 5,000lb and 10,000lb bombs interchangeable with conventional stores could be developed. These would manoeuvre with accelerations of 3.0 to 3.5g at sea level, and could carry a somewhat reduced weight of High Explosive (HE) than conventional stores, but, of course, with greater accuracy. A 1,000lb Blue Boar would be less economical, but could be used as a 'practice bomb'. Consideration was also given to a 'Special Blue Boar' of up to 20,000lb weight, of considerably lesser HE content than conventional stores of the same size – but simpler to control than multiple bombs amounting to that weight in a single aircraft. Guidance would be by television, but the largest versions could use H2S Radar with blind bombing capability, if the H2S could be made to work in the timescale.

Designed principally as 5,000lb and 10,000lb bombs for accurate bombing from 50,000ft, Blue Boar would be carried in the bomb bays of the V-Bombers (Valiant, Victor and Vulcan), flying close to the speed of sound (up to Mach 0.87).

Four stubby, rectangular wings, with trailing rear-control surfaces in two planes at 90° to each other, provided lift for its roll stabilised transonic 40° glide and for lateral control. In order to fit two 10,000lb, or four 5,000lb, or one 10,000lb and two 5,000lb bombs into the V-Bombers' bomb bays, the wings were stowed inside the bomb's cylindrical bodies. They would then 'flip out' to their respectively 62in and 78in spans once they had cleared the aircraft, immediately after release. The specification required Blue Boar to achieve a (50 per cent probability) miss distance of 100 yards, allowing a 6 second-long guidance period after breaking cloud at no lower than 10,000ft. For night-time bombing, a second (5,000lb) Blue Boar filled with flares would be dropped 3 seconds after the first HE bomb and glide parallel and above it, in such that the light from the flares would always be from above the bomb's nose-carried TV guidance system looking down at the target. The gyroscopically stabilised TV picture would be transmitted via an antenna pointing back up to the bomber, and the bomb aimer would point the camera at the target by transmitted control signals via the bomber's lock-follow antenna. The pointing demands would generate guidance signals that would then input manoeuvre signals to the autopilot, to steer the bomb. The 6-second period after breaking cloud was deemed sufficient for the bomb aimer to recognise the target and steer Blue Boar onto it. Blind bombing was envisaged for later development, employing H2S ground mapping Radar.

The Development Programme

This required a large proportion of flight trials for proving, as well as for operational verification to be conducted in Australia, and for Vickers to establish a trials organisation in South Australia utilising the facilities of the Woomera Rocket Range. There, besides large tracts being unpopulated, clear weather up to 50,000ft for Kinetheodolite photography could be guaranteed year round. The Vickers Australian trials team was established by Jack Redpath, who moved out to Adelaide, and for the regular ferrying of contractors' engineers and other personnel, the RAF ran a weekly run from Lyneham in Wiltshire to Edinburgh Field near Adelaide, using Handley Page Hastings transports. These Second World War-era aircraft flew at 200mph and 10,000ft altitude, for a noisy and vibration-prone nine days' grind, stopping overnight at RAF bases in Tripoli, Habbaniya near Baghdad, Mauripur near Karachi, Negombo near Colombo, Singapore, with an extra night for rest, then Djakarta, with a night in Darwin en route. Vickers engineers' contract terms for spells in Australia provided for weekly staff to be paid the grand sum of £2 12s 6d per day, and to be insured for £2,000 against death (other than as a fare-paying passenger!). Home leave was provided after three years at two days per month served. In the event, a number of engineers served shorter periods, down to one year.

One of the earliest trial needs highlighted by the Development Programme was to test the flip-out wing design on a 5,000lb bomb. This was executed at the Imber range, when dropped from a Lincoln bomber and successfully demonstrated the capability in 1950.

RAE Note No. GW 49 by F.G. Tarrant gives the Provisional Specification of Blue Boar[4] and Mr Tarrant's RAE Tech Note GW 95 of December 1950 specifies The Development Programme for Blue Boar.[5] Fred Tarrant became a familiar figure at Weybridge as the Ministry of Supply's project officer for Blue Boar.

The latter report indicates Vickers as the prime contractor, with EMI Engineering Development Ltd creating and providing the TV Guidance System; and Smiths Aircraft Instruments developing and providing the autopilot and control system. Hydraulics were provided by British Messier Ltd.

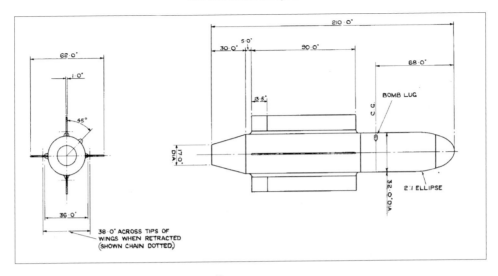

Fig.3.1 Drawing from RAE T.N. GW 166.[10]

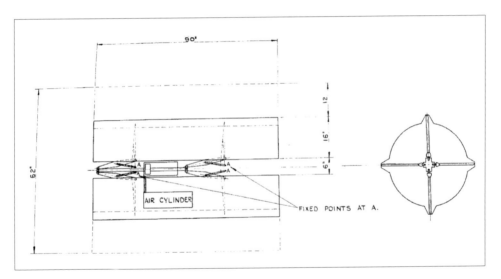

Fig.3.2 From RAE T.N. 141, Blue Boar wing flip-out mechanism.[10]

The programme listed a number of stages, employing test vehicles with BTV designations:

BTV1   To fly at M0.7 to M1.15. Ground launched by rocket booster up to M1.3 at Larkhill, ½-scale models of the 1,000lb 'ractice bomb', to determine the aerodynamic derivatives and control characteristics required for the larger missiles.

BTV2   Same size as BTV1, 1,000lb test vehicle for environment-generated vibration measurements. Ground launched by the RAE RTV booster and also air launched, using a Canberra from A&AEE at Boscombe Down, Wilts. These rounds also had to measure control surface hinge moments and the power generated by an air turbine.

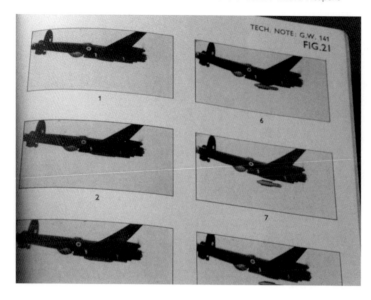

Fig.3.3. BTV11 5,000 lb. Flip-out wing round dropped from and RAF Lincoln over Salisbury Plain.

BTV3   Same size as BTV2 but roll stabilised, to develop the BTV4 system. Six rounds to be ground launched and six air launched by a Canberra bomber at M0.8 and 45,000ft altitude over Aberporth during the latter half of 1951. Radio Telemetry would be used for collecting test information.

BTV4   For air dropping as BTV3, roll stabilised but with the elevators fixed to achieve an approximately 40° glide angle for the final portion of the trajectory from up to 50,000ft. These air drops had a fifteen miles radius safety trace, so initially it was planned to conduct these trials entirely in Australia. As the programme proceeded, drops were also made at Aberporth. These rounds were designed to carry a television camera and 300MHz transmitter to explore picture quality, with the receiver at this stage being located at the ground station.

BTV5   These rounds were initially for testing control by the Autopilot and to achieve the required accuracy of the 40° glide path. Later trials would induce manoeuvres by ground-controlled command signals to the autopilot enabling trials to commence with the 300 MHz television equipment tested in BTV4. This test vehicle would function as a controlled Blue Boar, with the exception that guidance would be provided from a ground station.

BTV10 5,000lb bombs for air carry trials to test equipment functioning were initially carried in the bomb bay of a B-29 Washington based at Wisley. Even in this large aircraft, fixed-wing models had to be carried rotated 45° from their normal fight orientation, placing the wings in an 'X' configuration, and still they protruded beneath the aircraft. (See Fig.8). Operational Bomb test drops in Australia were planned from Valiant bombers, being the only available aircraft with the necessary high altitude and speed performance capable of carrying this large weapon in its bomb bay, together with the supporting electronic equipment. Initial trials would be with wings in a fixed position, before testing BTV11 flip-out winged rounds.

BTB12 10,000lb Operational Bomb tests could only be carried out with functioning flip-out wings, since no aircraft was large enough to accommodate the 78in wing span. After initial flip-out wing trial drops from a Lincoln at Aberporth, control trials were planned using Valiant bombers in Australia.

Television Equipment tests early in the programme required a Valetta aircraft as a flying laboratory.

Fuze, warhead and bomb carriers were not part of the Vickers design, since the Ministry's Directorate of Air Armaments was already developing similar items that could be adapted for Blue Boar. Similarly, a special bomb sight suitable for the longer gliding trajectory were required for adaptation from that for conventional free falling bombs.

Trials techniques and tribulations

In early 1952, when I arrived in the Trials Section, ¼-scale BTV1 Blue Boar models were being flight tested using rocket boosters fired at the Imber and Larkhill ranges on Salisbury Plain. For aerodynamic trials employing simple 'rounds' with fixed control surfaces, information was obtained by using a combination of short-firing pyrotechnic 'bonkers', giving the round a sharp lateral impulse, and accelerometers measuring the aerodynamic forces of lift in three axes and drag. As earlier indicated, scratch recording accelerometers were used, sometimes in conjunction with radio telemetry – and by Kinetheodolite photography from the range's ground stations. BTV 2 test vehicles were also being dropped over the Aberporth range on Cardigan Bay.

In order to keep test vehicles from landing outside the range boundaries, a Safety Trace was produced for each kind of trial, checking the trajectory and impact point for every possible failure mode. To shorten flight trajectories after the essence of a trial was completed, the test vehicles were broken into two pieces by a Cordtex explosive charge set off by a timer and thus rapidly brought to earth. The slower impact following break-up enabled missile-borne instruments to be recovered in good enough condition for analysis of the data. The safety trace naturally had to take into account the possibility of break-up failing to occur.

Before any rocket firing or air drop, trials engineers, assisted by technicians from the laboratories in the Pits, had to check all explosive igniter circuits for rocket motors, bonkers and break-up units with considerable care for their own safety, as well as all functioning elements of the test vehicles. They participated in the mechanics of rocket launches and liased with the RAE Range personnel who operated the Kinetheodolites and operated radio receivers and telemetry recording equipment. If all this worked according to plan, the trials engineer could later analyse the information back in Weybridge.

Recovery Systems were put into development, to enable the re-use of expensive test vehicles and these occupied a considerable part of the design and trials effort. Under Mike Still, a number of ingenious recovery systems were designed for the 1,000lb-sized test vehicles, employing various combinations of dive brakes and parachutes or combinations of them. These were designed to deploy at critical heights, and a large ballast weight would be blown off, before a main recovery parachute would deploy, before the remainder of the missile would stick into the ground on a spike, whose shape was designed to retard it at a constant 'g' with the minimum of shock. Requiring the same tolerance to high altitude, vibrations and high 'g' manoeuvres as an operational missile, the difficulties experienced in creating a reliable recovery system became comparable with the main development problems – and the recovery process probably never really achieved its cost-saving aim.

Considerable amusement accompanied one trial employing the dive brake system over the Imber Range, with Mac flying in Canberra WD935 to drop the recovery test vehicle from 37,000ft. After clearing the bomb bay, firstly a small parachute was deployed to start the recovery sequence, followed by the opening of the dive brakes, and after sufficient deceleration towards Salisbury Plain, the large nose ballast weight was to be jettisoned before deployment of the main troika of recovery parachutes. The test vehicle's travels through the spectrum of wind speeds and directions existing in the 37,000ft of sky was difficult to predict with accuracy, since the path of the bomb had to be estimated from last-minute meteorological data obtained by weather balloons released from the range. These factors had little effect on a normal, solid free falling bomb. But with parachutes and dive brakes slowing the rate of fall and catching whatever winds happened to blow on its way down, caused the trajectory to follow a complicated path. Using the Safety Trace I had calculated, allowing for the possible failures that may occur, I had to use the meteorological data, and while Mac was flying overhead, I had to calculate the trajectory and decide on the release point such that the bomb should not fall outside the range under any circumstances. Under the pressure of time limited control of the aircraft that also had to be pointing in the right direction at the release point, I worked my slide rule and drew diagrams on graph paper as fast as I could, finally choosing the release point which was advised to the Radar controller. Mac's Canberra was then directed to this point and the bomb was released.

The Kinetheodolites were primed and pointed at the aircraft to follow the bomb's descent, and at the numerous Observation Posts (OPs) around Imber Range, powerful binoculars were aimed towards the same trajectory. They all saw the initial parachute deployment and, after following the bomb down to around 10,000ft, it disappeared from everybody's view. Nobody saw where it landed. We hiked over much of Imber Range for the rest of the day, but there was no sign of our test vehicle, and with colleagues and a few stout spades, I returned the next Sunday for another search. Several more hours of hiking in the summer heat led us to an old disused farm next to the range boundary, and after breaking through the surrounding hedge, we noticed three little parachutes neatly deployed around a small hole in the ground. There was our Blue Boar buried up to the last inch of its length, only the white parachutes revealing its presence. The location was barely 25 yards behind an OP – where an observer had been training his binoculars, looking in the opposite direction.

Salisbury Plain is composed of chalk and digging was not too difficult, until placing a foot closer to the hole centre immediately compressed the loosened chalk into a solid

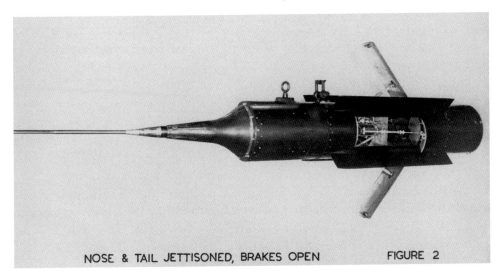

NOSE & TAIL JETTISONED, BRAKES OPEN   FIGURE 2

Above: Fig.3.4 1,000lb recovery test vehicle with wings deployed.[11]

Right: Fig.3.5 Recovered 1,000lb test vehicle as found after impact.[11]

mass once more. It took several hours of careful digging before we could extract the 8ft bomb for inspection. The ballast weight was still attached since the explosive bolts had failed to ignite, hence the failure to recover as planned. Now we could disassemble the bomb so we might recover the instruments on a panel within. These included a gyroscope, accelerometers and an altimeter, all looking in surprisingly good shape.

No glass was broken and the Smiths eight-day clock was still going, but running at least 5 minutes fast. My letter of complaint to Smiths about their clock's timekeeping a week after a 20g landing from 37,000ft was only slightly acerbic. However, this system could work as seen in Fig.3.5 above.

Another recovery system employing 'umbrella dive brakes' was tested on a spectacular rocket sled at the Proof and Experimental Establishment (P&EE) owned by the Atomic Weapons Establishment at Shoeburyness. This was a scale model of the larger dive brakes intended for fitting at the tail ends of 5,000lb test vehicles.

Fig.3.6 Blue Boar 'Umbrella' dive brake test vehicle, on Rocket Sled trolley. [12]

Fig.3.7 Umbrella dive brakes shown open, revealing the six metal brake elements, joined by nylon 'gores' to create the high drag umbrella effect for maximum retardation of the missile to be recovered. [12]

The approximately 400 yard-long rocket sled track used solid fuel rockets to accelerate the trolley and test vehicle up to about 800ft/sec. in a little over half the track's length. The test recovery system was set to deploy at the maximum speed, just before retro rockets fired to stop the trolley before it could run over the end. The force of the retro rockets sent the trolley hurtling back towards the start point again, but now the water scoops dipped into the water channels either side of the track. This brought the trolley, with its test vehicle, to a stop about halfway back along the track, accompanied by two spectacular fountains of water reaching some 100ft into the air. The whole process was completed in about 3 seconds from the first firing. Kinetheodolites places about the track provided cine-film of the whole trial, for later analysis of how the 'Umbrella' dive brakes operated.

Although trials of both recovery systems were successfully completed, the costs and time taken for this development became comparable with the main development programme, and conventional firings and air drops using expendable test vehicles probably overtook the desired money saving recovery methods.

The provision of power supplies and radio telemetry systems which could perform with reliability under the extremes of temperature, altitude, vibration and 'g' forces of rockets and manoeuvres became a major factor in trials. These items had to be designed to the same standards as the missile electronics, batteries and mechanical parts. Before the Transistor, high temperature, sub-miniature thermionic valves were the norm and it was necessary to conduct large amounts of heat out of electronic units, which had to be 'potted' in resins to withstand shocks and vibrations. Likewise for air drops, 'external' power supplies and batteries in the aircraft carrying the weapons had to withstand similarly severe environments, as well as be reliably switched to 'internals' in the missile before it was dropped. Consequently, in the earlier days of test vehicle firings and air drops, as many delays and failures occurred due to power supply, battery and telemetry problems, as due to problems with the missiles under test.

The accent on meticulously detailed design had to become an end in itself and pre-trials functional and environmental testing in the laboratory became of prime importance. Otherwise already expensive trials with expendable vehicles could become excessively wasteful, even considering that Blue Boar was a leading edge development.

To power operational Blue Boar, an air driven turbine was developed, relying on the speed of fall for driving an electrical alternator to supply power at 400Hz and at 1600Hz, and high pressure hydraulics for control actuators. Air turbines were also the object of ½ Scale 1,000lb BTV1 ground-fired trials in January 1952 at Larkhill. Considerable design work was conducted towards creating a suitable turbine 'prime mover' for Blue Boar's power system, with alternatives to air turbines including cordite driven turbines. These were offered (by Rotax), and while considered simpler, their disadvantage was the noxious efflux – particularly if run inside an aircraft's bomb bay.

The 1,000lb 'practice bomb'-sized test vehicles were initially ground launched employing rocket boosters to accelerate them to supersonic speeds appropriate to the terminal gliding speed of Blue Boar. Ongoing high-altitude 'carry over' trials and drops from Wisley-based Canberra bombers were conducted over the Aberporth range at Cardigan Bay. Initially, these were mainly to test the survivability of the electronic power supplies, autopilot and hydraulic actuators in a representative jet bomber environment at altitudes up to 48,000ft. Similarly, a great many trials were conducted at the Woomera Rocket Range in Australia. Here, in addition to the high altitude and low temperature end of the environmental spectrum, the test vehicles also had to perform in the Australian desert at 122°F (50°C) heat at sea level.

A succession of BTV sub-variants used for trials are referred to in Vickers progress reports in 1951 and 1952,[13] and indicate increasingly complex rounds as envisaged in Mr F.G. Tarrant's RAE TN GW. 95.[4] Besides the BTV1 air turbine vehicles mentioned above:

BTV2c   Recovery Test Rounds air dropped at Imber and Larkhill (some with smoke flares)

BTV2d   2,000lb Parachute Test rounds dropped at Imber

BTV2e   1,000lb Dummy Round with preset control surfaces

BTV2f   Dummy Recovery Round for BTV4d

BTV3b   Free Drop Roll Stabilised Round dropped at Aberporth

BTV3c   Free Drop roll stabilised round with 40° glide dropped at Aberporth and Woomera

Before continuing with later varieties of Blue Boar test vehicles, delays in the programme due to the already described problems, and due to aircraft unserviceability, should not be forgotten. These delays were a constant source of embarrassment to Vickers management, as the MOS were pressing us to meet their development plan schedule.

A critical trial

BTV3c had me personally involved in no insignificant manner, and it certainly made life at Vickers at least 'interesting'.

After tests of small-scale models at Larkhill on Salisbury Plain when 1,000lb test vehicles were dropped from the Canberra over Aberporth, their autopilot control systems had to hold the roll stabilised bomb steadily in its 40° dive, and at this stage of the programme Henry Gardner, our high and mighty chief engineer came down from his ivory tower and visited my humble desk: 'John, this trial MUST be a success – I have a Ministry meeting tomorrow and if I can't report good performance, or if we delay again, I'll be for it.' And somewhat menacingly, with a beady eye-to-eye contact, he added, 'So, I am relying on you!'

Not responsible for the vehicle's design or manufacture, at least I could, as usual, expect the experts who built the control system to help set up the autopilot, and other engineers to set up telemetry, power supplies and safely jack up the bomb and lock onto its bomb slip. I would concentrate on the trials engineer's job of checking the cockpit monitoring equipment, phoning Aberporth to arrange for Radar control of our runs and for the cameras and telemetry recordings at an agreed time-slot in their busy trials schedule. Once airborne, first after take off while within telemetry range of Wisley, and later over the trials area, my job was to continually monitor some twenty-four missile parameters besides numerous temperatures, to switch and monitor power and radio telemetry, exercise the missile's rudders and elevators to check their proper functioning, switch the aircraft's own cameras to record the drop, and – suppressing the youthfulness of a twenty-three-year-old – keep my head.

Early that morning, none of the usual Vickers engineers nor the Smiths autopilot experts had arrived. On my 'tod', I was left to fulfil all their functions, in between making telephone calls to Aberporth and getting kitted out to fly. After a frenzy of this unitary activity of tests and telephone calls and safely attaching the bomb to its 'slip' in the roof of the bomb bay, the pilot and navigator were ready to drive me to the range, neither being familiar with Canberras and visibly apprehensive. Once strapped in for take off, I explained to Bill Fell, the navigator who sat next to me, 'Bill, I would like you to do a couple of things when we reach the end of the count down. At minus 10 seconds, twist this knob to lock this inclinometer on your table – that gives a datum when I unlock the gyros, then at Zero, press this "tit" to drop the bomb'. He looked at me with the benign tolerance that air crew have for humble engineers and asked, 'Then why are you here and what are *you* going to do?'!

We took off, and amid my frenetic monitoring and other activities, I soon became conscious of pilot Stuart Sloan's ham-fisted use of pitch trim recently introduced with 'flying tails' on the latest jets. Every time he trimmed as we gained speed and height, the plane pitched down with stomach lifting negative 'g'. This continued throughout most of the 20 minutes to reach Wales and throughout our two racetrack-shaped circuits under ground Radar control, which involved constant steep positive 'g' manoeuvring to maintain an accurate track towards the target. The dummy run and then the live run being completed, I exercised the missile's elevators and rudders, did the final tests after decaging the gyro at minus 10 seconds, then 9, 8, 7, 6, 5, 4, 3, 2, 1, and Bill dutifully pressed the 'tit'. The bomb released and transmitted its telemetry information to the receivers on the range.

I had done all I could and the adrenaline quickly subsided, when I found myself thoroughly air sick, immediately throwing up enough to fill my oxygen mask! 'Don't take if off at this height, the cabin altitude is 25,000ft', Bill screamed as I went to remove the mask to shake the vile smell out. 'Stuart, reduce height for our return, John's been sick into his mask', he added with disgust.

'We can't come down, our fuel won't last unless we stay at 40,000ft', Stuart calmly informed us. It would have taken but a few insignificant seconds to shake the mask clear, but I did as I was told and endured the stench until we were close to landing. The autopilot had worked, the missile glided as required, before the actuators eventually ran out of oil before the round entered the waters of Cardigan Bay. Henry Gardner must have heard what happened and made a second descent from his Ivory Tower to my desk to give his thanks.

Pilots, navigators – and humble engineers

The trials engineer was always the 'junior boy' among test pilots and navigators, where prima donnas were not unknown. During returns from Aberporth to Wisley, the pilot would commonly radio to Flying Control, 'This is Lima Eleven, make lunch reservations for two in the Management Mess, and one in the Weekly Staff canteen'.

From the trials engineer's perspective, the test pilot did little else than drive to the range and follow commands from ground control. The navigator made sure we knew where we were and the heading to follow, before and after Aberporth Radar brought us under their control. The purpose and success or failure of the trial were entirely down to the trials engineer and the team of technicians who prepared the round and the aircraft for the trial. That team could take many days of work, including much tribulation with equipment under development, before a trial was ready to go ahead. We were, therefore, reliant on 'normal' aircrew to be ready at the appointed hour, when everything was primed and the range was ready to accept us, otherwise all the effort could be wasted and a later attempt would become necessary.

After a particular occasion when the test pilot arrived so late that the trial had to be cancelled, getting somewhat hot under the collar, I berated him for causing such a waste of our collective efforts. Soon after, I arrived for a trial at the usual time ahead of take off – near lunchtime – and found myself locked out of the parachute store where my flying kit was kept. Some frantic hunting around Wisley airfield finally enabled me to find a key and, as I was running towards the apron, zipping up my pressure-breathing waistcoat, I heard the Canberra's engine starter cartridges fire. I ran as fast as I could towards the aircraft, which began to taxi slowly towards the runway, the little aircrew ladder trailing from the still open door. With a great effort I caught up, climbed the ladder and closed the pressure cabin door behind me, whereupon Spud opened up the taps and the Canberra leapt towards the runway. By the time I had climbed into my seat, strapped on the parachute and ejector seat harnesses and connected into the oxygen system, we were at 2,000ft over Reading.

Nevertheless, we maintained a mutually bantering, if respectful, relationship and flew many trials together, but we also managed to take off on time for subsequent trials, albeit with barrel rolls over the runway after take off and en route, while my head remained down to concentrate on the Monitor Box and all those switches.

The logging of readings had to be recorded as the trial continued, by making notes on a 'knee pad' comprised of a fat shorthand notebook on a plywood base, fixed to my thigh with two heavy leather straps and buckles. Only pencil could be used to jot down these tables of figures, since pens would leak ink at the cabin altitude of 25,000ft. Back in the office, after landing from a typical 90-minute flight, we would arrange to obtain any telemetry recordings and Kinetheodolite films from the range and, following full analysis, eventually prepare a detailed report for management and to permit an 'inquest' into any problems the trial may have revealed.

Continuing the summary of Blue Boar test vehicles from BTV3c described earlier, others included:

BTV4a   Ground Viewed rounds for testing the EMIED TV head, for dropping at Woomera.

BTV4b   Autopilot and Servo Test rounds incorporating Recovery Gear, for trials at Woomera.

BTV4c   Ground Viewed and Controlled round.

BTV4d   Ground Viewed and Controlled round, Recoverable.

BTV5   The 1,000lb Practice Round

BTV10   5,000lb Fixed Wing round carried by the B-29 Washington over Aberporth.

'The Aluminum Toobe'

B-29 Washington (WW349) trials for the 5,000lb Blue Boar test vehicles necessarily took a different form. With gun turrets removed, two side windows in their place became locations for 'scanners', who sat one each side of the rear cabin and observed the engines. Their reliability left much to be desired, and it was the scanners' job to advise the pilot of any visible trouble. It seemed that on three flights out of four, one or other of the engines would leak oil and smoke, when the scanners would alert the pilot to shut the engine down before it could catch fire.

The flight crew – test pilot, navigator and flight engineer – sat up front in the large 'glasshouses', the many windows constituting the aircraft's nose. Once above cloud, the sun streamed in and heated the front cabin to a temperature that led to the aircraft's heating being turned off. engineers working the 'bomb' sat and froze in the rear cabin, where instead of the small, stowable 'Monitor Box' used in the Canberra's cramped cockpit, racks of equipment rose over tables, where we could set down conventional writing pads and try to write down our observations. I say try to write, because the vibration level made any legible writing virtually impossible. After the first trials, where we froze while we

Right: Fig.3.8 B-29
Washington WW349,
carrying a 5,000lb Blue
Boar test vehicle over
Wisley airfield.[33]

Below: Fig.3.9 Shows the
Field of View seen by the
TV guidance head in a
typical trajectory.

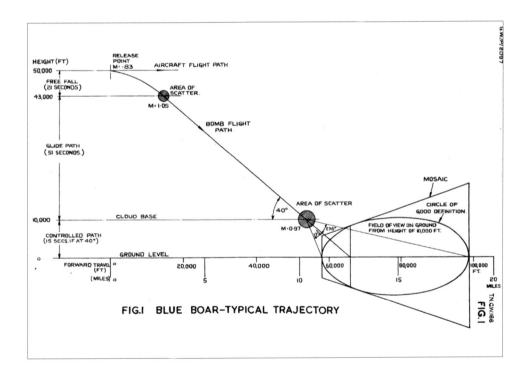

FIG.I BLUE BOAR–TYPICAL TRAJECTORY

could see the big 36in diameter and 62in (unretracted) wing-span bomb hanging in the
bomb bay through gaps in the structure, we were issued with electrically heated flying
suits. I found it one of the sweetest experiences, to get thoroughly cold and then to revel
in the warmth pouring into me when I turned on the heated suit.

The aft cabin was connected to the forward cabin by a long tube, the whole of it
being pressurised, enabling us to fly without continually wearing oxygen masks. 'The
Aluminum Toobe' nickname had long been ascribed to the B-29 by the USAF, and it was

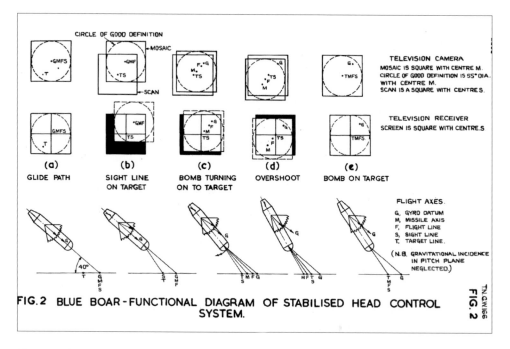

FIG.2 BLUE BOAR - FUNCTIONAL DIAGRAM OF STABILISED HEAD CONTROL
SYSTEM.

Fig.3.10 Shows TGW 166's Fig.2.

just possible to crawl between the cabins. On the way back from a trial, I foolishly tried out the tube and crawled forward into the front cabin. Foolishly, because had there been a pressure cabin failure at either end of the aircraft, I would have been fired out into the stratosphere like a bullet, in one direction or the other. The test pilot was not backwards in his metaphorical backside kicking, though I was allowed to crawl back to my position in the rear.

The principles of Blue Boar television guidance are illustrated in a November 1950 RAE Report by F.R.J. Spearman.[14]

Within this view, Blue Boar's flight path has to be controlled, with respect to the missile axis, its flight line, the sight line direction, the line to the target – all in relation to the gyro-stabilised datum on which the TV camera is mounted. The mathematical control equations to manipulate the bomb's flight path using these parameters were the subject of the control and guidance system design and the simulation of the bomb's response and trajectory to the target.

The thumbnail diagrams above show the circle of good picture definition in relation to the TV scan, and also the points where the different lines just mentioned appear as the bomb is guided onto the target. This guidance has to succeed within the 6 seconds available after the bomb breaks cloud at the lower limit of 10,000ft, allowing for the bomb aimer to recognise the target and then correct the trajectory.

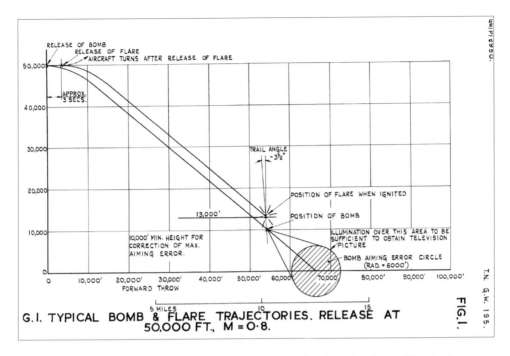

Fig.3.11 (RAE TN 195's Fig.1). Shows typical trajectories of such a pair of stores. The circular area of illumination around the target shows the Television Head's field of view.

Guidance by night

However, for night bombing with Blue Boar, an extra 5,000lb Blue-Boar round containing six banks of 250 flare candles, was to be dropped 3 seconds after dropping the HE round (either 5,000lb or 10,000lb). The Flare Bomb would be identically controlled on a 40° glide, remaining parallel to the HE store and always remaining above it.

The RAE as Design Authority for Blue Boar conducted the first trials in early 1952, to establish whether flares could be realistically used as a means of the enabling the Blue Boar gyro-stabilised TV unit to provide sufficiently clear images for guidance to be applied by the Observe in the bomber. These are reported in RAE Tech Note GW195 by F.G. Tarrant.[13] Firstly, trials were conducted by illuminating buildings with flare candles of representative power to check the performance of ground-based TV cameras at EMI's laboratory in representative conditions of illumination. Next, a Lincoln aircraft at 20,000ft air dropped flares timed to ignite typically at 12,500ft over Imber Range, using the town of Westbury in Wiltshire as a target. These trials all used readily available 300MHz interlaced scan TV receivers carried in a Valetta aircraft flying at 10,000ft, with the TV camera pointing down at the representative 40° angle. Now pictures were recorded to compare aerial views of Westbury by normal daylight photography, with the same picture degraded to represent TV theoretical image information clarity, then with actual TV pictures taken at night, by the illumination of the Flare Bomb.

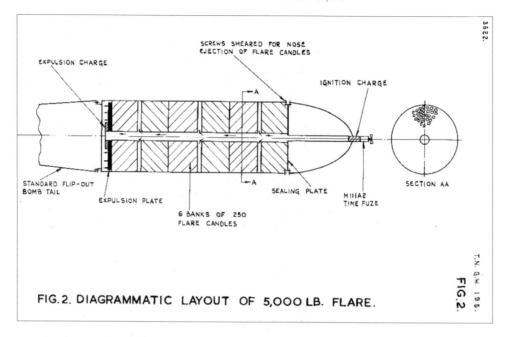

3622.

SCREWS SHEARED FOR NOSE
EJECTION OF FLARE CANDLES

EXPULSION CHARGE

IGNITION CHARGE

A

STANDARD FLIP-OUT
BOMB TAIL

EXPULSION PLATE

A

SEALING PLATE

6 BANKS OF 250
FLARE CANDLES

M111A2
TIME FUZE

SECTION AA

FIG. 2. DIAGRAMMATIC LAYOUT OF 5,000 LB. FLARE.

T.N. G.W. 195.

FIG. 2.

190·5"

32"

Above: Fig.3.12 Shows (RAE TN 195's Fig.2) how the 1,500 flare candles were arranged within a 5,000 Bomb body.

Left: Fig.3.13 Flare Bomb ready for aircraft (per RAE TN 195's Fig.3)

Fig.3.14 (RAE TN 195 Fig.18) Westbury photographed from the air, by daylight.

Fig.3.15 (RAE TN 195 Fig.20.) The degraded photograph to represent what could be expected from viewing a TV picture.

Fig.3.16 Actual TV picture as photographed from the TV 'scope. Details of Westbury are clearly visible and recognisable. Viewing by eye produces a far better and more precise picture than photographing the image.

It was concluded that pictures obtained by the ground-based monitoring equipment were satisfactory for 'clear nights' with six miles visibility and enabled the (Westbury) target to be recognised from photographs of the 300MHz pictures. Furthermore, the report stated that the clarity seen by eye (as would be the case for a bomber's observer) is significantly better than the photographs would indicate. Operational 5,000lb bomb-carried TV would use Millimetric frequencies for still higher quality, employing a cathode potential-stabilised Emitron.

Transmitting the TV picture back up to an aircraft could lead to multi-path wireless transmission of the TV picture to the aircraft, direct as intended, and by reflection from the ground. The interference caused by this could confuse the picture. This had to be overcome employing a microwave link and circularly polarised aerials, before completing the development programme.

The Imperial War Museum has movie films taken from such dives onto Basingstoke and onto an aircraft carrier off the Isle of Wight. Excellent footage clearly indicates the ability to impart guidance signals.

Fig.3.17 Meteor NF11 WM262 with trial Blue Boar television equipment made by EMIED. This aircraft executed a number of trials diving at 40°, to simulate the expanding television view to be received by the bomb guidance officer in the launching V-Bomber.

Bomb to bomber to bomb signal transmission

The video signal generated by the television camera in the nose of the missile is transmitted to the parent aircraft over the microwave radio link. At the aircraft, this signal is fed to a display unit to give the operator a reproduced picture of the ground, as viewed from the nose of the missile. The operator manipulates a joystick to keep the chosen target coincident with a fixed cursor, which represents the aiming point on his display. The joystick movement controls two command voltages, which are functions of the pitch and yaw errors in the flight path of the missile, and which are suitably encoded and relayed to the missile over the return microwave link. These command signals are detected at the missile and fed to the autopilot, which proceeds to correct the flight path until the missile is headed on the target.

The television scanning system was chosen to be sequential, having the same resolution as an interlaced scanning system if half of the flicker rate is acceptable. This had the effect of better resolving power and of reducing the susceptibility to jamming. A lower limit of 20 frames/second was applied, to avoid blurring due to picture expansion as the bomb falls. The resolution with a 425-line system and a 3MHz bandwidth was considered to be suitable for the purpose.

Fig.3.18 Meteor NF11 with Blue Boar TV guidance, ready for flight.

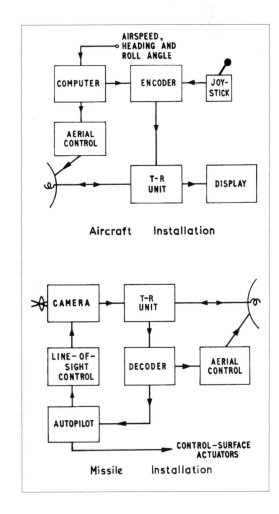

Fig.3.19 Simplified block diagram of Blue Boar Guidance System.[16]

The Aerial Systems designed to maintain contact between two rapidly moving points (on aircraft and missile) required a compromise between beam width and power transmitted. A 16in diameter paraboloidal aerial provided a 14° beam angle (at the half power points), while a helical feed with helical polarisation gave the necessary bandwidth. This helix gave some protection against multipath interference.

The computer of the day was, necessarily, an analogue electromechanical device of servos, and driven in relation to the gyroscopically stabilised space datum in the missile, to point the aerials correctly and to keep the television head properly aligned. Autofollow aerials were not used, to reduce the possibility of Radio Countermeasures (RCM). Gyroscopes of the spatial reference system were de-caged on release of the bomb.

This system assumed that the aircraft flew straight and level at the time of releasing Blue Boar, but was free to manoeuvre thereafter. Simplifying assumption in the computer design was that the bomb flew at a constant speed on its 40° glide. Combining the foregoing description with the earlier Functional Diagram of Stabilised Head Control (Fig.17) gives an outline of the problems being solved in the development of Blue Boar, to achieve the required 100 yards 50 per cent probability of accuracy from a height of 50,000ft, after breaking cloud at only 10,000ft altitude.

The reactions of a human operator while guiding the missile during the short 3 seconds following recognition of the target in the prior 3 seconds, initially required testing by simulation. Eventually, only full-scale flight trials with all of the elements of the system in place could verify the operational accuracy of the Blue Boar design.

An untimely end

Blue Boar trials in the UK and in Australia continued till August 1954, when the project was cancelled by the Ministry of Supply. Having completed such a large part of the development, Vickers felt that in view of the costs incurred over more than five years, the project should have been completed. The reasons for cancellation were never clearly stated, but were thought to have been related to the desire for a totally blind capability employing a Radar guidance head. However, the development of a long-range 'stand off' bomb Blue Steel (at Armstrong Whitworth Aircraft) to be carried by the V-bomber force, may have been the final reason to terminate the project. Nevertheless, the team at Vickers was now experienced and capable of tackling the additional work required to complete further complex Guided Weapons projects.

Not entirely irrelevant, trials in Australia were easily affected by miscommunication between Vickers teams in Weybridge and down under. Before the advent of the fax or email, the weekly newsletters plodded their way between the teams, only to result in more misunderstandings. These were superbly illustrated in a Design Office Dinner sketch, where a mangle represented the conduit for messages between two sides of a separating wall. After being 'mangled' through, messages read on the receiving side conveyed the exact opposite to the information being transmitted for the other party!

Chapter 4

A MATURING GW DEPARTMENT

Guided Weapons development covers many engineering disciplines, from aerodynamics, lightweight structures, rocket propulsion, autopilots, servos and hydraulic control actuators, guidance systems of numerous kinds, warhead design, overall lethality considerations, not to mention launching conditions from aircraft, meteorology, ground Radar systems and data communications. Perhaps that was the beauty of being in a team that covers such a wide field, seeing how a knowledge of mathematics can be applied over these many disciplines, and having to know something about each one. I was one of those fortunate enough, along with Bill Redstone, to be sent on a Guided Weapons Course for Industry at the (now Royal) Military College of Science at Shrivenham in Wiltshire.

The usual course was of a year's duration and, considering that I was told of being sent away on the day I returned to Vickers from my honeymoon, I was not a little pleased that our residential course was for only five weeks. However, the course syllabus required us to study the same breadth of ground covered by full-time students in a whole year. Perhaps we were rushed through some things, but without doubt we learned about Guided Weapons technology in some detail from A to Z, and once I had got over the dawn-to-late-night regime of lectures and private study, I felt invigorated with a great deal more knowledge. It enabled me to understand much more about our sub-contractors' designs for autopilots and guidance systems, as well as the design of rocket motors and warheads that were all well beyond undergraduate degree studies. Some late sessions in the Mess of this military establishment had us well oiled and singing all kinds of bawdy songs around the piano, in preparation for the next morning's early start. We even learned some hitherto unheard of technical terms, the best of which related to our exceedingly pompous Colonel Tumber, who covered explosives and propellants. By unanimous consent, the Universal Unit of Pomposity was thereon named 'One Millitumber'.

By the spring of 1954, the scale of Red Dean work, coupled with continuing work on Blue Boar, led to the completion of a purpose-built Guided Weapons Department building between the main Aircraft Design Office building and the Vickers Apprentice School. It also led to substantial expansion, both in its management and engineering personnel. The GW Building housed most of the technical staff in a large, open-plan office, with management offices along one side, a large manufacturing area with offices for purchasing and supplies a well as laboratories for electronics development, and further small laboratories on a lower floor to house some work originally conducted in The Pits. With Red Rapier coming to a close, relatively little GW work remained to be conducted from the original Aircraft design office, except for a considerable amount of drawings relating to trials aircraft installations.

The advent of new management

Initially, an electronic controls expert, 'Johnny' Johnson, and a high-flying mathematician, Bernard Hunn, arrived as Project Manager, soon to be elevated into a management-level position. He undertook the analysis and control of project designs, with a team of engineers who interacted with the functional engineering departments dealing with designs such as Mechanical and Hydraulics design (Mike Still, with Bill Redstone, Peter Rice, John Lattey, Chuck Fry and others), Aerodynamics and Propulsion (J.E. Daboo, who also made project studies), the Drawing Office and the technicians in the electronics laboratories (in The Pits, the W103 Hangar, the 'Flak Tower' and other labs in the new Guided Weapons building). Bernard was assisted by John Housego, Les Vine, Tom Curl, Gordon Alexander and other senior engineers. Besides Charles Fricker, an experienced controls engineer who came from Supermarine's Whitechapel Torpedo Works, a retired RAF Group Captain also joined in a supernumerary management role, to progress project programmes under Eddie Smyth.

A not unimportant consideration with these diverse personalities, and with Henry Gardner remaining sufficiently in touch to make visits to the new GW Building, was the matter of the Management Urinals. Bill Murdoch, in charge of facilities and allied problems, described in graphic detail how the height of the urinal bowls had to be tried, tested and demonstrated for the very differing heights of Henry Gardner standing at around 6ft and 'Johnny' Johnson, near to 5ft. When even more diminutive Dab was elevated to Management Staff, with a key to this high foluting lavatory, an even lower urinal had to be added.

As chief trials engineer, a colourful ex-Second World War Navy Lt/Cmdr Paul Leyton arrived from a similar position at Sperry's Guided Weapons operation in Hayes, Middlesex. Besides driving a throaty Alvis saloon while gritting a cigarette holder between his teeth, Paul inhabited a double-decker bus he had converted for his family of wife and four sons. This was parked on a site in Byfleet village nearby, and it appeared that he had lived in this for much of the time since demobilisation from the Royal Navy, and moved it from job to job. Eventually, on becoming secure in his position at Vickers, he bought a large Georgian house in Byfleet and the bus faded into the past. Sadly, Paul's arrival led to the disillusionment and departure of the long serving and effective Barry MacGowan. However, Paul became my boss and made me a section leader in the Trials Department, requiring me to head up Trials Planning while continuing with trials operations at Larkhill, Imber and Aberporth, with the attendant missile and aircraft operational equipment testing at Wisley, besides continued flying as trials observer and undertaking the analysis of trials

Fig.4.1 Paul Leyton (right) with Maurice Brennan, chief engineer of Saunders-Roe, at Woomera, on the occasion of the first successful launching of Black Knight (forerunner of a ballistic missile launcher similar to Blue Streak).[102]

results. Again, Paul was soon working at management level and a degree of politics became evident in his relationships with Eddie Smyth and Bernard Hunn. He proved to be an excellent and resourceful leader, where deserved, firmly supporting his subordinates through thick and thin, and he more than made up for any lack of technical knowledge with experience and acumen. Rumours spoken in hushed terms suggested that Paul was being paid a really high salary of £2,000 p.a.

Later, the energetic and experienced ex-Canadian with a wicked sense of humour, Frank Bond, joined from the Aircraft side of Vickers as group leader for trials under Paul, and I then reported to him. John Lambie, also a long-standing engineer from the Aircraft side, came into GW in a management position, along with the Scot, John Begbie, running development laboratories, after serving in Australia. Now, as a relatively experienced member of the GW team, the education of more senior newcomers about the test vehicle programmes and the trials situations often fell to me. This brought me into the wider orbit of the company's business, while assisting with the indoctrination of some of the new blood. As a section leader, I began to oversee other engineers, including John Whetmore, John Leaman and others, while John Curry and Alan Thurley, who had preceded me in the GW Department, as well as Bob Taylor, continued their work alongside. Brian Soan, who returned from several years heading the Australian trials section, moved on to other fields.

Around this time, Dab made one of his occasional visits home to his family in India, when he would be away for three weeks or so. Still a somewhat shy bachelor approaching thirty, he had no ties and could work his slide rule design and trajectory calculation into a red hot frenzy of even greater duration and intensity, before taking time away from the company. Already good friends, when he reappeared from Bombay, we detected a change of some kind, and he suddenly revealed that he had brought a wife back with him. Somehow, nobody could imagine Dab as a married man and soon it transpired that he had gone to India for an arranged marriage – to Amy, an equally diminutive Brahmin of high intelligence and education.

We were soon invited to visit them in a well-appointed flat at High Point (later Henry Gardner also occupied one) and saw Amy's ample dowry, including her trousseau of many diaphanous and colourful saris. There was clearly some serious money behind the marriage and when they projected the film of the wedding for us, it could have taken place in a Maharaja's palace, with all characters, including Dab, regaled in silken robes and turbans. Shy as he was, Dab looked decidedly uncomfortable sitting through the incantations, and now entertaining us for dinner in Weybridge, he was the same shy engineer as always, energetically supported by his new wife Amy. As a couple, we hit it off very well and a lifelong friendship followed. Of course, the Mobsby cartoons took little time to depict the couple sitting up in bed, with Amy playing a flute for the snake rising out of the snake charmer's basket in front of an obviously bemused Dab.

The Vickers Flying Club

In early 1955, the start of a subsidised Vickers Flying Club affiliated with the Fairoaks Flying Club near Woking, enabled me to achieve an important personal ambition. Most of my colleagues were as keen as I to join and learn piloting skills. Since the 90 per cent subsidy's ability to attract a tax break for the company was dependent on membership being by ballot, it was literally a 'toss up' as to who would win the benefit of learning to fly at a cost of only 7s per hour. An engineer's salary would certainly not allow me to pay for flying lessons at the full rate. At twenty-six, and with a small son, my wife naturally feared that light aircraft flying could be more dangerous than trials in a professionally piloted Canberra jet, and I felt my responsibilities. She knew the degree of my craving for learning to fly, after my boyhood days in the Air Training Corps, and felt her own guilt at the thought of preventing me. We tossed a coin over whether I should enter the ballot; I won and was among the lucky ones who were picked out of the hat. Between May and September, along with colleagues John Curry, Maurice Watson, Chuck Fry and others, I learned to fly, stall, spin, restart a stopped propeller by diving vertically, land and to navigate 'cross country' in the eponymous Tiger Moth, and gained a Private Pilot's License. My wife was one of my first passengers in the front seat on a windy day, while three months pregnant with our second son. Mac was another to trust himself to my newly learned piloting skills. In terms of job enthusiasm, an already exciting life in a stimulating and friendly team was greatly enhanced for everybody.

The odyssey of travel to Woomera

By late 1955, I was much involved in the Red Dean air-to-air missile programme trials, and this included the establishment of a Safety Trace for firings at Woomera. Paul Leyton agreed that I should visit Woomera, to negotiate this Safety Trace with the range authorities and plans were made for me to fly out on the RAF's weekly run with Handley Page Hastings aircraft, from Lyneham. Since I would be travelling with the RAF for nine days each way, as was customary I was given an RAF rank for the duration of the five weeks I was to be away. As a Squadron Leader, I would live in the RAF officers' mess at each of the staging posts and share quarters with RAF Squadron Leaders and wing commanders. Quite nice, but I had no spare cash whatever and envisaged evenings with these well-established and well-paid officers, without the means to buy even one round of drinks. Requests for an expense allowance were summarily tuned down by Henry Gardner, who took the position that the RAF would feed and water me, so why should I need an expense allowance? I was, after all, only a junior on the weekly staff. Monthly staff were allowed about £15 per day while travelling and enough to pay for a reasonable hotel room while in Adelaide.

After some lobbying, Gardner's personal assistant Jack Carter took up my cause and eventually extracted a big concession – I was to be given £1 per day during the nine-day journey, and could spend up to £30 (Australian) per week on guest house accommodation during my three weeks in Australia! Armed with my Safety Trace proposal and £9, I arrived at Lyneham and spent a cold November night in concrete-built room, corridors and ablutions, before an early departure for the RAF base in Tripoli.

I had bought a small world atlas in Woolworth's with a view to following our route to Australia. At only 10,000ft, once we were away from cloudy England, I should be able to follow our route and mark our track across the globe with relative ease. After the noisy 9-hour grind in the totally uninsulated bomber type 'cabin' at 200mph over France and the Mediterranean, my first arrival outside temperate Europe into the humid heat of a Tripoli night was quite a shock. RAF officers still had free service of 'batmen', and I received the usual attentions of bed making, shoe cleaning et al. A letter from Mary already awaited me – she must have sent it well before my departure and, sitting up in bed to write back, the sweat dripped all over my efforts, even though I was totally naked. Next morning we took off for RAF Habbaniya near Baghdad, and in another day's travel I was in yet another totally different world, with my batman ministering to my needs while wearing a Fez. Each successive stop at the now long abandoned RAF bases 'East of Suez' – Mauripur near Karachi, Negombo near Colombo in Ceylon and Singapore, followed by the RAAF base in Darwin – came and went like the views through an ever-changing window, like a tale from *Arabian Nights*. Little pencilled crosses plotted our path on my Woolworth's atlas, made by taking estimated fixes through the windows. Between the Persian Gulf and the Indian Ocean, the Hastings had to climb over mountains to 14,000ft near Sharjah and, not being pressurised, we had to don oxygen masks until we came down to 10,000ft again.

I found myself travelling with several Wing Commanders about ten years my senior, with significant responsibilities in the Air Ministry and the Ministry of Supply. Reggie Harland, project officer for Red Shoes (eventually to become the Thunderbird surface -to-air (SAM) missile), was my most frequent companion, with whom we whiled away many a laborious and noisy hour discussing the technicalities of our respective projects. A brilliant engineer of many skills coming from the Harland (of Harland & Woolf) family, Reggie also wore pilot's Wings and was not exactly short of cash.

With another letter from home received and answered at each stop, we proceeded on our journey to the other end of the world. Needless to say, I could not afford the taxi fare from Habbaniya into Baghdad as I had heard was normal for an evening out by more senior colleagues on their trips. We managed to share a rickety bus into Karachi, past the stench of the Indian Partition-era refugee camp of 500,000 into the city's teeming mêlée of humanity, some sleeping on the pavements and droves of beggars bearing deliberately maimed babies, holding their hands out. A persistent Fakir could not only make my Rupee coin slide up his arm, but when he held my hand it also gently vibrated up mine. Negombo's mosquitoes left my face and head covered in itching bumps, yet to my jealous chagrin my roommate slept through it like a child. Singapore afforded the crew an extra day's rest while I went sightseeing and shopping with Reggie Harland. While Reggie was buying jewellery for his wife, guarding my precious £9, I bought my father a carved coconut for £1. I would leave the tempting Chinese silk material which I planned for my wife until the return journey, when I may have enough money left for a few yards.

En route to Djakarta (in our office sometimes confused with 'Jack Carter'!), engine trouble brought us into the fabled island of Bali, where bare-breasted maidens were reputed to abound everywhere. The runway spanned a narrow peninsula in the island's south, ensuring that any overshoot would have the Hastings finish up in the sea. The women cutting the airport grass with sickles were all too well covered from our eagerly peering gaze. In the Transit Lounge, the Indonesians were most suspicious of our intentions after our unscheduled landing – the second occurrence in a week – and kept us corralled until the aircraft was ready to depart. Inviting elegantly slender carved hard wood Bali heads were cheap enough for normal mortals, but beyond my allowance, so with never to be forgotten regrets, I did not buy one. The next stop in Darwin's humid night was enlivened by the croaks of rugby ball-sized bullfrogs in and around our wooden cabins on high stilts above the marshes. According to rumours, these frogs sometimes emerged from lavatory basins as users lowered themselves onto the seat, so great care was in order. The final leg across the Australian desert to Edinburgh Field followed the recent arrival of our trials Canberra aircraft, which barely arrived against an exceptional head wind when its engines cut out on the runway immediately after landing.

Jack Redpath, Maurice Watson and others greeted me in the dazzling Australian sunshine as I deplaned, and asked why I had come! After explanations, they did everything to make my three weeks' stay as comfortable as possible, providing lifts for their 'poor relation' in their cars between my cheap digs in North Adelaide and their offices. The daily office finishing time at around 4 p.m. was explained by the 4.30 p.m. closing time of pubs in South Australia. Men were segregated from women into separate bars and as 4.30 p.m. approached, a menacing-looking Aussie policeman lolled against the exit door, providing a none too subtle hint that it was time to go. Consequently, in view of only a half hour being available for drinking, everybody downed as many schooners of Fosters as they could gulp, after which they got into their cars and wove their tipsy way home. Each morning on the way to the Vickers office, the succession of wrecked cars by the roadside bore testimony to the previous evening's consumption of Fosters before 4.30 p.m.

Eventually it was time to make the trip to Woomera, with suitably stringent security checks before the one-stop flight departed – and another equally stringent security check as we disembarked, just in case somebody had succeeded in boarding the DC3 in mid-air. Here in the desert heat, the beer arrived in quart-sized pitchers, which the Aussies downed as fast as I had ever seen pints consumed. Aircrews gave this a reluctant rest between Sunday nights and Friday afternoons, making up for their denial over the weekends. Before my meeting with the range safety officer to finalise the Red Dean Safety Trace, a compliant

Fig.4.2 Jack and Rosamund Redpath of Vickers (left), with Mr and Mrs Stan Joyner representing Saunders-Roe.[102]

RAAF Squadron Leader Foster acquiesced to my solicitations and allowed me to add one more type to my flying log by arranging for me to fly a Winjeel trainer. Not a bad day, and after another pair of security checks at each end of a non-stop flight, we were back at Edinburgh Field. Adelaide in the 1950s was deceptively neon-lit as seen from a distance, but at weekends all life appeared to die and there was little to see or do. Eventually, with everything settled and with another £9 (now in the lower value Australian currency) in my pocket, I boarded a Hastings for the return journey – spending most of Henry Gardner's 'generous' expense allowance on that Chinese silk brocade for my wife. I was home a few days before the Christmas holidays and in time for the annual salary reviews. Now, at long last, as a result of Paul Leyton's lobbying on my behalf, I was elevated to the coveted level of monthly staff. Had this been secured a few weeks earlier, I would have of course received the luxurious expenses denied for my travel to Australia as a junior on weekly staff. Everybody on the monthly staff seemed to be wearing smart tweed suits – quite a fashion, which became known as the Monthly Staff Tweed Suit (except by Sir George Edwards, to whom it was his 'racking suit'). I soon fell in line and bought one.

Paul became involved in local politics and topped the poll in the election for the Council, where he soon became chairman of the Highways Committee. Then he suddenly sold his big house in Byfleet and moved to Saunders-Roe on the Isle of Wight, to become chief development engineer on the Black Knight rocket programme. Very soon after his leaving party, the Council drove a road right though the site of Paul's house, which he had sold in good time, at a good price. His success at Sauders-Roe was somewhat truncated, when he fell out with his boss Maurice Brennan, whom he later described to me as a 'jumped up squirt'. Soon after Paul's departure from the Isle of Wight, Brennan also left – and came to us at Vickers in Weybridge. Paul could just as well have stayed!

The new top duo

The most significant new executive arrivals were into the very top echelons of Vickers Guided Weapons. George Edwards had not taken much personal interest since the early days of Red Rapier, leaving the management of GW to Henry Gardner and Eddie Smyth. With projects running late and remaining unfinished before they were cancelled, in 1957, Edwards, who was now managing director of Vickers Armstrongs (Aircraft) Ltd, offered the position of chief engineer (Guided Weapons) to the exiting Director of Guided Weapons Projects (DGW (P)) at the Ministry of Supply, Brigadier John Clemow. Clemow was an armaments and gunnery expert, who had unearthed some of the German Second World War Guided Weapon developments during the post-war occupation and had become familiar with US developments of the period. As an accomplished mathematician, he became an expert in most aspects of guidance, control and weapon systems in general, writing papers and books on the subject. His retirement from the Army and engagement by George Edwards was on the basis of Henry Gardner relinquishing his GW responsibilities and reverting to chief engineer (Military Aircraft), complementing Basil Stephenson who was chief engineer (Civil Aircraft). He recalls that he also insisted on getting, 'the best office, the best secretary and the best car parking location'. John Clemow expected to have additional responsibilities relating to aircraft, but many years later, the intentions and motives of George Edwards remained unclear and John Clemow did not receive some anticipated additional responsibilities. Nevertheless, his advent brought the total Guided Weapons effort under his authority, and he continued to weld a powerful team, while making significant personal contributions to design and to development policy.

Clemow's reputation preceded him and left most of the Vickers staff quaking in their shoes in anticipation. The reason for this can be found in his last tasks as DGW(P) at the MOS. Fairey Aviation had been in trouble with their development of the beam rider air-to-air missile Blue Sky, and Clemow was sent it to sort out the project. Apparently, a large part of the Fairey design team was fired during the process and a rebuilt team eventually made the project work well enough to bring the missile into the RAF service as 'Fireflash'. Next, John Clemow was sent in at Armstrong Whitworth Aircraft (AWA) in Manchester, to sort out the Seaslug (ship-borne anti-aircraft missile), when he had the personal support of Admiral Lord Mountbatten at the Ministry of Defence. By all accounts, Clemow reaped a similar whirlwind at AWA, with many AWA staff falling by the wayside. How safe would our jobs be at Vickers and would Clemow also wield his axe here?

John Clemow arrived on April Fool's Day, 1957 – ironically during a Vickers strike – wearing a jaunty bow tie, soon to be seen as daily de rigueur. He brought with him Howard Surtees, a brilliant engineer from the original Fairey Aviation team, and installed him as chief designer (GW), with the managers already mentioned reporting to him. Also an accomplished mathematician, Howard had a degree in electrical engineering and enormous expertise in missile control and guidance, and much down to earth engineering experience in the many disciplines required for guided weapon development. The group leaders heading departments reported direct to Howard or an assistant chief designer, with John Clemow mainly dealing with external policy questions, while continuing to oversee technical policy relating to the several development projects in hand. His highly efficient

Fig.4.3. Brig. John Clemow, just before retiring from the Army, to take up his post at Vickers on 1 April 1957.[86]

secretary/PA, known to everybody as Miss Jenkins, was the genial gate keeper at the chief engineer's door and his telephone, while producing reams of reports on wax Gestetner duplicating originals at breakneck speed. She also brought him regular top-ups of his favourite, strong black tea without milk, which he drank while it was hot enough to steam up his spectacle lenses. By this time in the mid-1950s, we gained our first photocopying machine – a wet process device that took several minutes to produce a copy and to dry, before it could be used. Pedestrian as this was compared with dry copiers by Xerox and the like to come later, it made a big difference to our lives.

With a wary eye on John Clemow's reputation, caution reigned among the lower ranks during meetings and when occasions for personal contact arose. He insisted that we should never flinch from 'grasping the nettle', and also made clear his distrust of (particularly self-proclaimed) 'experts'. Teddy Hall's tendency to present himself in this manner elicited Clemow's direct stare when expounding this dictum.

However, it did not take long to realise that our new boss was both approachable and totally open in all of his dealings. Like a breath of fresh air, I first experienced this soon, some time after his arrival, when I was promoted from under Frank Bond in the Trials Group, to head the Test Group previously headed by John Begbie. As a group leader I also acquired the 'rank' of senior designer, at which level it was customary to travel first class. I duly bought a first-class ticket for a train journey to London to a Ministry meeting, and on presenting my expense claim, Eddie Smyth sent it back with a note, 'you are not entitled to travel first class'. On tackling him as to why as senior designer I could not travel like other senior designers, Eddie said, 'Sorry, but there is a secret rule and until you comply with the secret rule, you have to travel Second Class'. He would not disclose the secret, but agreed that I could approach John Clemow. At a suitable opportunity, I raised the question and Clemow gave a big grin. 'The secret rule is that your salary must be at least £1,500 a year, and it seems that you are below that level'; it was actually nearer to £1,200! Taking a chance I replied, 'There is an easy solution to that, just raise my salary to £1,500 a year – Sir.' Clemow laughed and a couple of years later, it finally climbed over the barrier.

Howard Surtees gave the initial outward impression of being more intent on keeping things close to his chest and could also be distinctly acerbic with people who appeared to take him or the job in hand too lightly. However, once I had direct contact with him on any matter, he was totally open and straightforward, even if his manner was sometimes as brisk as it was friendly. His analysis of all matters was incisive, and though he gave credit where it was due, he did not hesitate to criticise constructively where criticism was due. Besides running all aspects of the GW Department's day-to-day business, Howard continually created new ideas of considerable mathematical complexity, which in the magic manner of top-class mathematicians, resulted in clear and simple conclusions. Thus, the top duo soon overcame our initial fears and the GW team became stronger for their advent in every way.

A new departure in missile testing

My later promotion to test group leader was an innovation in the philosophy of how Guided Weapons should be developed, in a manner that would overcome the natural tendency of project designers to think they had covered all contingencies in their designs. In the past, designers would serve up test vehicle designs and have them manufactured for trials, which would then result in ground-launched rocket firings or in airborne dropping and firing trials, with the expensive loss of many test vehicles. The remit I was given was to be totally independent of the design side of the department and report through a different channel direct to the chief designer. In my case this was via John Lambie, who was relatively unfamiliar with GW engineering after his background in aircraft design, so I had frequent access to Howard Surtees. Now, all test vehicle designs destined for flight trials were required to be independently tested in my laboratories, against overall performance specifications. I was free to conceive my own tests regardless of claims that 'this or that' problem had already been anticipated by the designers, and to conduct such tests as would independently establish a very high probability of flight trials being successful. Here, success was defined both as proper functioning of the test vehicle and the successful harvesting of trials results by the instruments carried.

In the W103 Hanger, my staff of about twenty engineers was divided into three sections. Development Test Section, under my old friend John Lewis, conducted operational tests to simulate the required functioning of test vehicles in flight, employing special laboratory rigs made for the purpose. Environmental Test, under Peter Inglis, operated a variety of heating/cooling, humidity and salt spray chambers, besides centrifuges and vibration rigs, drop testers and other impact devices. These had instrumentation for monitoring the test vehicles' correct functioning while they were exercised through appropriate environments designed to be sufficiently harsh that should they survive them, they would surely survive the rigours of a ground-launched rocket or aircraft-launched flight. George Errington's Test Gear Design Section created the necessary test equipment for both sections. A small private office with windows looking out on the laboratories was built for my use – my first experience outside the hurly burly of the open-plan general office. Now, leadership skills and interaction with other groups became as important as technical problem solving, and I had to admit to relishing my wider role. It was in this environment that for the first time, the move from cost, plus Ministry contracts, began to give way to company funded Private Venture developments. In the past, at my level we were totally removed from the costing of our work, which was left to remote Commercial departments and top management. Now I was expected to produce cost budgets for the labour and materials to be used for each given test programme, and obtain approval before commencing the work. I had much to learn.

A sense of proportion when testing missiles became evidently important early into my tenure, since we soon proved, for example, that sufficiently harsh vibration can break anything. Using stroboscopes, one could clearly see how equipment and the structures on which they were mounted would resonate at certain frequencies, inviting fatigue or simply causing an item to break free and fly across the lab. The trick, of course, was to make the structure resonate at a higher frequency than would be encountered in practice, rather than simply to beef up the strength. The proof of each pudding was in the eating, and then once out of my group's hands, further proof would come (or not) in the flight trials at Aberporth, Larkhill or Woomera. Minor clashes occurred from time to time, with designers who were used to getting their own way without such independent verification of their babies' deepest secrets. Nevertheless, the practice became embedded in the GW Department's psyche and continued with suitably reliable trials results. Coupled with this, the recently established concept of reliability engineering was brought into my orbit and this supernumerary responsibility had me attending industry wide meetings at other GW companies including our future partners in British Aircraft Corporation,

Fig.4.4. High-altitude trials continued, as photographed by me, through the Canberra pilot's canopy.[103]

English Electric at Stevenage and with the Ministry of Supply departments in London and Farnborough. This highly detailed consideration of standards for the wide range of electronic components used in missiles and their environmental testing was somewhat tedious, but later experience in the industry proved its importance. Without reliable and interchangeable components, all designs were flawed, however brilliant their concept and execution.

Chapter 5.1

RED DEAN AIR-TO-AIR MISSILE PART 1

The origins of Red Dean

The Air Ministry issued an early Air-to-Air Missile requirement in 1947, for rear attack against a 600mph target, but by December 1950, the Air Minister, Sir Ralph A. Cochrane GBE, KCB, VCAS, made it clear that the RAF was not interested in weapons that imposed manoeuvrability restrictions on the attacking fighters. A January 1951 Joint Naval/Air Staff Target 1056 called for an all-round attack long-range Guided Weapon, usable in all weather conditions at all heights up to 50,000ft, named Red Hawk, with a secondary role of bomber defence. Concurrently, Assistant Chief of Air Staff Air Vice Marshall C.B.N. Pelly wrote to the director General Weapons R&D, and for the first time envisaged giving the Red Hawk alternate a new name.[29]

In a letter of 18 June 1951,[17] Group Captain C. Scragg, deputy director Operational Requirements 5 (DDOR 5), recognising that the Red Hawk concept would be unattainable for many years, issued a draft Operational Requirement, which became OR 1105 for a purely air-to-air attack missile, to be called Red Dean. This Active Radar Homing missile was principally for two-seat and perhaps single-seat fighters. The particular aircraft envisaged to carry two Red Dean missiles was the Gloster F153D 'thin winged Javelin', with possibilities for use on the DH 110 Sea Vixen and the Supermarine Swift. Since the nature of the Operational Requirement (OR) indicated that Red Dean would need to be launched with the aid of an Air Interception Radar carried in the fighter's nose, single-seat aircraft were deemed unsuitable. The A.I. Mark 18 search and lock/follow Radar would need to be developed and integrated with Red Dean's launching system.

Initial work on Red Dean was done by Folland Aviation under the leadership of W.E. Petter, who had earlier designed the Canberra bomber at English Electric Co. at Preston in Lancashire. E.K. Cole was to design the Radar guidance system. However, by October 1951, Follands had become consumed by work on its new Light Fighter aircraft which became the Folland Gnat, and in November the company decided not to proceed with the Red Dean project. When the Ministry of Supply then asked Vickers to take on the project, the company also initially declined. However, considerable pressure was applied at Vickers Board level to persuade the company to develop Red Dean in the national interest. At the time, Vickers was already engaged on developing Red Rapier and Blue Boar, but although these programmes were behind, an later MOS memorandum[3] stated that Vickers was, 'the only firm really capable of undertaking this very important project and in whom the Ministry of Supply had every confidence'. Finally, the company agreed to take on the Red Dean project.

The July 1951 operational requirement[17]

The requirement thus required Red Dean to:

'Be of a size, shape and weight, for two to be carried by fighters of about 10,000lb all up weight, without undue restriction on the operational ceiling, rate of climb, top speed and manoeuvrability of the fighter.'

Attack Primary Targets of Bomber aircraft, including fighter-bombers, both piston engine and jet, operating at speeds up to Mach 0.95.

Attack secondary targets of Fighter aircraft of all types up to speeds Mach 0.95. However, if this were to introduce delays into the development programme, this requirement would be waived.

Operate in all weather conditions and at night in all possible theatres of war.

Operate at heights up to 60,000ft, with the caveat that if this were to impose excessive complexity, then the low level requirement would be waived.

Employ a guidance system of active pulse Radar homing and achieve a minimum lethality of 50 per cent per missile against unarmoured bomber types, employing a fragmentation (later changed to a blast type) warhead and proximity fuze of a size and type to ensure this lethality within the accuracy of the guidance and control of the missile.

Self-destruct in the event of a missed target, in order to avoid any threat to the launching or neighbouring friendly aircraft.

Be capable of attack from all-round directions, giving the fighter the greatest possible tactical freedom before and after launch. With fighters not able to carry AI Radar and computing equipment, the cones of attack directions would be 'as wide as possible'.

Have weapon range, avoiding a requirement to come no closer than 1,800 yards from the target.

Be launched automatically, individually, or in ripple, with the time interval between launching successive missiles to be as short as possible, consistent with avoiding mutual interference.

Discriminate between targets from any direction against aircraft in close formation, without the lethality of the missile being reduced by the proximity of other aircraft of the formation.

Take all reasonable steps against countermeasures, such that target evasion, counter-measures against the aircraft or the missile Radar and against proximity fuzes, which should not affect lethality.

The 'sting in the tail', as handwritten into the margin by the Assistant Chief of Air Staff (OR), was that, 'Operation of the weapon should not demand such concentration from the aircrew that a watch on the general air battle cannot be maintained.'

Additionally, the OR specified storage under already existing procedures, assembly and maintenance by semi-skilled personnel and that assembly of the missile from component parts should be on a 'go – no go' system basis requiring no more time than 1 hour, and to remain serviceable for a further 48 hours without further testing. Ancillary Equipment, packaging and a degree of compatibility with other operational systems such as AI Radar, blind firing for guns, collision-course computer for aircraft projectiles and beam-laying equipment for Blue Sky were required.

Blue Sky was an interim Beam Rider air-to-air missile being developed by Fairey Aviation. Once formally issued, the OR also referred to another (passive) Infra Red homing system by de Havilland Aircraft, known as Blue Jay.

In November 1951, the ACAS (OR) wrote a lengthy paper on the 'Future of Red Dean', discussing the form of Red Dean and the reasons, its installation on fighters, and concerning their performance and handling. This discussed target discrimination by the homing Radar and the warhead and its lethality. This again discussed the attack directions and ranges to the target(s) and the order in which relaxations in the requirement might be considered, namely: Discrimination, warhead and lethality, Range, Height band and Direction of attack. None of these would be seriously relaxed and the development should essentially be for all weather fighters. In a time before the advent of the transistor – and when even printed circuits were a new and relatively untried innovation – this requirement with a 1958 in-service date was nothing if not ambitious.

The contractor team and optimisation of the design

Vickers as prime contractor took overall responsibility for missile and weapon system design, for what was soon given 'super priority' by the MOS. The rocket motor design was undertaken by the RPD Wescott division of RAE. Guidance was by GEC (Electronics) Ltd at Stanmore, who had already undertaken similar active homing guidance studies relating to the Seaslug missile, after studies of semi-active Radar homing system were effectively ruled out by the OR. Autopilot design was by Smiths Aircraft Instruments in Cheltenham with British Messier hydraulics (both of whom were already sub-contractors for the Blue Boar autopilot). The proximity fuze design contractor was EMI Engineering Development Ltd (usually referred to as EMIED), at Hayes.

As with most Guided Weapons of the period, the initial designs commenced at the RAE at Farnborough, who often conducted aerodynamic wind tunnel tests and even rocket launched flight trials to establish a basic design, before handing the development over to Industry for development. Red Dean went through such a programme, including flight tests of CTV and other basic test vehicles. When Vickers took over from Folland Aircraft, a basic shape had been established but required considerably more theoretical design, wind tunnel work at Vickers (low speed tunnel) and at the National Physical Laboratory (supersonic tunnel).[29]

The Schlieren photographs below were taken later at the NPL with Red Dean models of the final WTV5 plan form, at Mach Numbers of 1.6 and 2.35. The earlier aerodynamic measurements were used to validate theoretical estimates, which were later further tested in rocket-boosted flight trials at the Larkhill Range on Salisbury Plain.

The above from a 1956 report is shown to indicate how Red Dean was to be used in operations, and although out of historical time sequence here, this basic concept was known from the beginning.

In the early months of the contract, the first priority was to make a general assessment of Red Dean's shape, size and weight, considering its requirement to deliver a suitably lethal warhead to within the miss distance expected to be achieved by active Radar homing, from a wide range of launching conditions over the height range up to 60,000ft (later reduced to 50,000ft).[19] This mathematical analysis[19] concluded that for a given lethality, a weapon with a large warhead was cheaper than a large number of weapons with smaller warheads. The remaining work therefore assumed a warhead weight of 100lb.

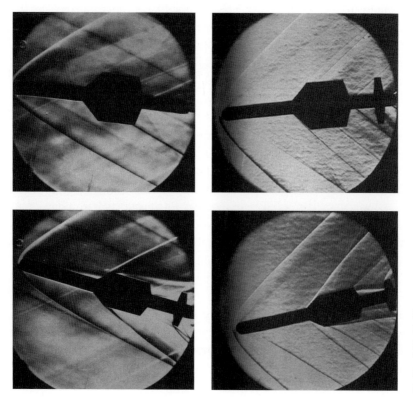

Fig.5.1. a and b Shock waves in the NPL Wind Tunnel at Mach 1.6 and Mach 2.35.

Fig.5.2. Red Dean as intended for mounting under 'thin-winged' Javelin aircraft in a wind tunnel.[18]

Aberration of the Radar transmissions due to the Radome at the nose of the missile was the next important consideration in confirming the general missile configuration. The fixed cruciform wing and controls configuration with a hemispherical radome was found to be less expensive than other configurations with otherwise the same performance. Furthermore, anticipated development of a more aerodynamic radome shape would further increase performance due to reduced drag, which became possible with shapes such as an 'ogive'.

A general analysis of various shapes and sizes employing the chosen configuration resulted in firm choices for weight: 650lb, Body Diameter (initially 15in, later reduced to improve low altitude performance) 12.5in.

Further considerations receiving early attention were the high-altitude performance to be available from adequate wing area to create up to 15g of manoeuvrability in each wing plane, the effect of minimum length and body diameter for optimum arrangement of internal equipment, and calculation of the aerodynamic loads for structural strength. Associated with this were the effects of aerodynamic heating which occurs at high Mach numbers, on the strength of the materials in structure. Besides these considerations, by way of mathematical modelling and design and the wind tunnel tests to obtain measurements of the aerodynamic characteristics, realistic flight testing was necessary to verify characteristics before the design could be regarded as firm. The initially chosen 15in body diameter was reduced to 12.5in during this analysis process, altering the flight trials models' scale from ⅓ to ⅖.

The first flight trials used several dozen ⅖-scale rocket boosted fired at Larkhill, to achieve a maximum speed of Mach 2.3. After aerodynamic separation of the consumed boost motors, the coasting missile was subjected to tests and internal instrumentation, and/or radio telemetry to ground stations provided readings from which the aerodynamic characteristics could be obtained. The missiles were finally programmed to fire an explosive Cordtex ring, causing break-up into two sections. This had the effect of slowing the parts' final descent to well within the calculated Safety Trace representing the boundary of

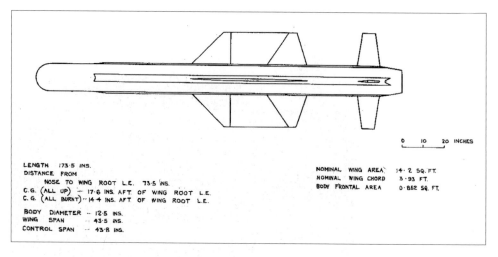

Fig.5.3. Red Dean WTV4 configuration and dimensions summarised in a February 1954 Report.[22]

possible ground strike positions, allowing for all foreseeable modes of failure. One of my first tasks after joining the Trials Section under Barry MacGowan was to design the rocket booster, compute the safety trace and to select the internally carried instrumentation for my own subsequent laborious analysis.

For rocket booster design, we were able to rely on various existing boost motors made by the Rocket Propulsion Establishment of the RAE at Westcott, and the Demon Booster became the unit of choice. The first question was how many Demons would be required to bring the Red Dean model test vehicles up to speed within the limits of the Safety Trace for the Larkhill range. At first glance, it would appear that the more Demon boosters used in an assembly to create the booster rocket, the faster the missile trajectory would be achieved. However, besides requiring sufficient thrust to accelerate the weight of the missile and to overcome its drag, the booster also had to accelerate its own weight and overcome its own drag. It also had to carry drag-producing tail fins of the correct size to ensure a stable flight, and all of this had to accelerate at something like 20g. A logarithmic law of diminishing returns soon showed that a booster assembly with two Demons was not quite up to the job, one with three Demons just about reached the required speed in time, but an assembly with four demons actually achieved a less satisfactory trajectory rather than a better one. My Mach 2 'plus' design therefore used a 'Triplex Demon' booster.

While Vickers technicians Teddy Pierce, Alan Jones, Don Wells and the missile's designer draughtsman Frank Howard were responsible for readying the test vehicles and their instrumentation, RAE range personnel operated the launching rockets and firing sequences, creating great trails of fire and smoke as the rockets literally leapt off the launcher. They also operated the Kinetheodolite cameras to record the test vehicles' trajectories and visible behaviour, as well as the telemetry receiving and recording equipment. Test vehicles carried accelerometers coupled with centrifuge calibrated 'scratch recorders' to measure the 'g' due to drag and lateral accelerations. This required painstaking recovery

Fig.5.4. Triplex Demon rocket booster designed by me, with ⅔-scale Red Dean model.[86]

of the missile parts after break-up and impact onto the range, and also required retrieving the delicate scratch recorder films for later analysis back at Weybridge. Our regular trips to Salisbury Plain in a company Austin A40 car involved overnight stays in 'digs' with a somewhat miserly budget of 15s per night (no hotels for weekly paid staff). En route, we would stop for any meals at the Linga Longa café on the A303, where our daily allowance of 3s 6d provided sufficient sustenance to supplement any sandwiches we may have brought with us. On the earliest morning arrivals, however, before going onto the range, we could pick great, tasty mushrooms in the fields to take home.

The WTV1A series
The WTV1A series of twelve firings on which I reported in 1952 and 1953 obtained preliminary aerodynamic information using both hemispherical and conical nose shapes, and established the ground-launched rocket firing techniques. Analysis of the Kinetheodolite films, that also precisely recorded the intersecting directions in which they were looking for triangulation of the trajectory's path, permitted confirmatory aerodynamic data to be calculated, and also provided a pictorial view of the missiles' behaviour during flight. The immediate results provided measurements of drag throughout the speed range, from Mach 1.5 during the decelerating 'coast' phase until break-up and other information enabling the next series of firings to proceed.

The WTV1B/1 series
The WTV1B/1 series of twelve more test vehicles in late 1953 enabled us to measure lateral aerodynamic characteristics. Measurements of cross-coupling rolling moments generated by lateral movements in flight proved to be affected by small wing misalignments and were not completed. In this series, test vehicle control surfaces were fixed at various offset angles to create the pitch and yaw forces that may cause cross-coupled rolling moments. After my initial firings, these were continued by Henry Hunt and John Curry.

Fig.5.5. H.P. Air-driven Gyroscope used for roll control of Red Dean ⅖-scale (5in diameter) models for Rocket Boosted ground-launched trials.[23]

The WTV1B/2 series

The WTV1B/2 series, starting in 1952 and comprising thirty-six test vehicles, overlapping the earlier tests, sought more ambitious results, using a gyroscope to stabilise the missile in roll and employing one pair of miniature actuator driven controls as ailerons. The other (pair of rudder) controls were fixed at various deflections. These more complex rounds fired between 1954 and early 1955 used Radio Telemetry to provide sixteen channels of information from accelerometers, the gyroscope and the actuators. In the days prior to the advent of transistors, the use of telemetry employing thermionic valves under severe vibration and 'g' forces, and the need to dissipate heat from the valves, added to any other reliability problems. The telemetry 'histogram' of the sixteen channels' data required calibrations of each channel to be consistent with the range of expected data variation. Added to the need for rapidly moving missile borne antennas to radiate sufficient signal to the ground station from widely varying trajectories, the telemetry instrumentation system of the day was as likely to cause abortive trials as the developing test vehicles themselves. These trials reaching into 1954 were reported by John Curry, Henry Hunt and Don Wells.

The Gyro rotor was run up to speed using high pressure air, fed in through the nozzle on the right of the picture. The nozzle also caged the gyro's gimbals until a couple of seconds before launch, when the nozzle was pneumatically ejected, automatically de-caging the Gyro. A voltage output from the potentiometer (bottom of picture) 'picks off' the missile's roll angle for control purposes and to feed to Telemetry.

These WTV1B range of test vehicles were subject to airflow incidences of up to 10°, and lateral forces of up to 6,000lb, requiring an increase in weight from 100lb to 200lb to avoid creating excessive manoeuvre 'g'. This consequently required the structure to be manufactured from high-grade steel instead of the light alloy used in WTV1/A. In order to boost these missiles up to over Mach 2.0, the Triplex Demon Booster was be used.

Disturbances to the missile's flight were used to measure its aerodynamic stability, by creating measurements of how lateral acceleration is damped out. The disturbances were produced by the firing of 'bonkers' – small explosive charges detonated by a timer, to create a sideways impulse. The resulting oscillations can be likened to the oscillations of a spring and, when recorded against a real time base provided in the Telemetry system, they produce a plot of the missile's lateral 'g' variations against time. These trials successfully measured lateral aerodynamic characteristics, although they were marred by the high level of telemetry failures.

Airborne firing trials of Red Dean were scheduled from Canberra B2 jet bombers – the only available aircraft capable of the required high altitude (up to 48,000ft) and the necessary high subsonic speeds. Canberra WD935 was already used for Blue Boar trials, and WD956 was added, both aircraft being fitted with under-wing pylons, electrical power and support systems for two Red Dean test vehicles.

Before airborne firing trials could be contemplated, wind tunnel tests were conducted on the aircraft/missile configuration. These were aimed at checking the effect of the missile on the aircraft's performance and the ability to jettison a missile safely. It was also necessary to test the rocket motor's satisfactory functioning in Red Dean test vehicles, and any damage to the aircraft structure due to the rocket efflux. After initial firings in a Static Firing Rig at RPD Westcott, ground-launched firings of full scale vehicles was the first step.

With WTV2C full-scale rounds between September 1953 and June 1954, ten ground-launched rocket firings were conducted at Aberporth, from a Canberra wing section with a pylon mounted rail launcher (obtained from the retrieved wing after a jet pipe failure on a Canberra requiring a rebuild). These proved the planned aircraft firing trials technique, initially with the 6,000lb-thrust Buzzard motor, and later for the operational 15,000lb-thrust Falcon rocket motor-powered Red Dean. In these trials, some test vehicles were tipped with an Ogival nose shape, representing a radome producing lower drag than the hemispherical nose initially anticipated. Radar aberration could prove to be problematical with a sharper conical nose, but it was anticipated that with an ogival radome, aberration would not unduly affect guidance. These trials provided realistic drag measurements for Red Dean up Mach 1.1.

Factors affecting the development of the weapon system

Flight trials relating to these factors are described later. However, theoretical assessments, wind tunnel test and ground-launched firings of Red Dean models were carefully interwoven and their results compared, in order to establish the accuracy with which performance predictions might be possible over flight regimes that could not be fully tested in flight trials.[24] Agreement was better at supersonic speeds than subsonic, with variations depending on the parameter in question. It was found that with certain factors applied as a result of these trials, predictions would be realistic and within 1955, it was possible to refine Red Dean's body, wing and control surface designs, towards the final shape of WTV5 and the Red Dean Prototype. Changes included the lengthening of the body and altering the wing plan form to align the missile's centre of pressure more accurately, with a more forward centre of gravity as the rocket motor fuel was consumed, and as previously underestimated component weights became better known. Telemetry failures with the scale model flight trials failed to give sufficient information concerning roll control (using the pairs of elevators and rudders working together as ailerons). However, studies indicated that even when the manoeuvring missile would be 'fighting' rolling moments due to large lateral incidences, a slightly increased control surfaces span would provide enough aileron control with only 7° of the available 30° control deflection being used for roll control. Their detailed shape was altered to minimise the effects of local centre of pressure movements with Mach No. and with incidence. Structural design of the total airframe went through the earlier stages of WTV2 and WTV4 for Autopilot flight testing, before the WTV5 design with new honeycomb wing construction techniques could be ready in 1956/57. More details of this are given in a later section.

The foregoing missile design parameters and details were all defined by 'Dab' and others, in the context of the wider requirements for the overall weapon system. These included the fighter's AI search and lock-follow Radar and launch computer, its ability to put the missile's mutually pulse locked guidance Radar onto the target(s) for its own lock-follow phase and the subsequent autopilot controlled navigation to one or more evading targets. The missile characteristics discussed above had to be thus integrated into a highly complex system involving all of these parts – and deliver Red Dean to within a maximum of 50ft 'miss distance', for its 100lb fragmentation warhead to achieve the required lethality. At each step of this process, a variety of problems and contingencies had to be addressed and interactions assessed, in order that eventual homing trials should result in the minimum need for modifications and re-testing. To assist this, simulations were conducted at the GEC's guidance laboratories in Stanmore. However, these were two-dimensional, requiring further simulation in three dimensions at the RAE using their Tridac Computer. These studies led to a number of important but acceptable limiting parameters, within which the fighter, the AI Radar and Red Dean had to operate.

For example, in order to ensure the fighter's safety after launching Red Dean, the range at firing was specified to be not less than 1,800 yards. In a stern chase, this was a limiting factor, while in a head-on attack, much greater ranges would apply, yet the maximum launching range could not exceed the Red Dean guidance head's ability to lock onto a target with an Radar Echoing Area of 10sq.m, representing the amount of energy reflected by the target. This was equivalent to returns from a 10sq.m plate at right-angles to the direction of view. Using Radar pulses of 50kW power, this maximum range was limited to 7,500 yards. Furthermore, the missile could be launched from a fighter pointing anything up to 15° off the target sight line. The achievement of a kill from these ranges depended on Red Dean's manoeuvrability, defined by the 15g in each of the horizontal and vertical control planes of a roll stabilised missile. This in turn depended on the missile's speed and the altitude of the attack trajectory – and, of course, the wing area available to generate the manoeuvre (at least 10g at 50,000ft). The Operational Requirement and the missile's capabilities merged into an attack altitude range between 10,000ft and 50,000ft, where its accuracy would depend on whether a single or multiple targets were being attacked – and on the separation between the targets. Discrimination of targets between 200 and 400 yards separations was evaluated, with the lower (more difficult) separation being found to be achievable over the required height range. It was determined that this could be more easily achieved if the missile started to manoeuvre during the 2 seconds-long 15-20g acceleration boost phase. The remaining coast phase of the trajectory could last another 8 seconds, during which the deceleration due to drag could be as high 8g (at low altitude). Within these parameters, the Homing Head Radar guidance system had to look through the varying thickness of the Radome, and as already indicated, the shape and material through which the beam travels can cause aberration errors, which either have to be measured and compensated for, or filtered out.

The reflections from the target normally contain an element of 'jitter', 'glint' effects and can even contain 'squint' errors, which together with any aberration problems inject 'noise' into the guidance system, causing both guidance errors and potentially destabilising effects in the missile's autopilot control loop. Vibrations within the missile during this rough ride can inject further instabilities, unless the detailed design can eliminate its effects. The simulations conducted at the GEC and at RAE provided enough information to indicate that the system can be made relatively immune to these effects and achieve the required accuracy. Nevertheless, the detailed design of the Homing Head and the Navigation Computer and Autopilot had to take these factors into account, before embarking on flight trials of the overall system.

The actual route between the launch point and the target, and the resulting need to manoeuvre at up to 15g was by means of a homing trajectory computed in the Navigation Computer. This used as its input, the angular rate at which the guidance system's auto-follow Radar sight line to the target was seen to change and applying a multiplying factor to demand an appropriately faster rate of missile manoeuvre. The greater this 'k' factor, the faster the missile will turn towards the target. With a 'k' factor of 1, the missile will always finish up in a tail chase. With k=2, the path will be circular, while with higher values, more manoeuvre occurs during early stages of homing, leaving more time for finer corrections, and more time to deal with targets which may themselves be taking evasive action with turn rates of up to 3g. Clearly its turning rate must be limited by the missile's structural strength and conversely, at high altitude, the available lift to create manoeuvre becomes limited. For these reasons, the value of 'k' needed to be chosen immediately before launch, depended on the launching speed and height. Initially, the missile was intended to conduct its manoeuvre after rocket burn-out, during the 'coast' phase. However, the studies again showed that better accuracy was obtainable over the whole range of launching altitudes, if a 'manoeuvre during boost' phase was utilised and the Navigation Computer had to be given different parameters for this 2-second period.

Thus, Red Dean underwent a series of design changes from the original Folland Aircraft design, through the several test vehicle series, toward the final design for the Prototype Red Dean WTV5.

This development process was carried out in the context of earlier memoranda, including that on 7 September 1951 from W/C Hunter-Tod, RAE project[31] officer, and the air officer commander-in-chief, Fighter Command[32] on 25 February 1952, concerning the question of height bands for guided missiles in the context of the (anticipated by 1957) threats arising from the Cold War, and how the weapon system should be configured with respect to Interceptor performance, AI Radar performance and the Armaments that would be required. The eventual change in the specified maximum operating height from 60,000ft to 50,000ft was accepted in the context of these papers and the many theoretical system studies referred to above.

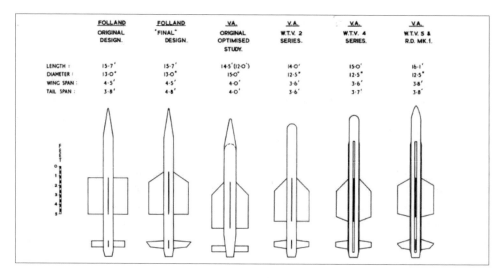

	FOLLAND ORIGINAL DESIGN.	FOLLAND 'FINAL' DESIGN.	V.A. ORIGINAL OPTIMISED STUDY.	V.A. W.T.V. 2 SERIES.	V.A. W.T.V. 4 SERIES.	V.A. W.T.V. 5 & R.D. MK.1.
LENGTH :	15·7'	15·7'	14·5'(12·0')	14·0'	15·0'	16·1'
DIAMETER :	13·0"	13·0"	15·0"	12·5"	12·5"	12·5"
WING SPAN :	4·5'	4·5'	4·0'	3·6'	3·6'	3·8'
TAIL SPAN :	3·8'	4·8'	4·0'	3·6'	3·7'	3·8'

Fig.5.6. Progression of Red Dean test vehicle designs.[24]

Structural considerations

Body, wing and control-surface design also underwent a progressive process, as analysis and design of the major component contents progressed: homing guidance head, autopilot, warhead, proximity fuze, rocket motor, the electrical and hydraulic power supply system, hydraulic fin actuators. The resulting overall weight and performance of Red Dean were analysed in ever greater depth as test vehicles for flight trials were constructed and first tested under vibration and other stressed conditions. Besides the various aerodynamic and propulsive forces becoming more firmly defined as trials progressed, factors to be taken into account included the important matter of kinetic heating at high Mach numbers during an engagement. A limitation to the skin leading-edge temperature of 250°C could not be exceeded without invoking the use of titanium and high-strength steel (which was nevertheless envisaged for later versions, particularly when launched from supersonic fighters at up to M1.7). Furthermore, during final stages of the WTV5 design, an aerodynamic simulator was constructed and investigations made[25] of structural aeroelasticity and stability of the design (resonances causing flutter and airframe distortions affecting alignments).

The Honeycomb Sandwich Wing design undertaken by A.W. Kitchenside in the Stress Office under Peter Stannard and Peter Mobsby in the GW Department, caters for the above effects while minimising weight, and is described in his report.[26] With this technique used in the (USA) Glenn Martin Co.'s Matador project, a honeycomb-filled structure with Durestos heat insulation was shown to create the lightest, thinnest and stiffest wing section without propensity to panel flutter, with a good surface finish and minimised weight. Relative ease of manufacture was also of great importance. The manufacturing technique employing high temperature Redux bonding and air drying required great attention to detail, involving the wing frame, wing skins, doublers, the honeycomb core and their assembly. The resulting wings were made and proved on test rigs, before use with air-fired test vehicles.

The black skin panels seen in Fig.5.7 are the Durestos lagging elements over the Aluminium panels between which the Aluminium honeycomb is glued. The development process underwent many changes of bonding technique, including the details of glue depth and glue line width, before arriving at the optimum design. The bonding process under high temperature also underwent changes, particularly the concentration of heating at the heavier root section and the speed of heating up to the required temperature, to avoid bonding properties being destroyed during prolonged periods of lower than required temperature. With the added use of rivets at the root sections, that also served as conduits for cabling between body sections, the required wing strength was achieved and the wing weight target of 20lb per wing was surpassed by this weight becoming only 15.3lb. In the final WTV5 design, the number of shear webs between the leading and trailing edges was reduced to two, relying entirely on the honeycomb for internal support over much of the wing area.

Body structure development also followed a development process, initially considering 'manacle joints', but finally ending up with the light-alloy monocoque tube body sections being locked together on assembly, by 'piston ring' joints. Body joint placings naturally followed the five main sections (from the rear): control surfaces actuator ring and the hydraulic and pneumatic bottles, rocket motor, warhead and initiator, autopilot and turbo-alternator electrical power pack, proximity fuze electronics, homing head and radome. The wing chord being of similar length to the rocket motor fixed that combination, with aerodynamic wing design being such as to match the centre of pressure to the missile's centre of gravity. The fuze aerial orientation requirement with respect to the wings was found not to be unfavourably affected as the contractor EMIED initially feared, and it was found possible to insert channels for the fuze aerials (remoted from their electronics) into extensions of the wing roots. This also minimised aerial distortion.

Besides development of the piston ring joints to achieve the required bending strength of the missile body under rapid manoeuvre 'g' conditions, considerable attention was given to heating caused by Mach 2 and higher speeds of the attack trajectories. While the radome tip temperature could be permitted to reach 250°C in the short time to target, and wing leading edge temperatures may reach similar levels, the heat would have to be dissipated rapidly enough for the wing structure not to exceed 150°C. Internal warhead temperature rise during extended carry before firing, was kept to 18°C by air insulation

Fig.5.7. Red Dean WTV4 with wing skin removed, to show honeycomb sandwich construction.[26]

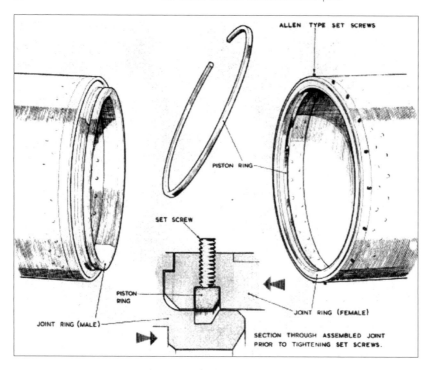

Fig.5.8. Details of Piston Ring type break joint.[27]

between the missile body skin and the warhead's outer skin. During the 10 seconds or so of the attack trajectory, the warhead would not overheat.

This kinetic heating question required considerable study and an Analogue Heat Flow Computer was specially designed in order to establish the heat flows that may be expected along the wing chord and the body, before structural design could proceed with confidence. This was initially a single-dimensional computation, and later with a design based on a RAE computer, two-dimensional heat flow simulation became possible. This major effort was a development programme in itself, involving both structural designer A.W. Kitchenside and the Electronics Laboratories. The aeroelasticity simulations and structural tests referred to earlier were intimately related, leading to the final designs for WTV5 and the Red Dean Prototype.

Practical details relating to Red Dean's handling and storage before a mission requiring design attention at an early stage included the need for the rocket motor to be non-propulsive. For the RAF, this meant that the Falcon had to be separately stored until the time of deployment. For use with carrier-based aircraft, the Royal Navy required the missile to be stored completely assembled for readiness, mounted on its fighters. This required provision for a missile already attached under the fighter's wing with the rocket motor in a non-propulsive condition, to be rapidly made propulsive by some means outside the missile's body. For aircraft carrier operations, Red Dean also had to withstand the salty and vibration-prone environment on deck, and to function properly after the shocks attendant to the fighter being launched by catapult. Safety of the warhead was another obvious stipulation, affecting the design of the initiator with provision to inhibit this until after the missile was in flight. In the event of a 'miss', a break-up charge had to destroy the missile, to ensure that friendly fighters were not destroyed by overtaking its exploding warhead.

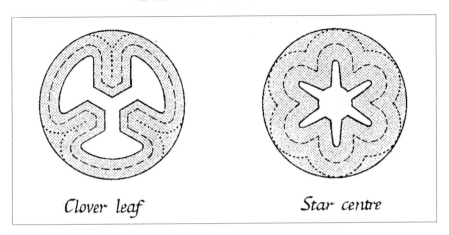

Clover leaf   *Star centre*

Fig.5.9. Typical rocket motor charge cross-sections.

The rocket motor propulsion system

Utility of all the foregoing depended on the solid propellant rocket motors designed by RPD Westcott. After initial use of the interim Buzzard motor providing 6,000lb of thrust for 4 seconds, the operational motor chosen was the more powerful Falcon, giving 15,000lb of thrust for the much preferred short missile boost period of 2 seconds. Cordite rocket propellant extruded into a 'star' section provided an approximately constant burning rate, as the inside surface of the star section burned away towards the outer diameter of its medium-weight rolled and welded sheet motor body casing. This produced a quasi-constant thrust during the missile's boost phase.

Burning rate depends on the chemical nature of the propellant, its temperature and on the pressure within the motor casing. The design of the rocket exhaust nozzle therefore has to balance the need to maintain sufficient pressure to maintain the required rate of burning and the creation of thrust by supersonic escape of the gases through the venturi cone-shaped nozzle. Consequently, the motor body has to withstand the pressure and temperature generated within, while prior to firing the propellant has to retain the required characteristics, after being subjected to the very wide range of temperatures inherent in the missile being carried by a fighter, anywhere from sea level in the tropics to 50,000ft altitude over the arctic.[28]

With both Buzzard and Falcon, since the rocket motors with venturi nozzles were positioned with the wings half way along the missile, a long tail pipe leading to the expansion cone in the tail end of the missile was required. This tail pipe would be surrounded by the compressed gas and hydraulic oil cylinders providing actuation power for the four missile control surfaces near the tail, and it was necessary to lag the outside of these to insulate them from heat generated in the tail pipe. Also, the tail pipe and expansion cone nozzle were therefore made from Durestos, rather than from steel (this changed later to Mintex with glass-cloth tape external reinforcement).

Rocket motors pose a severe safety problem, and besides requiring trials of their operation over the wide temperature range over which the missile must operate, the means of electrical ignition had to be both 'instantaneous' and safe. What is more, it was necessary to have means of testing the ignition circuits for electrical continuity before any trial or operational use, without risking premature ignition. As a trials team, we were not a little conscious of an accident whose gory details quickly made the rounds of the Guided Weapons industry. By all accounts, the rocket motor of a Fairey Aviation Blue Sky test vehicle had inadvertently ignited inside a test hangar, with the result that the missile flew disastrously around inside the hangar, disembowelling one or more trials engineers with its wings, besides burning up everything around its ricocheting trajectory.

The electrical current required to ignite the motor from the aircraft's 28 volts supply was, necessarily, very small. For safety, the firing circuit included a relay operated from this supply and its two independent contacts both had to close in order to complete the firing circuit. Additionally, a manually insertable safety plug would render the ignition circuit unable to pass current until it was inserted just before final continuity testing of the igniter circuit. Testing for continuity was essential to ensure that the missile would be sure to fire after its carriage to the trials range or the interception zone, and this test required current to actually flow through the rocket motor igniter. It is relevant to mention that while conducting a pre-flight continuity test, the trials engineer's head would be close to the motor blast nozzle! Although special safety ohmmeters were used, which were physically unable to create sufficient current to energise the igniter and rocket motor, when conducting a continuity test, we always combined meticulous care with earnest prayers for good luck!

These many factors in Red Dean's rocket propulsion design made it absolutely essential to work up to safe missile firings from an aircraft in flight, via a series of ground tests that would check all aspects of the motor's functioning within the missile's airframe. The first of these was by Static Firings, conducted by RAE/RPD Wescott during the early development stage of the Buzzard and the Falcon motors. These were followed by firings of a large number of simple (Vickers-designed) Projection Test Vehicles (PTV) in proving trials at Larkhill, to verify the safety of the rocket motors for air firings. These rounds carried chamber-pressure monitoring instrumentation and many firings were conducted after the motor and propellant had been 'soaked' at the extremes of temperature over which Red Dean had to be stored and flown. Following one failure of the motor head-end causing the missile to blow up (due to a crack in the propellant charge), each charge was thereafter X-rayed. The Buzzard and Falcon thereby completing their basic development, in the next phase firings were made from a fixed Canberra wing at the Aberporth range. These measured blast effects on the wing structure and provided flight information from the WTV2C1 test vehicles employing either cable telemetry or 600MHz radio telemetry. In firings between September 1953 and June 1954, the observed blast effects showed the need for blast protection of the Canberra wing structure and this became part of the Canberras' modification before air firings commenced.

Later in the programme to test the effects of motor firings on the fuze in 1955 and 1956, a Static Firing Rig was constructed at Wisley that supported a full-scale Red Dean airframe with its rocket motor. The rig was built to restrain the missile during motor firing, employing rubber in shear mountings and cables with spring-loaded dashpots. Thrust and vibration measurements were made with instrumentation relayed via three twelve-channel recorders wired directly to the rig. Telemetry transmitters were also able to make more limited recordings using the Wisley telemetry receiving ground station.

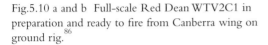

Fig.5.10 a and b Full-scale Red Dean WTV2C1 in preparation and ready to fire from Canberra wing on ground rig.[86]

Red Dean flight trials with Canberra aircraft

Besides external mild steel skin added to the blast affected areas, in order to proof the wings against the rocket motor blast as the missiles sped away, additional internal cleating of the skin to the wing ribs was necessary. However, before even the early air firings could be contemplated, besides making these modifications, the Canberras were fitted with pylons in a paired front and rear configuration. The missile's carriage was principally supported by the front pylon holding a launching shoe hung on a bomb slip. A smaller rear pylon provided stability and entry for the electrical motor ignition supply from the aircraft's 28 volts system.

Within the front pylon, a retractable Plug Base mechanism supplied the missile with its external power supplies as well as other operational commands needed before firing. It would later also provide hydraulic supplies for homing head cooling during the carry phase. The design was configured to enable ready jettisoning of missiles in the event of aircraft handling problems or other untoward situations. The launching shoe provided the missile with a suitably free sliding action of sufficient length to gain speed before becoming free of all restraint after the rocket motor was fired. Spring retractable crutching buttons in the missile body held the missile firmly to the launching rail until the missile moved forward on firing. In order to restrain the missile from forward or rearward motion during the carry phase, its movement was obstructed by a shear pin that protruded from the front pylon into the missile structure. The pin's shear strength at the narrowed diameter in the interface between missile and shoe was overcome by rocket motor thrust and, as the pin broke, the missile was released.

As will be later described, the shear pin design was not totally proof against incorrect assembly and after some successful firings it was replaced by a more complicated Retractable Latch Pin design involving a solenoid and micro switches to verify it had retracted, before power would be able to pass into the motor firing circuit.

WTV2A rounds without rocket motors were used in carry trials between October 1953 and May 1954, to check any handling effects on the Canberra over its operational height and speed ranges and to demonstrate safe jettisoning. In addition, the range of

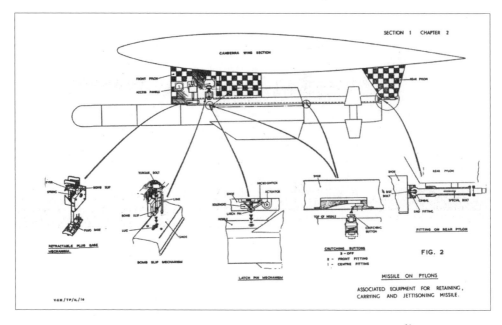

Fig.5.11 Red Dean installation drawing for mounting to Canberra B2, with details.[30]

temperatures within the missile during carry was investigated and the effectiveness of telemetry aerials was verified, for transmission to receivers at Wisley and the Aberporth range where successful jettison trials were conducted. The trials observers on most of these were Ron Jupp and John Curry.

I was lucky enough to fly one such carry trial, where the Canberra's acceleration performance was explored, while carrying the Red Deans. Flown at 15,000ft, this involved starting a run at 1.2 x stalling speed – about 130kts – and accelerating at full throttle up to 450kts. My hitherto best acceleration experiences had been on a motor bike that nearly pulled the handlebars out of my grip for a few seconds. Perhaps somewhat pedestrian compared with present-day jets with reheat, we were nevertheless pushed forcefully back into our seats and remained that way for more than a minute, until we reached 450kts. It was certainly exhilarating as the acceleration seemed to last for ever, without apparent reduction in performance due to drag from the missiles.

Jettison tests included the condition when the aircraft was deliberately yawed, to simulate an 'engine out' condition. They were completely successful and no excessive trim changes were required.

In Fig.12 opposite, camera pods are seen at each wing tip. These contained sideways- and forward-looking GSAP cameras used to record the jettison or firing of the missiles on 16mm film.

Following these trials starting in June 1954, after carry trials to investigate the effects of low temperature, buffeting and aircraft manoeuvre on the Buzzard rocket motor, WTV2C1 rounds were launched in early airborne firing trials. The first firing created a sharp yawing effect as the rocket thrust sheared the missile's retaining pin, but this was considered to be acceptable. However, the second firing led to a near disaster.

Fig.5.12 Canberra WD956 with two Red Dean test vehicles over Wisley runway.[33]

Flying at 45,000ft over Aberporth with test pilot Spud Murphy at the controls, the missile was fired, but failed to break the shear pin. The additional 6,000lb of thrust on one side of the aircraft immediately caused a large yawing effect and also began to accelerate the aircraft from its Mach 0.8 speed, towards the Canberra's Mach 0.82 limit for transonic buffeting. Applying hard opposite rudder to counter the yawing moment added to the already increasing rolling tendency due to the high yaw rate. This created an almighty rolling effect that turned the Canberra upside down and once more through 360°. Flick rolls are hardly normal nor desirable at 45,000ft and while upside down, the gravity-dependent fuel system no longer fed the engines, which both flamed out. At this point, Red Dean thankfully broke free and disappeared into the northern Cardigan Bay horizon. The old saying, 'there I was, upside down with nothing on the clock' really came true, but Spud quickly righted the plane and dived to lose height, while transmitting 'Mayday' signals to the nearest emergency diversion airfields at RAF stations Brawdy and Haverford West. At the 28,000ft maximum altitude at which it was possible to re-light the Avon jets, Spud managed to start one of them and brought the Canberra back to Wisley for a safe landing. I had the job of viewing the GSAP camera films taken in the wing tip pods and, realising that I could well have been on board, as with many other trials, grimly witnessed the horizon making one and a half awesome gyrations as the aircraft rolled, followed by the missile flying off into the distance.

Thereafter, some choice words flowed into the aircraft design office, assuring Henry Gardner that Spud would refuse to fly any more firing trials until the missile retaining system was redesigned to make such a hang-up impossible. The 'fail safe' Retractable Latch Pin retaining mechanism described earlier resulted from this near disaster, and after some months of design, survival testing under low temperature and vibration conditions, its operation in carry trials was verified by suitable monitoring of the pin's proper extraction during the firing sequence. Not only was firing inhibited until micro-switches confirmed the pin's removal from the missile, but they also lit lamps in the cockpit to verify its movement to the aircrew. After this necessary delay to the programme, three

Fig.5.13 WTV2C1 Red Dean mounted under Canberra WD956, ready for take off to Aberporth for firing.[34]

more WTV2C1 firings were successfully achieved over Aberporth without incident. With unrestricted movement of the missile along the launcher rail after extraction of the latch pin, launch was much smoother than when a pin had to be sheared, and disturbance in yaw no longer occurred.

Inspection of the pylon after returning from the hang-up revealed that the shear pin had been incorrectly fitted, so that its reduce-diameter 'neck' was not properly positioned at the missile to rail interface. Instead, the pin's full diameter section was in the gap and this was too strong for the Buzzard motor's thrust to break it. A fuel recuperator system was also fitted to the Canberras, to insure against engines being starved of fuel in any future manoeuvre. Talking of which, when Canberra WD942 was delivered to Woomera, it all but ran out of fuel en-route from Darwin. With fuel gauges showing empty for many minutes, a sweating pilot finally suffered an engine cut on touch down! An equally close shave.

See above (Fig.5.13) for how Red Den was carried on its trials Canberra aircraft WD956 (and similarly on Canberra WD935).

Missile electrical power system

In the context of a weapon system as complex as Red Dean, power supplies might be expected to represent no great part of the development problem. However, as with the other 'side issue' of Telemetry trials instrumentation, power supplies and batteries came with larger than life problems and complexities, equally affecting designers and trials engineers. Since operation of the missile entirely depended on its power supply being within tight limits throughout its wide operating range of height, temperature, and with attendant vibrations and accelerations, the importance of this supply can hardly be overstated.

From the beginning of Red Dean's development, it was realised that to power all of the electronics in the homing head, the autopilot and the fuze, the most suitable sources would be a gas-driven turbo alternator, supplying the variety of voltages and frequencies needed. In July 1952 it was decided to supply 2 Kwatts of power at a frequency of 2,400Hz, 115 volts single phase regulated to within 1.5 per cent and another 200 watts at 400Hz three-phase unregulated voltage. This AC power could then be rectified and controlled by power packs in the main electronic units to produce the required DC voltages needed in analogue electronic amplifiers and other units. Such units were being developed by de Havilland Propellers for the Seaslug missile, but although well advanced, they would not be available in time for early trials with the autopilot, nor for telemetry.

For WTV4A Smiths Interim Autopilot trials, tightly controlled DC voltages were nevertheless required and to be rated for 10 hours of ground testing, plus 30 minutes of carry by aircraft, followed by 2 minutes for missile flight. Supply of 1 to 2 watts at -100 volts DC, 20 to 30 watts at 12 volts DC for valve heaters (oh for transistors!) and 4 to 5 watts at 24 volts DC could be supplied by batteries. Regulator circuits had to maintain these voltages within ±1% and ±2% respectively. The 100 volts were supplied by resin cast Kalium batteries coupled with a neon stabiliser, and the lower voltages were supplied by a block of little Venner silver-zinc accumulators, both giving outputs well within the desired tolerances.

The additional requirement for 40 to 70 watts HT at 350 volts DC implied a very low output impedance, for supplying this power at altitudes up to 50,000ft and temperatures between +30°C and -40°C. In the early missile power supply system, this was provided by a rotary transformer with a shunt-type stabiliser, powered from the aircraft's 28 volts DC supply during carry. For the short duration of missile free flights, a bank of Venner silver-zinc accumulators provided this 28 volts power. Due to batteries' declining performance at low temperature, it was necessary to house all of these batteries in a heated box, thermostatically controlled at 25°C. During early trials, batteries nevertheless 'acted up' with a disproportionate number of failures, due to the more severe effect of intermittent power drain than with a normally steady supply and possibly due to overzealous pre-flight testing by cautious trials engineers.

Turbo-alternator power supplies were first used for Mk 1 Autopilot trials with WTV4B, employing the readily available MPU 302 Alternator. This was driven from compressed air bottles, co-mounted with the hydraulic accumulators and actuators for the rear-mounted control surfaces. For later test vehicles also requiring power for the GEC guidance Homing Head, the MPU 309 Alternator was used, again air driven from the rear-mounted air bottles through a forward-mounted pressure reducing valve. The 5in-diameter turbine wheel drove an axially disposed shaft carrying both the 2,400Hz and the 400Hz alternator elements, which were therefore equally frequency controlled by the 24,000rpm speed of the common shaft. With pneumatic valves, a special High Speed Changeover Switch, piping and associated electronic controller, the turbo-alternator assembly was formed into a cylindrical package, housed under the saddle shape cavity of the autopilot unit.

Since during carry, Red Dean's guidance system becomes locked onto the target, all control, navigation and the fuze systems must be operating on power supplied from the aircraft. The High Speed Changeover Switch was critical to affecting the changeover from external power to the missile's internal power supplies before launch. The maximum permissible duration without power input during this changeover was only 1.5 milliseconds. Power supplied from the aircraft was also produced by (oil-driven)

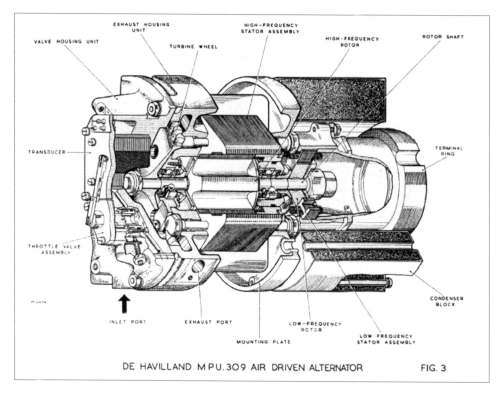

DE HAVILLAND M.P.U. 309 AIR DRIVEN ALTERNATOR   FIG. 3

Fig.5.14 Internal construction of the Red Dean Turbo Alternator.[35]

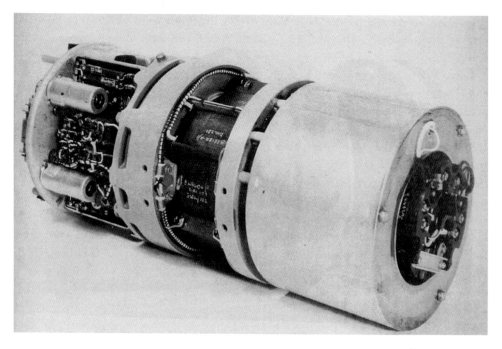

Fig.5.15 Red Dean's DH M.P.U.-309 Turbo Alternator package, including controller.[34]

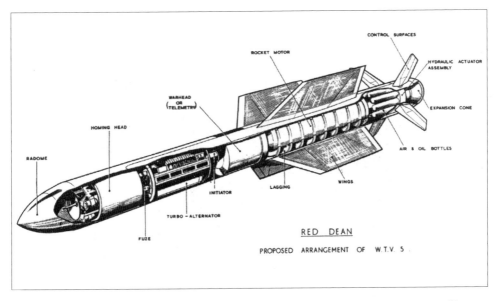

RED DEAN

PROPOSED ARRANGEMENT OF W.T.V. 5

Fig.5.16 Layout of components and overall design for WTV5, prototype for Red Dean Mk.1.[35]

turbo-alternators, one for each of two Red Deans to be carried, and another for the Fire Control, AI Radar system and all the ancillary sequencing and associated systems comprising the overall weapon system.

The illustration and photographs on the opposite page clearly indicate the complexity of the DH Propellers Turbo Alternator design needed to meet the Red Dean requirement.

In the diagram of the Red Dean Mk.1 design, the positions of the main components can be seen, including the MPU-309 Turbo Alternator nestling beneath the Smiths Aircraft Instruments Ltd Autopilot.

While WTV5 did not reach the trials stage, mock-ups of the design were completed and besides the development of the main components, autopilot and navigation computer, guidance homing head, warhead and proximity fuze were well developed. The installation designs for Red Dean on the F153D 'thin-winged' Javelin and its fire control system were taken to an advanced stage, as well as detailed planning and preparation for the final missile proving and RAF acceptance trials at Woomera, against representative targets through the operational spectrum.

In part two of this history of Red Dean, we can now look separately at the overall system design, developments and the trials completed by Vickers Guided Weapons Dept, and development of the above components made by Smiths Aircraft Instruments Ltd (SAI) with British Messier Hydraulics, the General Electric Co. (GEC) and EMI Electronics Ltd (EMIED).

Chapter 5.2

RED DEAN AIR-TO-AIR MISSILE PART 2

The Red Dean Navigation and Autopilot control system

Autopilots may not be an exciting subject for everybody, possibly conjuring up images of a robot wearing a leather helmet and flying goggles, his scarf trailing in the wind, jerkily controlling a flying object. However, in this narrative, the central function of its place in the workings of a guided missile system lead me to risk boring the less technical reader, who may not already be familiar with gyroscopes for determining an object's orientation in space and accelerometers, which measure the objects' motions. These finely tuned instruments are the heart of autopilots, which use equally finely tuned electronic circuits to achieve control of the missile.

Smiths Aircraft Instruments Ltd (SAI) had already been working with Vickers, providing the autopilot for Blue Boar. Under a similar sub-contract to Vickers, SAI was able to take advantage of some basic control system similarities, but now much complicated by the wider and harsher range of missile manoeuvres implied by air-to-air homing – the navigation (homing) course to be followed in response to the Radar homing head's sight line inputs. Considered separately from the Navigation Computer that gave the missile its manoeuvre demands, the autopilot responded to these demands by moving the missile's hydraulically operated control surfaces and ensured that, regardless of altitude and speed within the operational ranges specified, the missile remained stably under control on the desired flight trajectory.

In designing the autopilot, Smiths took into account the altitude range of 10,000ft to 50,000ft, the launch speed range between Mach 0.8 and the supersonic Mach 1.1 and the maximum manoeuvre rates in each wing plane, of 15g (reducing to 10g that is possible in the rarefied air in the stratosphere at 50,000ft). Besides this, the missile's high roll, pitch and yaw rates and accelerations in response to control movements were fed into the mathematical equations representing the missile's motions and its ability to exercise control. This control had to be accurately exercised under conditions of high vibration (which could affect the performance of the instruments) and of course, the missile's manoeuvre accelerations. It will be remembered from the previous chapter that, 'proportional navigation' is in response to signals from the homing head, giving the rates at which the sight line to the target moves – and that these are in the form of rates in the wing planes, the true horizontal and vertical measurements depending on the missile remaining stabilised to a constant roll position.

The navigation computer calculates the lateral and vertical accelerations required of the missile, to pursue the target at a suitably faster multiple of the target sight line rate, this multiple being the proportional navigation Constant. The autopilot causes the missile to achieve this acceleration by moving the hydraulically operated control actuators. The control parameters, particularly the autopilot gain (responsiveness), are further adjusted for the launch conditions of height and speed.

Partly for these related reasons, the rocket propulsion was arranged to give a short as possible boost period (2 seconds), initially leaving the navigation to be achieved during the longer coast phase after burn out. Original design was based on the assumption that it would not be possible to navigate during the boost phase, due to the instruments being adversely affected by the attendant vibrations. This placed restrictions on the obtainable miss distance. As the development testing and initial trials proceeded, it was found that the instruments would be sufficiently accurate during the boost phase, to permit manoeuvre during boost, thus improving overall lethality. The nature of this manoeuvre would, however, only be truly determinable after trials with the homing head showed the extent to which its sight line rate signals might be themselves affected by rocket motor vibrations and Radar noise. A compromise navigation regime during boost was to be used in early homing trials, where a constant 'g' manoeuvre rate would be demanded, its value depending on the initial aiming error at launch, but unaffected by excessive Radar noise that may occur in a fully closed loop system during boost. A significant launching aiming error had to be tolerable if the fighter was not to be unduly restricted in its manoeuvre. Changeover from boost navigation to coast phase navigation was considered to be most reliable, using an inertia switch to sense the end of boost, and this was successfully laboratory tested.

The proportional navigation constant itself would need to take account of the direction of attack and this was fed into the navigation formula by applying another factor, the missile's velocity along the sight line. Ideally, this would have been a measurement of the Radar range rate to the target, but this measurement was considered to be in danger of being denied by jamming signals from the target. Another compromise allowed an approximation to be used, namely a fixed value or range rate to be set in, dependent on the direction of attack (from the rear, side angles, or head on). The effects of Radar jitter and radome aberration causing noisy inputs to the navigation computer required further attention, and after studying various solutions, a simple 'bracketing filter' was chosen. This had the effect of filtering out the noise, but at the same time inserting a time lag into the control system. A careful balance between these two effects was necessary, and could only be finally proved in firings where the GEC homing head was giving real-time signals to the navigation computer.

Without going into the mathematics of missile navigation and control, a brief study of Figs 5.17 and 5.18 readily show the nature of the geometrical parameters that are handled by the autopilot and navigation computer electronics. In Fig.5.17, the missile's roll, yaw and

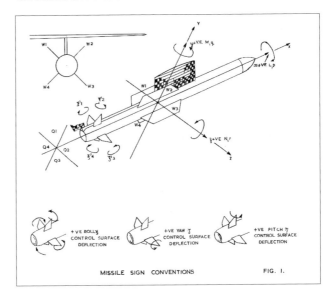

Fig.5.17 Missile orientation diagram for autopilot control.[36]

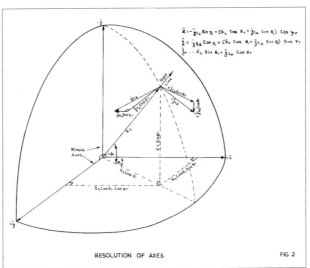

Fig.5.18 Geometry of missile sight line relative to the target.[36]

pitch axes and its rotations around these axes in response to the control movements can be qualitatively seen. The mathematical symbols represent the parameters handled by the autopilot's control system. In Fig.18, the missile's resultant accelerations are shown relative to the sight line towards the target, and these are the prime movers of the homing equations mentioned above. The angles and directions have to be resolved from measurements by the instruments – gyroscopes and accelerometers – and this all depends on the missile remaining roll stabilised to a constant orientation around its longitudinal axis.

At a first look, roll would most readily be stabilised using the reference of a roll displacement gyro and this was Smiths' first method during development of the Interim Series 4 Autopilot. Between January and September 1955, test firing of the WTV4A test vehicles were conducted over Aberporth, after an extensive series of carry trials to check the telemetry and its heating and switching systems. On these being cleared, firings were conducted in progressive steps of complication, starting with purely roll-only control flights and followed by firings with control in all three axes and applying varying manoeuvre demands during the coasting flights.

Although three of the early rounds of seven fired lost control, the series was successful in determining the need to include limiting filters to the roll control loop, to prevent instability due to saturation of the control servo amplifiers. Including lateral manoeuvres, all objectives of these trials were achieved; one related to a change in the method of roll control in subsequent autopilots.

Stabilisation in roll required a 'phase advance' signal to be applied to the control loop in addition to roll position as measured by the displacement gyro. This electronically created signal effectively provided a roll rate, to damp any oscillations of the loop. However, it was found that uneven (non-linear) response of the control actuators reduced the control margin to the point where it was desirable to redesign the roll control system. Thus, the Series 5 autopilots tested in later WTV4B missiles used a Roll Rate Gyroscope and an Integrator, to create the roll displacement value. The use of rate gyroscopes was in any case a necessary part of the lateral control loops, reducing the number of instrument types to be developed and proved. Accelerometers needed in the lateral control loops were carried in different locations on different WTV4A firings, to find the position where vibration effects would be minimised.

As Observer/trials engineer on a successful firing after three carry trials between 20,000ft and 40,000ft, my Observer's kneepad log for 26 August 1955 shows WTV4A/9 firing off smoothly, with the trajectory noted as being 'down a bit'. The retractable latch pin system worked well. The eighth round of the series was never fired, due to an unrelated minor accident with the Canberra WD935 that became the source of amusement in the GW Department. The Wisley runway ended relatively close to the A3 arterial road running across the landing direction. Consequently, the Surrey County Council placed a large 'Sudden Aircraft Noise' sign by the road side, to warn drivers who might otherwise be frightened into an accident as our Canberras took off over their heads. On a day when I was away on a brief visit to Aberporth with trials colleague Bob Taylor in the company's DH Dove transport aircraft, piloted by Dizzy Addicott, another pilot was practicing take-offs and landings on this runway. After a large number of landings, his brakes overheated. Failing at the critical moment, the Canberra finished up with one wing spread across the A3 – clearly visible from the Dove as we circled to land. Next day, our resident cartoonist Peter Mobsby produced a drawing showing this scene and the Surrey County Council's warning sign. However, the word 'Noise' was boldly crossed out, leaving an all too truthful warning, 'Sudden Aircraft N̶o̶i̶s̶e̶'.

The instrument heart of SAI's autopilot was now the Rate Gyroscopes, whose voltage output to the electronic control circuits were proportional respectively to the rates of missile roll, pitch and yaw, and the Accelerometers which measured the pitch and yaw manoeuvring accelerations.

The gyroscopic effect depends on the spinning rate of a rotor remaining sensibly constant. In a displacement gyro, the rotor is mounted in two sets of gimbals mutually at right angles to the rotor axis, such that if the missile body moves about the gimbals, the rotor axis remains fixed in space. In this manner, the gimbal angles represent the angles

Left Fig.5.19 Flight observer's view of knee pad (after fifty years).[37]

Extreme left: Fig.5.20 Cockpit record of missile firing.[37]

through which the missile has moved in the other two axes. Such angles are 'picked off' by potentiometers to produce error signals to the control system. Ensuring very small friction of the rotor bearings and the gimbal bearings is critical to avoiding drift away from the rotor's original axis in space. This is similar to the gyro shown in Fig.5.5.

Differently constructed, the SAI rate gyroscope's dynamically balanced rotor contains a stator mounted on a fixed spindle, fed with 115 volts, 400Hz three–phase AC (alternating current). The 400Hz electromagnetic field induced in the stator by this current rotates at that frequency and creates an electromagnetic drag, driving the surrounding rotor to follow it. The result is known as a hysteresis motor, running at 400 rotations per second – 24,000rpm. If a torque is applied to the gimbal of any gyroscope, the rotor's spin axis is caused to precess in a mutually perpendicular direction. Thus the rate gyro works by applying the necessary amount of torque, to cause procession against any rotational movement of the missile. The amount of torque required to keep to the rotor spin axis steady is a measure of the missile's roll rate. If the missile is controlled to a zero roll rate, the rate gyro axis and its gimbals remain in their original orientations. One of the two spindles connecting SAI's gyro gimbals to the missile frame incorporates a torsion bar, which provides the torque to precess gyro at a rate corresponding to the rate at which the missile is being turned. The resulting deflection of the gimbal is measured by an electro-magnetic pick-off, providing an electrical signal that can be electronically integrated to create an analogue of the roll displacement for control purposes.

The roll-rate measurement and the roll displacement signal were combined in a suitable control loop equation (transfer function), applying demands to the control actuators enabling the autopilot to control to a constant roll angle, with sufficient stability to avoid unwanted oscillations.

Today's gyroscopes, employing ring laser techniques, are mechanically much simpler, yet much more accurate than was possible to conceive in the 1950s. SAI's design was

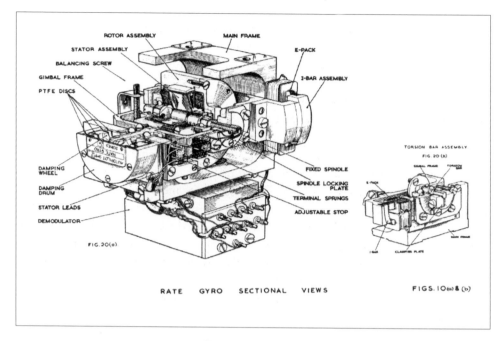

Fig.5.21 SAI Rate Gyro sectional views.[38]

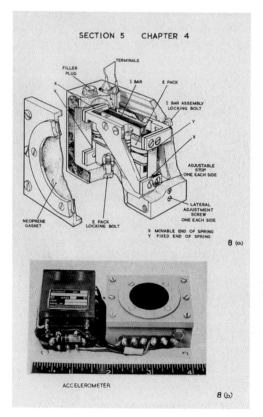

Fig.5.22 SAI accelerometer and sectional view.[38]

nevertheless able to meet the requirement, with the help of special measures.[38] These were incorporated to eliminate the effect of differential expansions between the elements due to temperature changes and also to provide damping of gimbal movements by employing a damping wheel in silicone fluid.

One rate gyro was used for roll stabilisation and one each for control in pitch and yaw. These latter control planes also required accelerometers as already mentioned, and a further accelerometer to measure accelerations along the missile's longitudinal axis.

Simple in principle, accelerometers rely on the movement of a spring-suspended mass, when subject to acceleration in the direction of sensitivity. The spring rate and maximum deflection are chosen to correspond with the ±25g range chosen for measurement – well within the ±15g maximum manoeuvre demanded of the missile, in order to maintain linear outputs. The mass formed the 'I' bar of an 'E and I' pick-off that was fixed relative to the missile body and supplied with a 115 volts-single phase 2,400Hz input by the missile's alternator. Movement of the I-bar under acceleration produced a differential change in the alternating voltage in the two halves of a secondary winding and this signal was converted to DC, to form the output signal for insertion into the transfer functions of the autopilot. Damping of the mass was provided by a temperature-compensated silicone filled container. The performance of such instruments can be affected by vibration, and some of the WTV4A trials already mentioned enabled this, minimised by the choice of accelerometer mounting positions.

The autopilot unit structure changed between the Series 4 and Series 5 models, the latter placing the three gyroscopes in a self-contained semicircular unit. Photographs of the two different configurations are shown below.

The Series 5 Autopilot also contains the Navigation Computer, for incorporating into the WTV4D vehicles carrying the GEC Homing Head. Thus, the WTV4D missiles

Fig.5.23 Series 4 and Series 5 autopilots. Series 5 (on left) has gyros mounted in the black section.[38]

are designed to complete the guidance and navigation loop for homing trials against airborne targets. This autopilot also incorporated the means of system loop gain variation, dependent on launching height, the gain being variable between 1.0 at 15,400ft and 0.48 at 47,000ft. The corresponding acceleration demands also vary over a roughly two–one range, suitable for the lower accelerations possible at the greater altitude.

Refinements included were the Vibration Filter already mentioned, which was designed to reduce effects due to the 72Hz–second harmonic of the main missile body vibration resonance frequency. The vibration effects were further reduced by locating the accelerometers on a vibration node, as verified in the WTV4A firings mentioned earlier. Another refinement was to place limiters on the angular demands made to the control fins. These limiters restricted the fin movement demands to ±20° in pitch or yaw and ±10° in roll, together amounting to the ±30° range of fin movements possible. Fin angular position was fed back to the autopilot from inductive pick-offs on each control surface shaft, completing the fin servo control loops and these fin control-surface movements were the final output of the autopilot in controlling the missile.

British Messier developed the rear-mounted complex of Hydraulic Actuators and the compressed air-driven hydraulic pressure accumulators that supplied the fluid to the actuators. This complex of mechanical engineering additionally supplied the compressed air to the forward-mounted DH Alternator for missile electrical power and the oil supply to the GEC guidance homing head's hydraulically operated Radar antenna dish. The compressed air and oil supplies ran forward under the wing fairings to those units.

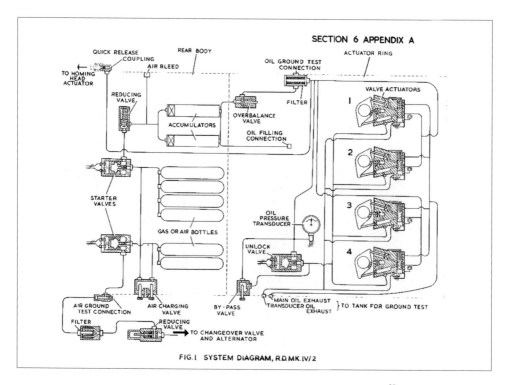

Fig.5.24 British Messier Actuation and air/oil supply system schematic diagram.[39]

The diagram shows an energy source of two gas or air bottles pressurised at 6,000psi (shown lower), supplying the Turbo Alternator through Starter and Reducing valves and via an aircraft supply changeover valve (not shown). Shown above these, four similar air/gas bottles pressurise the two hydraulic accumulators via a Pressure Reducing Valve. This high-pressure air forces a piston in each hydraulic accumulator, creating (via an Overbalance Valve) a 4,000psi supply of oil, respectively to the four fin actuators (on right) and to the homing head Radar antenna dish actuators (shown towards the left). Oil pressure is also used to actuate a Fin Unlock Valve (shown centrally), when it becomes safe to make manoeuvres soon after firing takes the missile clear of the aircraft. The starter valves and the changeover valve operate before missile firing, to bring the missile to independence from the aircraft. The air-charging valve, oil filling connection prime the system, while various test connections and filters allow for air and oil quality tests and system tests during missile preparation.

This complex system had to fit into the limited space between the rocket motor blast pipe and the minimum internal diameter of the rear body back to the tail of the missile, where the control fins were positioned. Within this space, the available volumes of the air/gas bottles and the hydraulic accumulators determined the total working 'duty cycle' of power available for driving the turbo-alternator, the control fins moving at up to 1,500°/sec, and the homing head antenna dish actuators. In the event, 91 per cent of the originally pessimistic estimate of this duty cycle over the missile's 10 seconds' flight duration was achieved and considered to be acceptable.

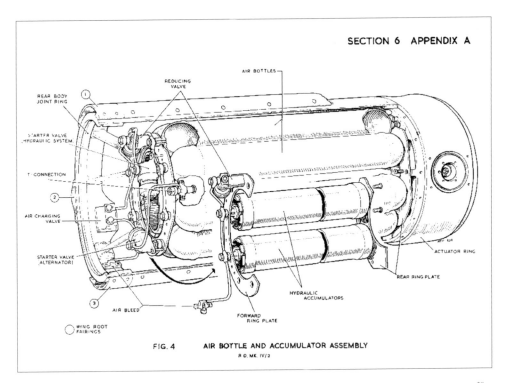

FIG. 4   AIR BOTTLE AND ACCUMULATOR ASSEMBLY
R.D. MK. IV/2

Fig.5.25 Assembly of air/gas bottles, oil accumulators, fin actuator ring and associated components.[39]

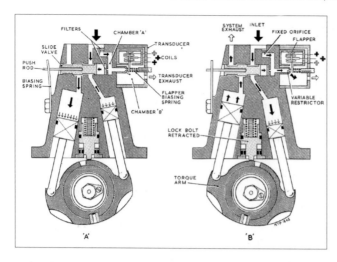

Fig.5.26 Shows oil flow between anti-backlash pistons driving the fin to rotate in each direction.[39]

The mean hydraulic demand of the system amounted to 12hp., resulting in the total expulsion system of bottles, gas, accumulators, oil and associated valves weighing 42.5 per cent of the complete hydraulic assembly. The end of flight oil pressure was calculated to drop no lower than 3,700psi, the actuators retaining their specified torque down to 3,200psi.

Unanticipated effects involved a number of detailed design changes in some components. For example, air supplied to the turbo-alternator under the autopilot well forward of the wings suffered a 100psi pressure drop over the pipe length involved. Consequently, the reducing valve had to be moved forward from the main British Messier assembly, close to the alternator, where the correct pressure could be supplied for the turbine. In this unheated part of the missile, the valve had to operate at temperatures down to -30°C, necessitating redesign of this valve's damper, using silicone fluid. This in turn led to having to change the material of the seals to natural rubber. The performance was finally checked down to -50°C in a cold chamber.

Structural integrity of the assembly and stiffness of the fin mountings were provided by a cruciform light-alloy casting. The fins had to be detachable and were therefore mounted in rotating sleeves in ball bearings, to permit the rapid hydraulically actuated movements in response to the autopilot. In order to eliminate all backlash, the three-way actuating mechanism incorporated two opposing pistons, one permanently pressurised. This mechanism was controlled by a spool (slide valve), which opened ports for the oil to flow into the cylinders housing the actuating pistons.

Spool-valve design involved the optimisation of 'valve overlap', to open and close valve ports at the best time. Sudden pressurising of the hydraulic system when the Starter Valve was actuated before missile firing was capable of causing a kick to the control surfaces, which could have caused the missile to roll while still on the launcher rail. The actuators therefore were positioned to prevent this and only allow pitch and yaw control surface movements when pressure was first applied. The Starter Valve itself was initiated by a small gunpowder charge in a paper capsule, fired by a suitable igniter. These had to be coated with a suitable high-melting-point wax.

Safety considerations included fatigue due to repeated gas bottle inflations following ground testing and completed carrying without firings taking place. The bottles were cleared for 100 pressure cycles to pressures in excess to the specified 12,000psi proof pressure, giving a large margin of safety. Corrosion of bottles and valves due to moisture was another consideration, as well as the possible auto-ignition of oil, leading to the use of nitrogen, while the effects with air remained to be proven. A multitude of detailed developments with pneumatic and hydraulic components were completed in arriving at a working system that was proved under laboratory and simulator conditions before flight testing with missile firings was possible. The introduction of roll-demand limits in the autopilot servo loops referred to under that section was the result of this development and was eventually proved by firings of WTV4A rounds.

WTV4D-p rounds, boosted by Falcon rocket motors, were used for flight testing the Series 5 autopilots powered by the turbo-alternator system. Between June and November 1956, carry trials were mounted, followed by firings. By this time, we had the benefit of a permanent RAF presence at Vickers, in the form of No.3 Joint Services Trials Unit (JSTU), headed by W/C Joe Dalley and engineer officer S/LDr Jim Scruby. Joe flew as test pilot on many Autopilot trials in the Canberra, while Jim liaised closely with the total technical picture and with the Trials Team.

With Joe Dalley on three and one each with test pilots Steve Harris and Jasper Jarvis, between June and September I flew as Observer on five carry trials over Aberporth at altitudes mainly around 45,000ft. These exercised the test sequences and checked power supplies and the gyros. The autopilot worked more or less according to plan, between occasional power-supply problems. The firing sequence was tested, including the changeover from aircraft power supplies to missile turbo-alternator powered operation, retraction of the Plug Base carrying services from the aircraft into the missile and the already proven latch pin retraction from its missile restraint position. This proved to work satisfactorily, until a firing attempt with Joe Dalley on my sixth WTV4D-p trial, when everything went well until the firing sequence failed, as Joe pressed the firing button to no avail and we had to return with the round. During and after this 'work up', when the missile and the aircraft-firing sequence equipment were cleared of earlier faults, Observers Ron Jupp and Russell Thornton had better luck, when a total of eight of our of nine rounds were successfully fired between July and November.

The first two firings, at 42,000ft and at 15,000ft respectively, proved roll stabilisation, including 50°/second roll-rate demands in each direction. The next two firings at 44,000ft and 14,000ft proved successful lateral stabilisation in the presence of roll demands. These were followed by three firings (one trial was repeated due to a roll control fault at ±9 g levels) to exercise lateral manoeuvre demands producing ±6g in pitch, then ±3g in yaw at 43,800ft, and at 15,000 ft. The seventh successful firing at 15,000ft manoeuvred Red Dean simultaneously in yaw at ±5g and in pitch ±14g. The eighth and final firing of the series placed a sustained ±5g demand in yaw, with ±15g superimposed in pitch. This firing was made at 35,000ft, since theory indicated that this height would be the least favourable in the creation of unwanted cross-couplings in roll. This was found to be causing no instability. With high manoeuvre-rate flights, the induced drag due to high incidences brought the missile speed down to below the minimum specified Mach 1.25 at strike, before control was lost. A useful outcome was to show a small degree of overshoot in roll, due to valve overlap in the hydraulic fin actuator spool valves, which could be corrected. Overall, these trials were considered to have proved the autopilot and its air-driven alternator and hydraulic system of actuators to considerable degree of satisfaction, under excessively severe flight conditions.

The Red Dean Homing Head guidance system

The GEC's design of the Homing Head for Red Dean interacted with earlier studies by RAE and by Vickers during the 1951/52 period.[40] The first basic principle of the Radar's design was to use the same X-Band (3cm wavelength) as for the AIMk.18 airborne interception Radar also being developed by the GEC at Stanmore. This simplified the necessary combination of these two elements into an overall Red Dean Weapon System, and also allowed for the possibility of using either Active Homing, where the missile became totally independent of the fighter after firing, or Semi-Active Homing, where missile guidance would depend on target signals received from continued illumination of the target by the fighter. GEC's report[41] on the comparison between these alternatives indicated that while an active homing head would be heavier and would require a larger Radar antenna dish than a semi-active one and consume more power, active homing would be more accurate against multiple targets, and that the development problems in association with the AI Radar would be much reduced. The semi-active system placed undesirable restrictions on the fighter's freedom to manoeuvre after launching Red Dean, and was, therefore, already precluded by the Operational Requirement. Yet considering the many elements and unknowns influencing this development, the ability to revert to semi-active homing was worth keeping open.

Both Radars utilised the well-tried method of angular tracking targets by means of 'conical scanning'. This rotated a slightly (3°) offset Radar beam 40 times per second (40Hz), to create a 55° half-angle conical coverage ahead of the missile. This was designed to track a target, towards which the sight line could move at a rate of up to 10°/second. Continuous Wave (CW) or pulsed Radar energy options were considered, CW appearing to have some advantages, but limited experience with this led to the choice of the better-known bat-like pulsed transmissions system. The level of reflected power from a distant, 10sq.m echoing area target being governed by its range raised to the fourth power, the minimum 10,000-yard range at which Red Dean would need to acquire targets, required a minimum Magnetron transmitter pulse power of 50kW for pulses to be detected. These ½µS (microsecond) pulses were transmitted at a repetition frequency (prf) of 2,000Hz. The nominal X-Band wavelength of these pulses corresponded to a frequency of 9,750MHz, but in order to permit several missiles to operate in close proximity, five separate frequencies were envisaged.

Limited by the missile and its Radome diameter and the required angles of look, the dish diameter was chosen at 8.5in, allowing its gimbal mountings space to move while tracking. Discrimination by this configuration permitted an angle between targets as small as 14°. Tracking was also necessary in range and this was arranged to operate up to a maximum of 16,200 yards,[42] to give an adequate margin over the design requirement for a maximum range of at least 10,000 yards, or five nautical miles. For head-on attack, a minimum tracking range of 2,500 yards was necessary and the tracking system had to cope with the range varying, due to relative velocity to the target of up to 4,500ft/second (around Mach 4), as well as acceleration along the sight line up to 1,000ft/second/second, or 30g.

As with all electromagnetic receiving systems, the signal-to-noise ratio would determine a receiver's ability to detect echoes well enough to drive the tracking systems. Red Dean's receiver and antenna system were designed to provide an overall gain of 110dB, with a dynamic range of 90dB achieved by the combination of Automatic Gain Control (AGC) and a fixed 'drop-in' attenuator, to ensure the correct output level. With an allowance of 10dB for manufacturing tolerances, the system could thus track reliably at a signal-to-noise ratio of +3dB.

The homing head based on these criteria had to provide outputs to the Navigation Computer and Autopilot. The rate of sight line movement was represented by a voltage proportional to the rate of turn of the conical scan axis up to 3°/second, at which the maximum control acceleration demand on the missile would occur. Tracking rates were actually possible up to 10°/second, to avoid loss of angular lock as the missile approached very close to the target. Range and range rate were also provided as voltages, in the scales already given.

In assessing the overall missile's performance and stability, it was necessary to consider the nature of autopilot control in combination with the guidance homing head. As already discussed in the section relating to Smiths' autopilot, the choice of rate gyros with accelerometers became an important feature of stabilising the missile's trajectory. Furthermore, the variation of missile response to control demands (gain) needed to be varied with the height of the engagement, since the overall gain could otherwise vary by a factor of 2.6, as air becomes more rarefied with height. Variation of gain with missile velocity would have given even better performance, but this was not sufficiently practical and therefore not implemented. All these factors were studied at Stanmore with the aid of a simulator, as well as at Smiths and Vickers, with the conclusion that developing the hardware for such a system would lead to satisfactory response of a missile, whose weight had increased since the early studies.

The effects of a real-life target echo subject to angular noise, 'glint' effects and linear (range) noise could seriously affect missile trajectory stability and, consequently, miss distance. Since the Radar signals have to pass through the Radome, aberration of the apparent signal direction due to passing through irregularities in radome's material and finite thickness would further affect performance. The only reason for considering the use of hemispherical radomes was to minimise aberration, with the penalty of greater aerodynamic drag, and its knock-on effect on missile range and the weight of rocket motor to compensate with extra thrust. A radome of ogival shape offered a close enough representation of the ideal conical aerodynamic shape, and early measurements indicated that aberration effects should be small enough to approach the guidance accuracy expected with a hemispherical radome. Successive simulations varying these factors were necessary to arrive at an ever-improving performance and the corresponding detailed equipment specifications.

Aberration was measured as the rate at which the apparent signal direction varies with the angle of look at which the signal passes through the radome into the receiving antenna dish. Simulations indicated that an aberration ('slope') of 0.01°/degree off missile axis would be tolerable, so long as a time lag was introduced, reducing the missile's guidance natural frequency to 15 Radians/second (2.4Hz). This criticality was different, between the aberration slope being positive or negative.

The most critical conditions were when the missile's aerodynamic incidence (angle to the relative airflow) was highest, while responding to severe manoeuvre demands at high 'g'. Aberration measurements were therefore needed with both radome shapes. Further investigations were made in regard to the effects of rain erosion at high speeds on the radome material, which was expected to be most serious with the blunt hemispherical shape. The greater the fineness ratio of an ogive, the lower the drag and, incidentally, the less it would be affected by rain. Firing conditions (and the highest speeds) causing rapid ablation of material could only occur at the minimum operational altitude of 10,000ft and above. Such very high (1in/hour) rainfall would only be likely below 15,000ft and in conditions such as in monsoons and along steep coastlines or mountainsides, or in cumulonimbus clouds. Thus, only the more extended durations of carry conditions under a fighter at much lower speeds before missile launch were likely to become a design imperative.

Much design work on the materials, structure and manufacturing methods of radomes ensued, together with laboratory measurements of the actual aberration angles for different radome shapes. These covered a range of ogive fineness ratios used in other missiles, from the hemispherical (0.5) to 3.0. Drag results were compared (mostly already estimated by Vickers from aerodynamic studies and measured in full-scale ground-launched firings at Aberporth) and with the aid of more simulator studies, G. Gordon reported[43] conclusions in late 1955. Aberration factors were found to vary from 0.01°/degree of look angle, to 0.06°/degree, for a very elongated radome of fineness ratio of 3.0. For Red Dean, a fineness ratio of 1.4 (as in the earlier Fig.5.16) would halve the drag relative to that of a hemisphere and his simulator studies indicated that such a radome's aberration slope would be 0.03°/degree. He concluded that this level of aberration would be satisfactory, provided that the homing head oscillatory response bandwidth were held to no greater than 0.8 cycles per second (Hz).

Vickers undertook radome manufacturing techniques development, which extended from mid-1952 to October 1956. Initially focussed on hemispherical radomes that could be used for the trials programme prior to homing trial firings, they ranged over a variety of polyester glass/compositions and foamed sandwich constructions, which were more able to withstand the pressurisation required by the microwave components of the homing head without leaking. The latter radomes were put into limited production for the WTV4D homing trials due in 1957. A number of ogival radomes were nevertheless made and flight tested for drag measurements as described above. Before foamed sandwich ogives were produced, the 17lb weight was well over the target of 10lb. With nominal wall thickness of 0.34in varying by ±0.03in, aberration slopes were within acceptable limits. Later in early 1956, foamed sandwich ogives of 1.44 fineness ratio were made and now, by reducing to two layers of glass reinforced skins over the long cylindrical portion of the radome, the weight came to less than the specified 10lb. Greatly improved electrical performance also resulted in acceptable aberration measurements. These considerations

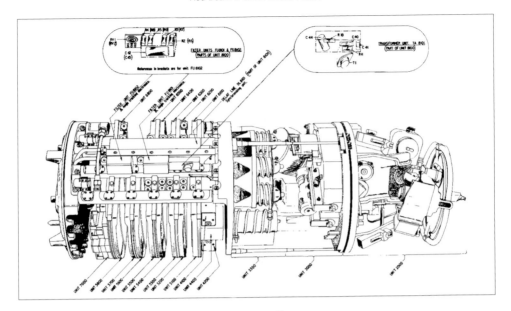

Fig.5.27 Overall view of GEC guidance homing head.[44]

might appear to be peripheral to the greater problems associated with achieving low miss distance homing guidance, yet their proper solution was a necessary evil precursor.

An additional means of reducing the effects of radome aberration was introduced into the Autopilot/Navigation Computer system, by means of a non-linear 'Bracketing Filter' and a variable constant time lag. Any propensity for missile oscillations to diverge into instability were thus greatly reduced.

Potentially destabilising effects of Radar noise entering the receiver, with the main target signal, were the subject of more simulation studies and their effects on the guidance process were raised in an April 1952 memo by then Col. J. Clemow, assistant director GW in the MOS. This memo commented on assumptions for noise (glint) under two different hypotheses being examined, namely (a) Constant Linear Noise and (b) Constant Angular Noise, and referred to American experience with the Falcon weapon being based on (a). (Col. Clemow was later director of GW Projects with the rank of Brigadier and, eventually, from April 1957, as a civilian, chief engineer Guided Weapons at Vickers). Of considerable importance, the somewhat related matter of Electronic Counter Measures (ECM) or jamming became the subject of a lengthy memo in the second half of 1955, which considered different Radars for the AI Mk.18 and for the Red Dean missile, employing CW transmission and frequencies at J-band or Q-band. However, during the main development period of Red Dean and its guidance system, intended to remain within its desired timescale to achieve homing trials in 1957, these alternatives were too far off for short-term consideration and will be covered later.

The general configuration of the homing head is visible in the diagram of WTV5 shown in Fig.5.16. Here above in Fig.5.27, it is seen in greater detail, showing the antenna/mirror assembly on its stabilisation platform at the right and the electronic circuit modules and wave-guides behind it.

The design of the guidance head required choices to be made for the Radar dish (or mirror) and how it should be independent of missile movements, so as to maintain a space stabilised sight line to the target. In a similar way to that described for the autopilot, any such stabilisation depended on the use of gyroscopes for stability in space.

Among detailed variations, GEC configured and laboratory-tested two main designs. The first series employed a 'direct-on-gyro', in which the antenna dish was mechanically linked to a gyroscope, which stabilised the angle of look and where the antenna was steered by precessing the gyroscope. The second main series utilised small gyros to indicate mounting gimbal angles and angle measurements were used to control servo systems to steer the antenna onto the stabilised slight line. The ultimate system for WTV4D trials and for WTV5 was chosen as a two-stage hybrid of these arrangements, where the Radar beam was stabilised over all angles by two small gyroscopes. The antenna gyroscopes assembly on a gimballed platform was controlled by a hydraulically servo, to follow movements of the gyro gimbals and preventing their being out of line by more than 10°.

The central hole in the mirror is for the spinning microwave antenna feed that creates the conical scan. As with light mirrors, the reflection of an incoming beam is at a similar and opposite angle to that to the mirror surface. Thus, the reflected beam moves through twice the angle through which the mirror has moved. However, whereas with a plane mirror, light reflection moves at this double the change of mirror angle, with a parabolic mirror as shown, the reflection or beam-switching ratio is smaller and the mechanical linkages had to be carefully matched at 1.8:1. This ensured that the mirror moves by the correct amount, for a stable lock onto the light line.

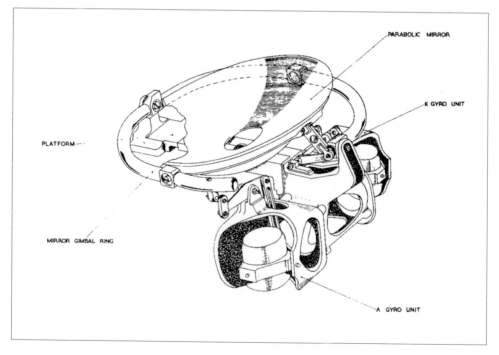

Fig.5.28 Platform with gyros in two spatial axes carrying the antenna mirror/dish in gimbals.[45]

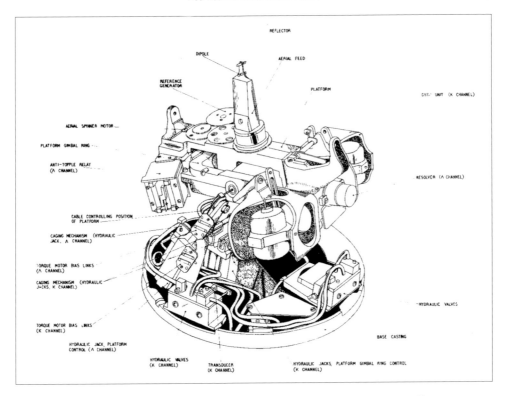

Fig.5.29 Mechanical configuration of stabilisation system for the antenna mirror/dish.[45]

The complexity of the complete mirror control system is evident from the above Fig.5.29, shown without the mirror itself.

The spinning dipole feed to protrude through the dish is seen at the top, with its spinner motor. In addition to the two gyroscopes on the platform, as in Fig.5.29, the hydraulic jacks for platform control in the two axes are seen near the bottom, level with the hydraulic valves on the base casting. Gyroscope torque motors for precession, caging mechanisms and angle resolvers and electronic transducers are also visible.

The design and engineering of the homing head was largely encompassed by the details described above. Within the resulting constraints and not detailed here, the design of the transmitting Magnetron, X–Band wave guides, rotating joints, automatic gain control (AGC), automatic frequency control using an appropriate intermediate frequency (IF) amplifier required, signal receiving and conditioning electronic units, automatic range tracking and many associated modules, resulted in an equal amount of design engineering and laboratory testing. Another necessary part of the effort was development and engineering of the hydraulic cooling system for the guidance system electronics, which contained some 120 sub-miniature valves and the 50kW peak power Magnetron consuming almost 1,000 watts of power.

In this process, the first airborne trials were undertaken in a modified Vickers Valetta aircraft, before homing heads installed in WTV4C and WTV4D missiles could be tested. In these Valetta trials between April 1954 and July 1955, the earlier WTV4C type circuits were being tested, with the tracking antenna and microwave transmit/receive system that could be housed in pressurised pods and radomes looking ahead, or out of the aircraft's starboard side. Test procedures and recording methods were verified in these first airborne trials of strengthened laboratory models, followed by trials against aircraft targets. These included measurements of Radar noise seen in the angular tracking circuits, as reflected from single and multiple targets and the effect of range to the target on signal strength. Later trials required 'putting on' when the antenna was deliberately misaligned to determine the amount of misalignment possible without adversely affecting target lock-on. These trials assisted the development of the later model guidance head for the WTV4D firing trials scheduled to follow later.

Between the following September and November, WTV4C heads were then flown in twenty-one missile carry trials under Canberra WD956, using a Valetta, Firefly and later a high-speed Supermarine Swift at 30,000ft as targets. With the help of Aberporth Radar control, the two aircraft were positioned to enable locking on at ranges at about 8,000 yards (held against the Swift up to 20,000 yards). However, at the 15,000ft trial altitude limit of the Firefly target, the Radar ground echo at the corresponding 5,000 yards range interfered with tracking of the target echo. In furthering the development of the WTV4D 'final' version of the guidance head with these early airborne trials, brief interruptions of the power supplies to simulate power changeover before missile firing was shown to permit functioning during the complex procedure of target acquisition.

WTV4D carry trials followed in 1956, with the missiles being fitted with all components for complete autopilot and homing head closed loop guidance, in trials that were planned for subsequent firings. The whole range of ground test equipment for the Red Dean system was developed to enable preparation for such flights and to be the precursor for operational test equipment.

The initial WTV4D-1 rounds were built to feed target sight line-rate outputs to the navigation computer, without closing the control and guidance loop, the autopilot remaining isolated. WTV4D-2 rounds would close the guidance loop for homing trials involving the range of attack conditions.

However, during 1956, the F153D 'thin-winged Javelin' aircraft for which Red Dean was intended was cancelled. This led to a gradual run down of the Red Dean contract, yet during the period beyond the cancellation fin into 1957, WTV4D carry trials continued. These mostly proved satisfactory functioning of the homing head and the navigation computer. Trials were generally monitored by Telemetry, to verify power supplies and the outputs of the guidance head and navigation computer. In a later section, I will describe advanced work also undertaken to develop the proximity fuze, the Fire Control System with AI Mark 18 in the F153D, and the associated aircraft development rigs.

As the trials engineer/Observer who conducted the very first Red Dean trials – rocket-boosted ⅔-scale model firings at Larkhill in 1953 – the last trials with WTV4D-1 enabled me to fly in Canberra WD956 for the last Red Dean trials. Initial carry trials were flown on 23 March, and two on 26 March, against Canberra WD935 as target. Fortunately, since the complications of sequencing with Red Dean and because of the many items requiring to be recorded on board, we had developed an Auto-sequencing unit and an Automonitor. These replaced the purely manual sequencing operations and the forty parameters monitoring box I had used in Blue Boar trials. Nevertheless, the Observer remained rather busy with pre-flight checks and after take-off.

I had been responsible for Trials Planning for a couple of years, while much of the flying had moved over to my colleagues, resulting in my making less frequent flights. Now I had to come up with a flight plan that would enable the two Canberras to find each other in a simulated stern attack, while remaining within the limited telemetry range for transmissions to Wisley. To stray outside this area of about 20-miles radius would cause all information except for my cockpit observations to be lost.

Pre-flight before rolling for take-off, my plan called for me to switch Generators 1 and 3 on line, then Nos 5 and 3 Inverters, followed by heating and cooling systems. Finally, auxiliaries, the Automonitor and Auto Observer master switches went on. Telemetry Low Tension voltage went on as we started to roll and Telemetry High Tension voltage at 'unstick', ready for an early telemetry reception check. Three minutes after take-off, telemetry was switched off and Ancillary LT went on. Once in the trials area, a dummy run started with the Master Arming Switch, telemetry LT and Ancillary HT at -6 minutes. Thirty seconds later, telemetry HT went on and at -3 minutes, a thermal cutout and crystal protection were switched. At 10,000-yards range, the Sequence Start was initiated, ready for locking onto the target in range. A short run was made with the Auto Observer at -1 minute. Live runs followed a similar procedure, additionally recording oil temperatures in the oil tank and in the homing head.

On the first of these carry trials, the operating altitude of 25,000ft for the trial runs was reached 11 minutes after take-off, the whole mission including sightings by, and of, the target lasting 70 minutes. Some malfunctions had occurred and we flew two more trials a couple of days later. It was intended to lock onto the target in range and angle, so that the latter could be tested at the high rates which occur as our aircraft breaks away from the chase and the target is passed. It was also planned to make the changeover from aircraft power supplies to missile internal power supplies as would occur just prior to firing. The pilot's gun sight, intended to enable locking on for angular tracking, gave trouble, and while I managed to detect target echoes at ranges varying between 2,000 yards and 7,000 yards, range lock did not hold, and angular lock was not possible. The results were all telemetered and subject to the Auto Observer's recordings.

The final carry trial was with pilot Steve Harris and navigator Don Bowen on 27 March 1957, and its detail could be considered worthy of some additional description.

Without the benefit of Radar control usually provided by the Aberporth Range, the trial over the Wisley area had to be accurately enough positioned to ensure telemetry reception there. We had to be in the right 'piece of sky', while WD956 with Red Dean closed on our other Canberra WD935 which was the target. Closing in a tail-chase had to commence some 10,000 yards behind the target and continue, remaining within telemetry range long enough to lock on at 7,000 yards and hold lock while overtaking the target. Using his gun sight, the pilot could help by correctly pointing the aircraft and its wing-mounted Red Dean. To achieve this with two aircraft of identical performance presented a challenge, since the target would fly at its slowest speed – about 150Kts – while in WD956 I would be overtaking at 450Kts.

The flight plan was consequently somewhat complicated, and involved several minutes of alternate right and left high-rate turns at roughly 15-second intervals, to keep down

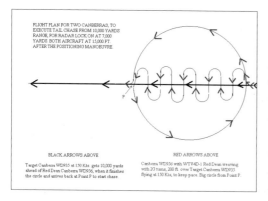

Above: Fig.5.30 Representation of my flight plan for Homing Head carry trial with lock on at 7,000 yards.

Right: Fig.5.31 Cockpit log pages, last Red Dean homing trial. The diagonal line signifies that the report was transcribed.[46]

to the pace of the target Canberra WD935 a couple of hundred feet below us. These presented me with a mostly vertical horizon and a doubling of my weight, except during the short periods of straight and level flight in between. While I managed to avoid toppling my own internal gyros, I had to execute the same procedures and recordings as in the earlier trials and, after the succession of steep turns, I could enjoy the luxury of 2 minutes in a more gentle orbit, while completing the pre-live run sequences. The manual operation of the Radar A-Scan remained to be executed as we chased down the target aircraft. The diagram indicates the nature of the flight regime, to harmonise the movements of a slow target and an overtaking attack aircraft over a precise spot in the sky.

In this way, we covered the same ground as the slow target aircraft until it reached the base Point P. Then we flew our large descending circuit, timed to arrive back at P and at target height when it was 10,000 yards ahead. At the 300kts excess speed, we raced past the target after merely another minute's flight.

The A-scan Radar display shows two horizontal traces, the lower trace displaying the Range Strobe and the upper one displaying the target echo moving to the right as range increases. These signals show as a small 'blip' rising from the respective traces, and as the target range decreased towards 7,000 yards, the target blip grew stronger and less noisy. By the 7,000-yards point, I was able to lock the strobe onto the target echo and observe how the strobe followed the echo, providing the Range value for feeding into the Navigation Computer. Successful Telemetry reception from our carefully defined piece of sky over

Wisley resulted in useful recordings of the required data, and the on-board Autorecorder also logged its required data.

Nearly fifty years on, reviewing my original cockpit record of this mission makes interesting reading. Thirty-five minutes after taxing out for take-off and all systems working (after an alternator tripped out and restarted), I had seen the ground echo, ran the Auto Observer and locked onto the target at an excellent range of 9,000 yards. In the dummy run, I had locked on at 7,000 yards, but lost tracking to the larger ground echo at 5,000 yards. Increasing range to the target from 4,000 yards, we locked on successfully, but once more lost lock to the ground echo on passing through 5,000 yards. Fifty minutes into the flight, a further -8 minutes point started another run in which we did not see the target return, due to misalignment of headings, while the Auto Observer was run for the last minute. The 8-minute point for the Live Run commenced 64 minutes into the flight.

Following this Live Run, my notes read, 'Internals run & sequence appeared satisfactory. 'Permission to fire' OK., target not seen on Radar, although in gun-sight at about -20 seconds.' We landed after a total time of 1 hour and 25 minutes.

The untidy nature of these digitally photographed pages (one whown in Fig.5.31) results from a combination of haste and the flying conditions under which the notes were taken, the use of pencil (ink was not possible at high cabin altitudes) and the author's all too naturally less than copper-plate handwriting.

The main outcome of these runs was that as the target range decreased to 5,000 yards, a much larger echo corresponding to our 15,000ft altitude then took over. This had happened during the Valetta trials with the WTV4C's earlier homing head design, but WTV4D exhibited the same inability to overcome the stronger ground echo. Clearly, attacks at greater than 30,000ft altitude would not be affected in this way, since the ground echo would be at a greater range than the maximum 10,000 yards attack range. The ground echo's amplitude would also decrease at the higher altitudes. However, at lower altitudes, all but short-range attacks requiring Radar lock below 3,300 yards would be affected, limiting Red Dean's operating spectrum. The GEC maintained that the side lobe problem was capable of solution, but there were no more flight trials to prove this could be mounted after this time.

The Red Dean Proximity Fuze and Warhead

Where a direct hit is hardly in question and the weapon system is designed for a 50 per cent probability missile miss distance of 30 to 50ft, achieving a high lethality depends entirely on accurate detonation of a suitably lethal warhead. Early design studies related in previous chapters led to the choice of a 100lb warhead, initially of the fragmenting type. Employing proximity fuzing by microwave radiation and reflections from the target as the means of measuring closing range, this would need to be detonated at a near optimum position in relation to the target, over a wide range of approach directions. From dead ahead, through beam attacks to stern attacks, the fuze would also need to take account of widely differing relative speeds between missile and target. Lethality was required to give a 50 per cent kill probability with single firings, rising to a statistical 70 per cent probability with two missiles fired in ripple sequence and this was thus dependent on effective matching of the warhead and the fuze. Studies at the RAE during 1949-1951 and by EMI engineering (EMIE) fuze contractors for a number of GW2 weapons from 1951, led to further lethality studies by Vickers Armstrongs in cooperation with the RAE assisted by the use of simulators.

The assumptions for miss distance under varying amounts of Radar noise during homing were largely unproven in the absence of representative trials information and, similarly, the fuzing distance errors due to aircraft shape and approach direction were difficult to estimate with any reliability. Nevertheless, the fuzing distance error was unlikely to exceed 20ft. Under these conditions, while estimates of absolute values for lethality under various conditions were not expected to be accurate, the relative lethalities for different kinds of warhead and given fuzing errors could be compared and enable choices to be made with some confidence. An important criterion among the assumptions was the nature of fuzing time delay. An optimum triggering time delay would require knowledge of the instantaneous closing range and range rate – and this was known to create considerable complications for the guidance equipment. The alternatives were to select discreet delays appropriate for given attack directions giving less than optimal, but good approximations to the optimum – or a simple fixed delay that would have to give reasonable satisfaction over this wide range of approach conditions.

Up to this time, a 'category A' kill on a TU4 bomber was considered to occur if both pilots were killed, or two out of its four engines were put out of action. This was subsequently increased to three engines also being disabled. However, with such large aircraft targets, the vital areas were far apart and engines on the remote side of the attack direction were shielded by the fuselage. This led to the conclusion that for high lethality, only the pilots in the nose section were worth attacking. To achieve this over the range of attack directions, the fuze would need to trigger at only 5ft range in a head-on attack, yet at 95ft in a stern attack. The corresponding diversity in closing speeds would require fuze delays ranging from 2 milliseconds in head-on attack, to more like 100 milliseconds in the stern attack.

Studies using the above variables were made at Vickers Armstrongs, for fragmenting and also for blast warheads. The latter had an advantage in being less sensitive to fuzing delay, and consequently permitting wider choices of how fuzing delays would be implemented. The Vickers assessments during 1955–56 showed a distinct, if modest, advantage to the blast warhead under optimum, fuze time-delay conditions with and without additional fuzing errors. Furthermore, since three quarters of a fragmenting warhead's destructive effect was due to blast, any reduction in blast effect with altitude would affect both kinds of warhead almost equally. After initially attempting to hedge bets in early 1955, by requiring Red Dean to be designed for either type of warhead, the complications and delays this would bring to a programme that was already behind schedule focused a decision in early 1956, to adopt only the blast warhead.

This was incorporated into the structural design of the Red Dean airframe, in the section forward of the Falcon rocket motor.

As mentioned, the warhead temperature was an important factor in the missile's environmental specification, to be kept under 70°C under long-term carry conditions under the F153.D fighter. warhead design was under the auspices of the Armament Development Establishment (ARDE) at Ford Halstead in Kent, where trials were conducted on warheads for all weapon systems. Nevertheless, EMIE laboratory

Fig.5.32 Mock-up
of Blast warhead for
Red Dean, showing
the Initiator.[47]

environmental tests involving temperature, drop and vibration tests and the Vickers static firings trials programme provided initial verification that the fuze operated satisfactorily under vibration and rocket motor shock conditions; to a limited extent this was representative of actual airborne firings.

The EMIE Fuze design dated back to the 1951 prototype, to meet the GW2 specification. Alternatives were considered for Red Dean, but in order to comply with the development programme timescales, this specification was nevertheless chosen. It used the well-proved National Bureau of Standards, Phase modulated Microwave (NBS PM-MW) design operating at X-Band radiated from the linear wave guide antennas mounted ahead of the four wing roots. The fuze system was designed to operate on a low-signal return from the target.[48]

This design used a Klystron for modulation of the X-Band radiation at under 1MHz. The phase of this transmitted signal was compared with the phase of the target return as the measure of range. Signal processing and output to the Initiator were executed in the third harmonic of these signals, since at this frequency, the side bands could contain the Doppler returns indicating range rate.

After laboratory development and consideration of other mechanical designs, the FM-1 Experimental Fuze became the preferred design for airborne missile trials.

The FM-1 Fuze contained a number of sub-units, which were not initially encapsulated ('potted') for shock and vibration protection. These units used wire-ended miniature valves and conventional wiring techniques of the time. In consequence, compensation had to be applied to reduce the effect of voltage drifts that otherwise caused pre-operational use warm-up problems. Power supplies for the final weapon fuze were to be received from the homing head. For trials purposes at the WTV4 stage, stabilised DC power supplies were not available due to the lack of stabiliser-valve ruggedness. Consequently, a battery power supply had to be designed and employed, and this provided satisfactory service, without producing spikes that could have caused spurious triggering.

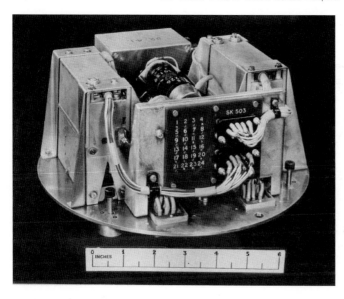

Fig.5.33 EMIE
Experimental FM-1 Fuze
with 'potted' sub-units, for
WTV4E2 and later trials.

Antenna configuration was, of course, central to target detection and range measurement by the fuze. The earlier description of missile structure already indicated the positioning of antenna elements in the fore body, along lines interspersed between the wing planes. This was to provide an 'equatorial' radiation field pattern about the missile and enable fuzing to occur at any angle of approach to the target. The field 'polar diagram' was required to cover a forward-looking included angle of 140°, to direct the field as precisely as possible within the available axial length of the missile and match the warhead's blast pattern. Slotted wave-guides were mounted in pairs for respectively transmitting and receiving in the two wing plains. Being flush with the missile body, additional aerodynamic drag was avoided. Forward tilting of the beams was achieved by careful positioning of the wave-guide slots. Antenna coverings were chosen, using fibreglass tape bonded to the radiating surfaces with epoxy resin, after investigating a variety of means to minimise the effects of skin temperature changes and of wind drag.

Missile carry trials and firing trials of the fuze were subsequently made using telemetry instrumentation, employing WTV4E1.3 with a non-radiating fuze and WTV4E1.4 rounds with a radiating fuze. These trials between October 1955 and March 1956, towards the end of the contractually possible trials programme, were satisfactory in a number of important respects. The trials were designed to show that the fuze survived the period of the missile engagement time, that it did not fire spuriously under realistic flight conditions and that it passed a firing signal to the initiator at the required range from the target. A gradual improvement of component survival and performance was obtained during carry trials, in which it was determined that no spurious firings of the fuze occurred due to reflections from the carrying Canberra's structure.

Two WTV4E1.4 uncontrolled rounds were fired over Aberporth. The first was fitted with a non-radiating missile forebody and the fuze was programmed to fire at regular intervals, with complete success. A second round fitted with a radiating forebody was fired with preset controls to induce a barrel roll creating a 9g constant lateral acceleration.

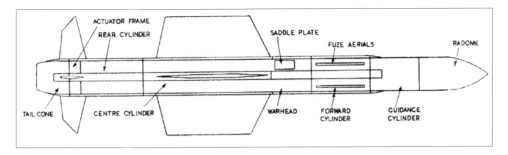

Fig.5.34 Disposition of Fuze Antennas as shown for the WTV5 Red Dean Prototype design.

The fuze again fired successfully at the prescribed intervals, and when finally the missile approached the sea, the fuze correctly triggered off the sea return. This correlated well with the characteristic sea returns obtained with earlier sea clutter tests using an experimental fuze in a Lancaster aircraft. Satisfactory as they were, these results were not considered to be altogether representative of conditions in the WTV5 Red Dean Prototype still to be tested. Work continued on fuzes for the planned later missile test vehicles WTV4E2 fuze trials and WTV4F to be used in homing with fuze trials. Now, sub-miniature valves in Aluminium blocks, potted by resin encapsulation and also etched wiring were used, simplifying manufacture and greatly reducing the unit volume as well as, most importantly, improving heat dissipation. Such were the joys of engineering design before the advent of transistors, let alone integrated circuits.

Besides detailed design development of the fuze to improve its functioning and layout, further mechanical redesign became necessary to allow more space for running hydraulic lines to the homing head and for better mounting details for the homing head itself.

The Red Dean Initiator
Along with the warhead, ARDE was responsible for the Initiator, but unlike with other GW2 specified projects the initiator could not be housed inside the fuze unit, due to the high temperatures generated by heat dissipation inside it, and the danger of premature operation. The maximum safe temperature at the time was considered to be 70°C, and although this was due to increase to 100°C, the initiator and warhead were moved outside the fuze compartment.

The initiator's primary function of detonating the warhead was circumscribed by mandatory safety requirements. Thus it was necessary for arming and detonation to be impossible, unless the missile had first executed its rocket launch and travelled a safe distance ahead of the carrying fighter. The missile, therefore, had to execute a minimum longitudinal acceleration for a period of time sufficient to fly Red Dean ahead by a safe distance, which nevertheless would be short enough for a rear attack from the minimum 1,800-yard range. Furthermore, in the event the target was missed, the missile would have to self-destruct, before it became a danger to friendly aircraft. The initiator contained the inertia mass and time-delay mechanisms to bring these conditions about.

While Red Dean was also specified for carrier-based fighters, their steam-catapult launch accelerations were a potential conflict in this safety requirement. The acceleration

Fig.5.35. Mock up of WTV5 Red Dean Prototype containing all the components.[35]

of Red Dean on firing the Falcon motor was at least 14g, while the specification for rocket-assisted take-offs was set as high as 13.5g, although in practice these did not exceed 7g. Longitudinal steam-catapulted acceleration of Naval aircraft did not exceed 9.5g, so there was a minimum safety margin of 4g. However, before attempting any live warhead trials from carrier-launched aircraft, trials would be required to verify the likely higher accelerations within a missile while mounted on the wing pylons during catapult launch.

These would certainly contain a short duration of higher 'g' transients. The initiator was of course designed to discriminate against these short transients, and in order to arming until a safe forward distance ahead of the fighter was reached, the rocket boost would first have to be propelling the missile for at least three quarters of a second. In the event, the requirement for naval use of Red Dean was cancelled before confirmatory trials could be mounted.[50]

RED DEAN AIR-TO-AIR MISSILE
PART 3

Attack profiles of Red Dean, fired from the Gloster F153D 'thin-winged' Javelin

In early 1956, new studies were made at Vickers-Armstrongs by Les Vine and John Housego, to analyse any problems due to restrictions of Radar view by a missile launched from the side of the fighter opposite to the target direction, and to consider typical homing trajectories.[51]

The delta wings of this aircraft brought the pylon and its Red Dean well behind the nose of the aircraft, limiting its Radar view across the fuselage in the 'away' direction. In order to lock the missile's guidance Radar onto the target before launching, while it was possible to gain increased viewing angle by rolling the fighter, some limitations were bound to remain, particularly if the fighter's freedom to manoeuvre was not to be inhibited.

Allowing for a maximum aircraft course error at launch of 10° for steering (allowable due to the missile manoeuvring during boost) plus 5° for tactical freedom to manoeuvre, the Radar semi-beam width of 3°, when added to the Maximum Ideal Kinematic requirement of 36°, would lead to an ideal Semi-Angle of view of 54°. The actual angle available round the nose of the Javelin is nearer to 32°, leaving a region of sky effectively obscured as shown in Fig.5.37. Obscuration of course only happens in one direction, the second missile on the other wing benefiting from a completely unobscured view. With firings being specified, using both missiles in 'ripple' sequence, the overall effectiveness of a Red Dean attack would be considerably greater than these questions might otherwise indicate.

This limitation of attack angles could be mitigated by two methods indicated by the study. Firstly, if locking on the Radar could be delayed until the missile has travelled just 14ft, it would have a complete view in all required directions. GEC and Vickers considered this to be feasible, but trials would have been required to verify the missiles' late lock-on capability before it could be relied upon. Secondly, the launching and the aircraft break away sequence could be so arranged that automatically, the aircraft would be rolled a couple of seconds before the instantce of launch. The roll angle required would range between 5° when turning ahead of the target, to about 25° when turning behind it. Fighter pilots would

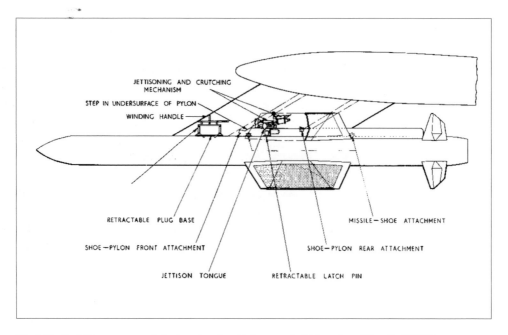

Fig.5.36 Red Dean, proposed single pylon installation on the 'thin-winged' Javelin F153D.

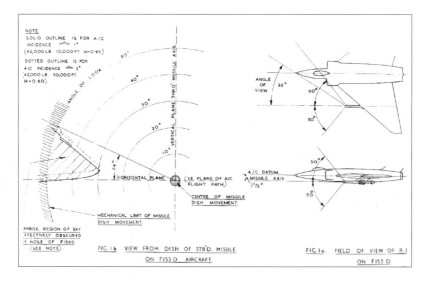

Fig.5.37 Angles of look for Red Dean's Radar when mounted on F153D swept wing pylon.

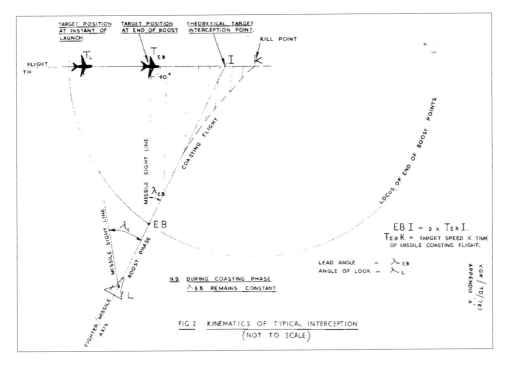

Fig.5.38 Typical Interception courses showing the homing trajectory during boost and coast phases.

undoubtedly have strong views about any constraints imposed by such tactics, and would evaluate what they consider to be acceptable during the proving trials.

The studies[51] summarised above brought the weapon system development to an increasingly realistic condition as the programme drew to its ending. Besides the main F153D host for Red Dean, designs were underway for its use with the highly advanced Canadian CF105 supersonic fighter (prior to its cancellation by Canadian Prime Minister Diefenbaker despite successful flight trials of this fighter).

At speeds up to Mach 1.7, Red Dean would be carried inside the CF105's fuselage weapons bay and be ejected at a downward angle to the aircraft's centre line, for safe clearance at launch. From the CF105 with a developed AI 18 Radar, Red Dean could attack in all-round directions against 10sq. m echoing area targets flying up to Mach 1.1 and 20sq. m targets flying up to Mach 1.4. At these supersonic launch speeds, Red Dean would be effective up to 55,000ft. With some modifications, it was considered likely that Red Dean on this aircraft would be (somewhat less) effective against targets up to 65,000ft. Studies by 'Dab'[52] were taken to the point of considering alterations to the weapon-launching computer in the CF-105. All the above conclusions were relevant when there was no enemy jamming, such as by Carcinotrons being developed by all sides in the Cold War.

Special tests and system rigs for the weapon system development

Pre-flight trials Development Testing was undertaken for all the main missile components described in earlier sections and ensured the proper functioning and mutual compatibility

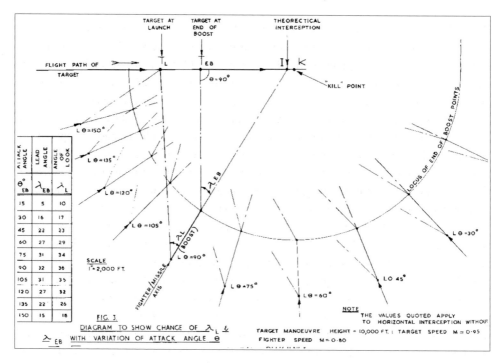

ATTACK ANGLE $\theta°_{EB}$	LEAD ANGLE λ_{EB}	ANGLE OF LOOK λ_L
15	5	10
30	16	17
45	22	23
60	27	29
75	31	34
90	32	36
105	31	35
120	27	32
135	22	26
150	15	18

FIG. 3.
DIAGRAM TO SHOW CHANGE OF λ_L &
λ_{EB} WITH VARIATION OF ATTACK ANGLE θ

NOTE
THE VALUES QUOTED APPLY TO HORIZONTAL INTERCEPTION WITHOUT
TARGET MANOEUVRE HEIGHT = 10,000 FT. : TARGET SPEED M = 0.95
FIGHTER SPEED M = 0.80

Fig.5.39 Variations of Missile Sight Angles for attacks from directions around the compass.

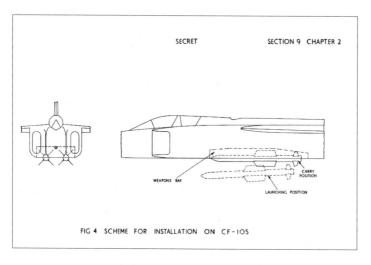

SECRET   SECTION 9 CHAPTER 2

FIG 4 SCHEME FOR INSTALLATION ON CF-105

Fig.5.40 Scheme for launching Red Dean for the Avro Canada CF-105 supersonic fighter.

of power supplies autopilot, homing guidance head and the pneumatic/hydraulic units that served the control surface actuators. This work required a custom-designed missile trolley, as well as a number of specially constructed test and monitoring rigs, some being mobile. Operational Field Test Equipment design was also undertaken in parallel with missile and other systems' design.

A special wing rig[53] was constructed in 1955, with the aircraft's operational equipment required to support Red Dean test vehicles, initially WTV4B/E autopilot rounds and

WTV4D-p homing head rounds. This enabled representative testing before embarking on airborne trials, for proving the aircraft's ability to operate the missiles during carry and prior to firings. In a hangar in Weybridge, a complete Canberra wing section was fitted with a pylon as a nucleus. With the exception of the primary 28-volts supply normally provided from two engine-driven P3 generators, all of the wiring and cables were made in the same size and length, as were to be installed in the aircraft. Identical panels and test units as those to be used in the aircraft were installed. Two banks of high pressure air supply were fed into the hangar and these were connected to the wing-mounted ('externals') alternator through exact pipe lengths and geometries. Similarly, high-pressure air was provided for the missile alternator through the ground test connections of the missile. Missile hydraulic supplies were similarly provided from a ground pump set. An installation was made such that trials with the WTV4E (Fuze) could be represented by its own representative wiring, which could be switched from the WTV4 wiring as needed. A fuze control panel and auto-observer were installed and could be tested with a dummy fuze.

In February 1956, the wing rig was re-engineered for the WTV4D installation. For this, the wing structure had to be augmented by two soundproofed cabin-like structures on two levels. The lower level was in two parts – the 'Engine Room' contained homing-head cooling rigs and hydraulic pumps, and the 'Bomb Bay' contained fire control equipment. The upper storey consisted of a platform level with the top of the wing enabling easy access onto the wing for installation and maintenance of the equipment inside it. Monitoring equipment was housed in a small soundproofed room. For greater accuracy of simulation, the 28-volts supply was now provided from four aircraft-type P3 generators housed outside the hangar. An aircraft-type de Havilland 2.4KHz oil-driven alternator was built into the correct wing position. By August 1956, tests began with totally representative wiring looms, cables, hydraulic pipes and supplies of high-pressure air, oil actuation and cooling systems. By allowing the homing head to 'look' out through the hangar's opened doors, it was possible to take testing to the point of homing head functioning against a Radar target.

This wing rig exercise enabled the location of over 200 faults which were rectified by ground testing, before committing to expensive flight trials that could have led to time consuming and expensive aircraft modifications.

Environmental testing of Red Dean was to a large extent conducted by carry and firing trials from Canberra bombers, where vibration and heat environments under rocket burn conditions and due to aerodynamic forces in free flight would be realistically applied. These have also been mentioned in connection with the Static Firing Rig at Wisley Airfield and the ground-launched trials from the wing section at the Aberporth trials range. In parallel, laboratory environmental tests were conducted involving drop tests and centrifuge tests – some at GEC with the homing head – and both vibration tests and stratospheric environments on complete full-scale missiles.

Vickers' great 25ft diameter x 50ft long Stratosphere Chamber[53] built in 1946 by Barnes Wallis, is capable of creating altitudes up to 70,000ft and temperatures down to -65°C, together with winds of over 70kts. At the time of writing in 2004, within the Brooklands Museum, it contains a complete Valiant V-Bomber's pressure cabin, leaving plenty of room to spare. In its time, it has tested complete aircraft and a model trawler for the build-up

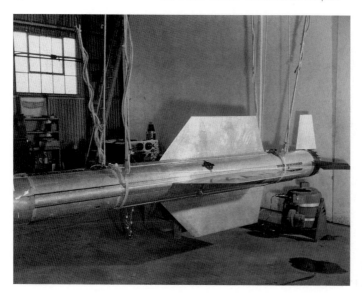

Fig.5.41 Vibration test
on full-scale WTV4A test
vehicle, applying vibration
to the tail section.[54]

of ice that caused several capsizes in the Atlantic. With facilities for operating electrical equipment and monitoring of missile electronic and hydraulic functions, it was used to test a full-scale WTV4D/1/1 test vehicle, containing functioning Autopilot and control actuators, homing head and power supplies. Besides being able to operate the missiles' systems during representative low temperature and pressure conditions, some sixty-nine thermocouples placed in strategic structural locations were monitored during trials. The main purposes of the trials were, firstly, to measure the transfer of heat through the missile skin under simulated flight conditions, in order to verify the accuracy of heat transfer equations used in the design. Secondly, they were to measure temperatures in and around the various missile units under simulated equivalent flight conditions.

Two test runs were carried out at ambient temperatures of -50°C to -55°C, with wind speeds of 72kts at the missile nose and 62kts at the tail. The first test revealed a number of faults which required modifications, including a cracked homing-head transformer, a burnt-out Autopilot wiring loom, unsuitable damping fluid in the Alternator-reducing valve, and frozen latch-pin assembly used for the safe carriage of the missiles and withdrawn before firing. After servicing the missile and making suitable modifications, a second test run proved successful, including satisfactory operation of the autopilot-controlled fin ring actuators and power-supply change over tests to the internal turbo-alternator. Now it was possible to verify the acceptable heat flow through the structure.

Strange phenomena in such testing were not unusual, such as John Lattey's thermocouple for measuring radome temperature that generated enough of its own heat to read 400°C when the ambient chamber temperature was -15°C. Perhaps this was a first in microwave ovens!

The use of these various rigs – in themselves quite complex, combined with the detailed development and environmental tests that were pursued throughout the development of Red Dean – enabled design and development to proceed towards carry trials and live firings with relatively few failures in the air. The GW teams had enough challenges and

Fig.5.42 Red Dean
WTV4D under
test inside the
Vickers Stratosphere
Chamber.[53]

headaches in the pursuit of leading-edge design, development and flight testing, to require the parallel work described throughout these chapters.

A Canberra high performance fighter variant with Red Dean

Besides plans for Red Dean to be mounted on the F153D and the Canadian CF-105, English Electric at Wharton (later joined with Vickers and The Bristol Aeroplane Co. in the British Aircraft Corporation) also made studies of a fighter version of the Canberra bomber. This was with a view to using Red Dean as its main missile armament.

The latest Canberra Mk.8 was studied for modification into a high-performance fighter to carry Red Dean or Blue Jay together with the AI Mk18 Fire Control Radar and Weapon aiming system. It would also carry secondary armament in the form of a 4 x 20mm gun pack.

Studies[55] showed that such an aircraft's interception performance with Red Dean combination would be superior to other existing fighters. This was due to the high performance intended for Red Dean and the ability of the Canberra to carry the complete system to adequate speed, just short of buffet and other transonic problems, without suffering the endurance, stowage and other limitations of supersonic fighters. The Canberra's unswept wings permitted wing-tip installation and this Canberra would have sufficient endurance for standing patrol and take full advantage of Advanced Early Warning. Much higher altitude interceptions would also be possible, particularly with a Napier rocket-motor installation and the use of later marks of the Avon engine. English Electric considered that a prototype could be equipped for trials by March 1958, and an operational squadron could be ready in 1959.

Besides the Red Dean and AI Mk.18 total weapon systems, the proposed design made comprehensive provision for all other weapon systems' equipment and for the necessary modifications of the Mk.8, including the PAS Mk.1 sight, Red Dean weapon release and jettison facilities, a rocket pack and Aileron power controls and Auto-Stabiliser and

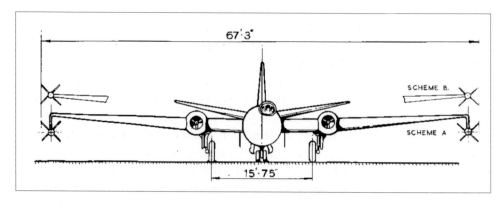

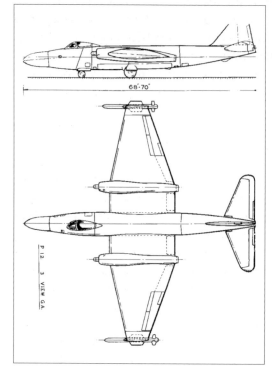

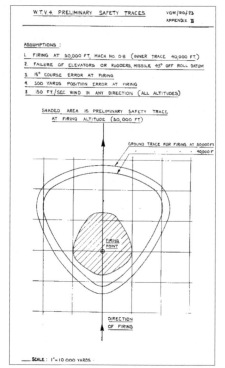

Top and above left: Fig.5.43 Canberra P.12, the all-weather fighter proposed by English Electric Co. in March 1956.[55]

Above right: Fig.5.44 Red Dean Safety Trace,1954, clipped from the original (faded) report.[56]

Power Controls for the rudder. The English Electric proposal brochure[55] also fully reports design considerations, including equipment cooling and ventilation and power supplies, the cabin arrangement, the aircraft controls and stabilisation system, power plant, strength and stiffness, and weights. Operational Performance: The latter considered Interception Possibilities with subsonic and transonic fighter speeds and the effect of target manoeuvre. These were presented as kinematic attack diagrams, similar to those produced by Vickers for the F153-D Gloster 'thin-winged' Javelin.

Nevertheless, as with so many Government-related proposals, the idea appears to have fallen by the wayside, even while the Red Dean programme was in full swing and before cancellation of the Gloster F153-D.

Meanwhile, plans for homing trial firings to be followed by fuze and warhead trials, and eventually proving trials, were well advanced in Australia at Woomera, in readiness for Squadron Service by the RAF. I made the journey to Woomera in November 1955, to negotiate agreement for the final Red Dean Safety Trace with the Range authorities.

The Long Range Weapons Establishment's Planning Specification of April 1954,[56] besides listing range instrumentation, safety, missile and aircraft preparation facilities, security and transport requirements, fully detailed the trials programme and the number of sorties in all directions of attack, against target aircraft. These included Jindivik drones, Lincolns, Meteors and Meteor pairs, amounting to a total of 100 sorties for completing development and a further 300 sorties for the MOS Evaluation Trials Programme through to the end of 1957, and trials of Production Weapons during 1958.

The Production Study[57] for manufacturing to meet all trials and later service delivery programmes was produced in a comprehensive form by GW Works Manager Peter Tanner, and J. Wastling, in April 1955, following a letter to Henry Gardner from the Ministry of Supply in November 1954. This indicated a service requirement for the first 2,000 weapons to be delivered by mid-1960 and a total of 5,000 by mid-1962. In order to cater for fluctuations in service requirements, estimates were required for production of 1,000 missiles, 2,000 missiles and 3,000 missiles on day shift only, night-shift work being held for reserve. Vickers was required to give detailed requirements for floor space, labour, machine tools, shop, stores and processing equipment, special materials and general facilities including canteen, packaging and so on. Similar information was requested regarding 'Embodiment Loan' items from the outside contractors Smiths Aircraft Instruments (autopilot), GEC (homing head), and British Messier (hydraulics). Separate exercises were to cover the rocket motor and warhead and Initiator items to be manufactured by Ministry departments at RPD Westcott and ARDE at Fort Halstead respectively, and, similarly, for the alternator and the fuze from de Havilland and EMI respectively.

While the study did not extend to the point of estimating the costs (or prices) of missiles to be delivered from production, the estimates covered all personnel and the cost of factory facilities that would be required at Vickers, GEC, Smiths and British Messier. Clearly. Commercial quotations would have to follow completion of the development programme. Labour assumptions were based on a fifty-week year with two weeks' holiday then current and 50-hour working weeks including 6 hours of overtime beyond the current practice of a 44-hour working week at the time.

The table overleaf is part of an extended sheet in this report, the increasing batch sizes of missiles to be manufactured for successive phases of manufacture from prototype WTV5s, through modifications, arising after acceptance trials, through incorporation of the first production modifications to batches of 1,000 with all serious modifications incorporated.

The planned build-up of missile production starting in early 1957 showed the manpower requirement peaking near the end of 1959, with missile production rate levelling off at about thirty per week or 1,500 per year, within two years. The RAF would receive 2,000 missiles by mid-1960 and it would have received 5,000 missiles by mid-1962.

BATCH	NO. IN BATCH	CUMULATIVE TOTAL	DESCRIPTION
B1	50	50	AS WTV 5
B2	75	125	BASIC MODS FROM ACCEPTANCE TRIALS NOT INCLUDED
B3	275	400	FIRST PRODUCTION MODS INCORPORATED
B4	600	1,000	ALL SERIOUS MODS INCORPORATED

Fig.5.45 Table of Red Dean batches planned for build up towards series production.[57]

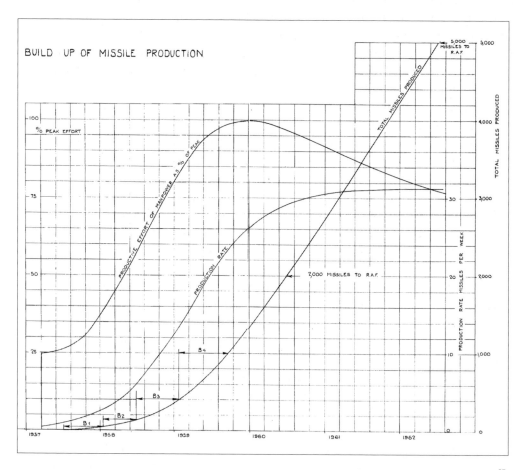

Fig.5.46 Graphs of production effort, missile build rate and total missiles to be produced for the RAF.[57]

The Red Dean programme can now be seen in its intensive and complex totality, right through from early requirement specifications through development, trials and production planning for RAF service. The more the pity that with the cancellation of the F153D, and in Canada, the CF105, even with English Electric's credible proposal for its P.12 Canberra fighter, Government support was cut off, with only limited budgeting for the final homing head trials already described in March 1957. So near – but not near enough!

One area of development that had not been adequately covered related to the possibility that effectiveness could be affected by enemy jamming – a technology being developed on both sides of the Iron Curtain. This problem was under consideration at Vickers and at GEC, in conjunction with ideas for Red Dean's successor – Red Hebe. That project will be the subject of a later section.

Consideration of changes to the guidance Radar, to counter enemy jamming

It was in July 1955 when Dr Cockburn, director general of Electronics (DGL), asked GEC Stanmore Laboratories to review the application of Q-Band Radar (instead of X-Band) to the AI 18 and Red Dean weapon system and to recommend whether development of the weapon system on this frequency should be started. Any such review had to be mindful of such a major programme change would have on the in-service date for Red Dean, which was already well on the way towards completion and commitments for final design, evaluation trials and manufacture for service.

The question of Radar noise effects on guidance accuracy was raised in an April 1952 memo by Col. J. Clemow, then assistant director GW in the MOS. Related to this, the vulnerability of the AI 18 – Red Dean weapon system to Carcinotron jamming had been discussed in a note by J.G.W. Munns of the RAE, with resulting concern and consideration of changes that might alleviate its effects. Electronic Countermeasures (ECM) had long been seen as a generic problem with most weapon guidance systems and 'Counter Counter Measures' (CCM) were a continuing development effort in all advanced defence industries worldwide. This aspect of weapons technology, essentially leading to the leapfrogging of one counter measure over the next, carried some of the highest security classifications, for obvious reasons.

This highly technical subject mainly concerned (in the case of Radar guidance) the effect of Radar 'noise' on tracking Radars used for acquiring and auto-following targets. The very nature of Radar returns from distant objects is such as to contain spurious signals (noise) in various forms. They can appear as superimposed waveforms and spikes resembling angle changes or 'glint', which can be likened to optical glint from a shiny object (angular noise). They can also appear as 'jitter' on the Range signal, making for difficulty in tracking the target altogether. I have discussed this in the section on the GEC guidance Homing Head and pointed out how this can affect the stability of the target sight-line angle measurements, on which the homing system relies. Excessive noise can destabilise the smooth tracking required of the target and can lead to oscillation in the missile's control functions and in its trajectory, resulting in an increase of the 'miss distance' – at which the warhead has to be lethal.

Jamming signals are designed to increase these problems and usually take the form of noise transmissions over a wide frequency range in the electromagnetic (Radar frequencies) spectrum; jammers pump out as much power as possible, in order to override or saturate the weapon system's signals. In the case of X-Band (3cm wavelength or around 10,000MHz frequency), noise modulated jamming is effective against Radars which employ 'conical scanning' of the Radar beam as the means of determining and tracking target direction, if the noise modulation frequencies cover the frequency of the conical scan. Conical scanning was the most commonly used means of tracking, and until solid-state, phased array scanning antennas were perfected, it remained in frequent use – and is still often employed on current-day Radars. Some protection by means of filtering is possible, but depending on the power of the jammer, so the difficulties can mount. In this context, noise jamming can be by modulations over a wide frequency range (to affect systems of characteristics unknown to the jamming party), they can be modulated at exactly the (Radar antenna spin) conical scan frequency if that has been determined, or they could be noise modulated and switched on and off at intervals.

The study looked at effects on the AI 18 in steering the fighter to the correct launching point, consistent with the all-round attack launch ranges specified for Red Dean. Primarily range information is required and in the face of ECM, whose effect is to require an even longer basic range capability than specified, in order to provide this parameter with certainty throughout the pre-launch period. The AI needed range information up to 30,000 yards for accurate launching after fighter manoeuvre to 10,000 yards. In the face of jamming, this was considered to by more effectively available using Q-Band Radar of 0.8cm wavelength. Moreover, it was considered possible to achieve missile release with sufficient accuracy without the use of range information up to the latter phase of the interception course, so long as Radar ranging was provided in the terminal phase using Q-Band and any excessive release error position could be compensated by missile manoeuvre during boost.

With X-Band missile guidance, while it would have been possible to home without range information relying only on angle information and this would work against continuous noise-modulated jamming, if precautions were taken against signal mixer saturation. Against spin-frequency amplitude modulated jamming, further guidance circuit complications would be needed, and against randomly switched intermittent jammers or non-radiating targets escorted by jammers, the jammer would need to be destroyed first.

The adoption of a Q-Band homing head would impose limitations and time delays in the introduction of enemy jamming systems, particularly because the power available to jammers at Q-Band would always be less than at X-Band. A Q-Band missile guidance antenna would also have a correspondingly four-fold narrower beam width, reducing the signal power density at the target. Another advantage of this frequency is that 'Window' (metallic foils showers) are less effective. The study indicated that a Q-Band homing head could be developed within a reasonable timescale – though longer than that available within the current Red Dean development programme for in-service readiness. Furthermore, Q-Band is excessively absorbed by rain and this could limit Red Dean's lower altitude operations to a minimum of 15,000ft. There were further questions concerning excessive weight and power requirements. Perhaps a more important factor militating against changing from X-Band was the limited engineering effort available – although this would be definitely be considered for future projects with later timescales. Further studies indicated that converting Red Dean's homing head to Q-Band and better anti-jamming capability might be best achieved in the interim, by changing microwave components, with minimised system changes.

These issues were further complicated by the coming projects for a supersonic fighter F155T, to OR329 with a new X-Band AI. In order to provide Radar ranging in the presence of jamming, the most likely solution considered was to add a Q-Band Radar ranging set in addition to the AI Radar and several aircraft designers were considering provisions for two radiating dishes. If this were to require two different frequencies, leading to the further problem their aircrafts' radomes, which are usually only suitable for one Radar frequency.

A successor to Red Dean, Red Hebe was already in the study stage at this time, mainly for the OR329 supersonic fighter successor to the F153D. This was foreseen to use continuous wave (CW) as opposed to pulsed Q-Band Radar guidance. For any change of Red Dean's homing head to Q-Band, deeper circuit and system changes beyond microwave changes would be better left for the subsequent development of Red Hebe. Such an interim Q-Band Radar for Red Dean was considered feasible at least two years earlier than the advent of Red Hebe. However, the estimated timescales between the projects were somewhat uncertain, being based on relatively early state of the latter's design. Depending on that outcome, should Red Dean receive the Red Hebe guidance head?

In 1955, improved versions of Red Dean Mk.1 were being designed, with the aim of improving performance and reducing weight. The arguments between the different Radar frequencies for an improved Red Dean with better resistance to jamming discussed above, led to the likelihood of upgrading to a CW Q-Band guidance homing head. J-band (1.5MHz) was also considered but rejected for various reasons, yet eventually for Red Hebe, J-Band became the proposed frequency. Transistors had for the first time become well enough developed and known for their use in developed Red Dean guidance and autopilot systems to become a likely reality. Whereas Red Dean's GEC homing head weight was 105lb, by using transistors and other refinements, GEC could reduce this to 90lb. If the guidance system were redesigned altogether to utilise semi-active guidance relying on the AI Radar for illuminating the target, the weight could be further reduced to 60lb, with very much lower power requirements. But semi-active systems were not proposed, since this would have required fundamental redesign of the AI 'lamp set'. Nevertheless, cumulative weight reductions from the WTV4D style guidance system and power supply systems would greatly improve performance. These ideas and designs morphed into the Red Hebe studies and led to an overall design along the lines of the drawing overleaf.

Red Hebe was to be a larger missile and versions were slated to carry a nuclear warhead. However, as the F153D Javelin and the F155T aircraft were cancelled – not unconnected with the infamous Sandy's 1957 defence white paper, which so inaccurately forecast the demise of all manned aircraft for defence – both Red Dean and Red Hebe were also cancelled. In March 1956, contracts for modifications to Canberra trials aircraft were still being issued and the full development programme continued until August 1956, after which a run-down programme continued into March 1957, when I flew the already described last guidance carry trial in Canberra WD956, using Canberra WD935 as the target.

The cancellation of Red Dean might have occurred in any event. As director of Guided Weapons (Projects) at the Ministry of Supply, our future chief engineer, Brig. John Clemow, had a low opinion of how Vickers and its team of sub-contractors – mainly GEC and Smiths Aircraft Instruments – had handled the complicated missile project. In the time it had taken since commencing development in 1952, the ambitious and complex

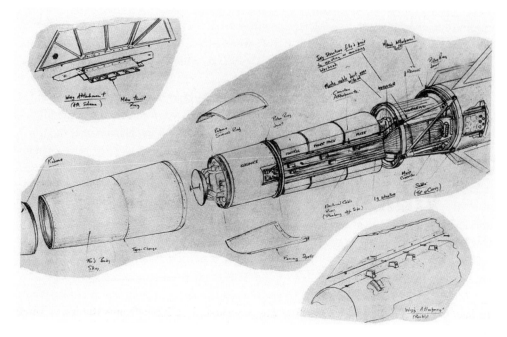

Fig.5.47 General arrangement of Red Hebe front-end components.[35]

programme had taken longer than anticipated, and yet still had a distance to go. As already seen, not only was the Radar guidance head suffering from the effects of antenna side lobes which caused ground reflections to take over from the target echo, when tracking through the range equal to the missile's altitude, it was expected to be susceptible to jamming by Electronic Countermeasures becoming available. Needless to say, it was John Clemow who signed off the cancellation – and later, ironically, become head of the very team thereby put out of the government's Guided Weapons plans and projects.

Blue Boar and Red Rapier having been cancelled in 1954, the Vickers GW team of some 800 people faced drastic cuts, even though we had started designing the Visually Guided Light Anti Tank, or VIGILANT wire guided anti-tank missile. Described in the following chapter, this was a company-funded private venture project, based on evident needs of the Infantry and the Royal Armoured Corps.

In a Ministry of Supply letter of 16 April 1957, it was proposed to issue Vickers with a contract for £20,000 per month, initially until 30 June. In the light of relevant work already proceeding on Vigilant, this included Hot Gas Driven Actuators, Quick Start Gyroscopes, Simulator work on guidance and control problems and environmental testing, besides some short-term radome work. I suppose this was in the spirit of pragmatic governmental contrition, after failing to support the completion of three major Guided Weapon development projects that had reached advanced stages.

Chapter 6.1

VIGILANT ANTI-TANK MISSILE PART 1

In late 1956 and early 1957, following the cancellation of Red Dean – the last of three major projects undertaken since 1951 – the advent of new management to the Guided Weapons Department coincided with Vickers' decision to undertake a private venture development. This would not be dependent on Government funds administered by the Ministry of Supply, and the Vickers Armstrongs (Aircraft) Board under George Edwards approved substantial funding. Staff numbers under the new management team led by John Clemow and Howard Surtees were now considerably reduced from the 800 or so at the peak of our handling three projects. The numbers were nearer to 150. However, this highly motivated and well-balanced team was able to deal in a professional manner with John Housego's ideas on his personally perceived requirement for the Infantry. He had checked the ideas with John Clemow when he was about to arrive at Vickers GW.

Tanks had always been a kind of nemesis for Infantry, whose light weapons and speed into action were effective against similar enemy forces, but who were almost powerless in the face of heavily armoured tanks. Anti-tank guided missiles had been developed for the Wehrmacht during the Second World War, but, fortunately, not soon enough to affect the conclusion of the war. These missiles, as well as air-to-ground versions, had been successfully tested using wire guidance, which had the advantage of being virtually impossible to counter with jamming, in the way electronic counter measures could be used against Radar and other electromagnetic spectrum guidance systems. To Vickers GW management, the Infantry's need was unquestioned, and armoured personnel carriers such as scout cars also faced heavy tanks, where a guided anti-tank missile could greatly improve effectiveness, compared with the best of armour piercing field artillery. With its ear to the ground and utilising its enduring contacts with government departments and the Army itself, Vickers decided to develop a British wire guided anti-tank system – Visually Guided Light Anti Tank, or VIGILANT.

While the government ministries – Treasury, War Office and Ministry of Aviation – had consciously decided to let Vickers 'wither on the vine', without prospects of further contracts in a Guided Weapons industry that was regarded as having excessive capacity, this development would require co-operation from the Ministry of Supply and from the Army.

Co-operation was needed for testing at the trials ranges on Salisbury Plain and for the development of the rocket motor and the warhead, usually the province of Ministry establishments and Imperial Chemical Industries (ICI). Nevertheless, these pyrotechnic items had to be specified to match overall performance requirements of Vigilant, including its range, speed and aerodynamic characteristics, including controllability and lethality.

Discussion with the Infantry led to the following overriding requirements for the missile system to be capable of:

Carrying and rough handling by soldiers, remaining effective under all kinds of battle conditions;

Rapid preparation from deployment in its protecting carrying container, to firing within about one minute;

Separation of missile launch position from the location of a guidance controller, by 50 yards;

Full activation of all propulsion and guidance systems within ½ second of firing action;

Guidance to hit stationary and moving 'hull down' tank targets at ranges between 200 yards and 1,500 yards;

Lethality against hardened, sloping tank armour with penetration up to 20.5in;

Guidance by average soldiers, after only modest time in training;

Guidance controller to facilitate viewing of long range targets and for rapid 'gathering' of missile for guidance against short-range targets;

High reliability and high direct hit rate, approaching 100 per cent;

Maximum range flight time of about 10 seconds;

Rapid firing rate of multiple rounds;

Missile in its rugged carry box and 70 yards long controller cable weight below 50lb;

Total system weight including sight controller under 60lb;

Guidance signals to be transmitted from the Controller, by wires unspooling from the missile during rocket boost and the subsequent rocket-sustained flight;

Sighting assistance by means of a flare carried at the tail of the missile;

warhead arming only after specified safe distance travelled down range after firing;

Controlled climb away from potential friendly positions in the event of guidance failure.

The imperative of delivering a large enough warhead over a nearly one mile's distance created the main missile parameters, established in assessments by John Housego, who first conceived the idea of a man-portable Infantry Anti Tank Missile and J.E. Daboo ('Dab'). An outline aerodynamic design had been established, using short-span cruciform wings (to fit into a small carrying container) and employing a two-stage rocket motor for boost and sustain phases of flight. They made the first visit to the Summerfield Research Station of ICI,[52] to discuss the required rocket motor. The rocket motor would have to be in the wings section about halfway along the length of the missile, so that the centre of gravity would remain near the centre of wing lift as the rocket motor fuel was consumed.

The warhead behind its fuze and crush button are seen at the front of the missile (Fig.6.3). The rocket motor is at the forward end of the wings section, with the blast pipe extending rearward, allowing room for the surrounding control actuators near the tail end. The short wing span was chosen so that the wings would fit within the corners or

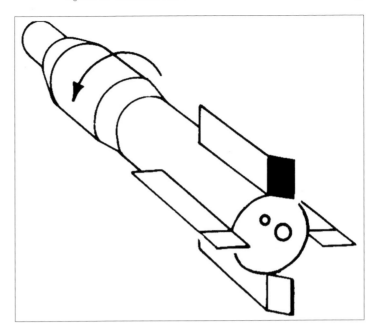

Fig.6.1 Outline design of Vigilant missile in rolling flight, showing controls deflected as rudders.[53]

a simple, square section carry-box/launcher, from which Vigilant would be fired when it was tipped up to the 20° launch angle, as supported by its hinged down lid.

Vigilant had to be inexpensive to manufacture in large quantities, an initial target being about £500–£600. Compared with Blue Boar and Red Dean, Vigilant would be a simple missile – and this was the first project where we had the benefit of Transistors, while multi-layered printed wiring was becoming a norm. Without this, it would have been impossible to create a missile within the stated parameters.

The privately funded nature of this project and its technical challenges required considerable courage on the part of Vickers management. As will be seen later, even after three years or so in 1960 and beyond, neither the Army nor the Ministry of Supply (later Ministry of Aviation), let alone the all-powerful Treasury, had confirmed that a requirement existed. At the same time, to the extent that a requirement was under serious discussion, Vigilant would be in competition with French Entac, SS10, SS11 (later to adopt a velocity control system emulating Vigilant's), the Swiss Moskito and the German Cobra missile. The much larger vehicle-mounted Australian Malkara anti-tank missile also affected the situation, and the Orange William project for another large anti-tank missile with a much larger separation between the guidance operator and the launching point was running into the sand. In this busy environment of anti-tank missile projects in Europe and America, the UK government appeared to remain aloof from such a British development.

Thus, the hiring of (ex-Ministry of Supply director of GW Projects) Brig. John Clemow to run a greatly depleted Guided Weapons Department and the commitment to fund a new 'blue sky' development was a true act of faith. George Edwards (by then a Sir) left John Clemow and the GW Department very much to themselves, though correspondence among Ministry departments[58] shows that Vickers' unfunded position and George Edwards' attitude to the Government's lack of support, even after three years

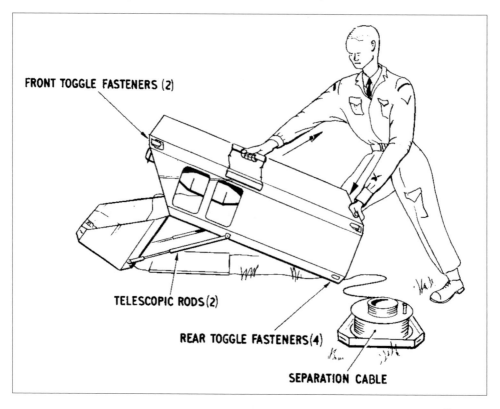

FRONT TOGGLE FASTENERS (2)

TELESCOPIC RODS (2)

REAR TOGGLE FASTENERS (4)

SEPARATION CABLE

Fig.6.2 Outline drawing of carry-box launcher and associated separation cable to the missile.[53]

of private investment, was not far from his mind. When the Permanent Secretary of the Ministry of Aviation visited Vickers on 25 June 1959, his private secretary, G.W. Clark, minuted:

> … he spent some time in discussion with Sir George Edwards. One of the points made by Sir George was that Vickers have had no GW project from the Department since the cancellation of Red Dean and that he could see no future project emerging. He was therefore disposed to cut his losses and disband the team.

In consequence, the MOA reviewed, 'the extent to which the Department is now using Vickers in the GW Field and what use we see for the team in the short and long term'. Nevertheless, even at this stage, the Vickers team was not disbanded, but continued with development. It was unfortunate that, having sowed the Vigilant seed in some detail, John Housego was enticed away by a lucrative job offer in America.

warhead lethality was, of course, the prime and mandatory parameter, along with the rocket motor to deliver the missile to the tank target. Both items were outside the usual remit of Vickers GW and, in the absence of any Government support, in late 1956 Vickers contracted with ICI's Summerfield Research Station for the rocket motor, and offered a Swiss-made warhead by CML. The latter was more effective than Malkara's

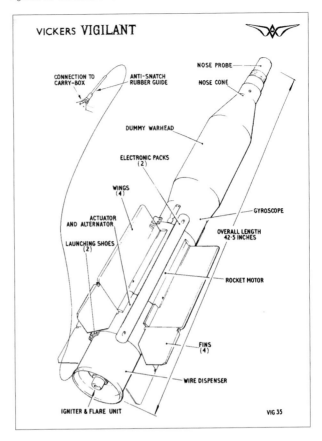

VICKERS **VIGILANT**

NOSE PROBE

CONNECTION TO CARRY-BOX

ANTI-SNATCH RUBBER GUIDE

NOSE CONE

DUMMY WARHEAD

ELECTRONIC PACKS (2)

WINGS (4)

ACTUATOR AND ALTERNATOR

GYROSCOPE

OVERALL LENGTH 42·5 INCHES

LAUNCHING SHOES (2)

ROCKET MOTOR

FINS (4)

WIRE DISPENSER

IGNITER & FLARE UNIT

VIG 35

Fig.6.3 Missile details per
'Instructors' Handbook'.[74]

High Explosive Squash Head (HESH) warhead, but less effective than some other
'hollow-charge' warheads. I had been made aware of hollow-charge warhead designs and
capabilities back in 1953 during my GW course at Shrivenham, and more recent tests of
in the USA had shown its superior armour-piercing capability. However, the Ministry of
Aviation's Armaments Research & Development Establishment (ARDE) at Fort Halstead
was in charge of any developments with hollow-charge warheads, and without hand in
glove co-operation, Vickers did not have rights to develop it for Vigilant. Thus, the Swiss
warhead was an 'off the shelf' option which may or may not eventually be acceptable to
the Army. Nevertheless, Vickers established a detailed design concept leading to detailed
development.

Dab's missile aerodynamics and general design would accommodate the Swiss
warhead with an arming fuze and the rocket motor was specified to provide two stages –
a 2½-second boost phase giving 180–200lb of thrust achieving a speed of about 500ft/
sec., and a sustain phase giving 30lb thrust for a further 10 seconds, taking the missile
to its maximum 1,500-yard range in a maximum of 12 seconds. The rocket motor body
would be the structural anchor for the four cruciform wings and a gas tapping from its
combustion chamber would power hot gas actuators in the rear of the missile, for the
aerodynamic steering control surfaces. For minimum dispersion during the 'gathering'
phase after launch, the missile control system was designed for rolling throughout flight,

with control surfaces acting as rudders and elevators in the proportions appropriate to the instantaneous roll angle, as measured by a gyroscope and commutators or resolvers. This, and a second gyroscope, provided azimuth and elevation references for yaw and pitch. These miniature gyroscope rotors were hot-gas driven from a cartridge and had to blast up to between 50,000–60,000rpm in half a second from firing initiation (a soldier pulling a trigger). The gyroscopes were key elements of control, together with electrical guidance signals transmitted from the soldier's optical sight controller via a thin cable of two wire pairs, continually dispensing from a spool around the motor blast cone. The signals were processed by two transistorised electronic packs constituting 'fairings' mounted outside the rocket motor body, between the wings. Electrical power within the missile was provided by an alternator, which was also driven by rocket motor gases.

The actuators and the alternator just behind the rocket motor were squeezed into the annular space around the rocket motor blast pipe, a hot area even before allowing for the motor gases being used to power these units. Behind this, the wire dispenser can be seen around the end of the blast pipe and the motor igniter at the very end, coupled with a flare, for easier sighting at long range during guidance by the infantryman. The connection of the wire spool to the carry-box for routing to the guidance controller is shown with an anti-snatch rubber guide – all seemingly relatively simple but, as usual, the devil is in the details.

The concept of guidance was naturally cardinal to the effectiveness in enabling a 'simple soldier' to steer the missile and the warhead to the target. With the infantryman hunkered down behind a convenient bank or other cover, and the missile in its carry-box launcher deployed in the open up to 60 yards to one side, the basic need was to see the missile as early as possible into its trajectory, to gather it onto the target sight line from its separated position and then to steer it accurately onto the tank. Our designer/resident-artist Peter Mobsby created a realistic scene that depicts a typical attack on a tank, though showing a smaller than maximum separation between infantryman and the missile launch point.

An absolutely cardinal factor in the design of the control and guidance system was the use of 'velocity control' employing gyroscopes, rather than acceleration control. This was determined by Harry Fryer and his team's simulation work. Later, it vitally led to acknowledgment by the Army and the ministries as providing superior control and guidance. Later again, the simulator was adapted for the training of guidance operators.

Guidance signals are created by the operator's thumb-controlled 'joystick', while sighting the missile and steering it towards the target. Long-range visibility is enhanced by the monocular sight and the bright flare carried at the tail of the missile.

The sight controller was developed to use a monocular instead of the binocular sight shown above, and its final form is shown at the right.

The basic technique to be developed with the aid of the electronic simulator assumed that the launcher box is aligned towards the expected target direction. To allow for targets coming from different directions, a heading switch can set the natural flight path 20° left or right of the firing direction, and within the limits of guidance, the missile can be directed over a 40° arc either side of the selected direction. Thus, a total of 80° angular cover is available, with the carry-box launcher's azimuth setting being at the centre of this arc. Likewise, the missile's natural control without guidance signals is such as to make it level out after its initial 20° climb, ready for guidance in azimuth to commence.

Fig.6.4 Artist's impression by Peter Mobsby, showing a Vigilant being fired against a distant tank.[60]

Fig.6.5 Infantryman operating guidance controller.[71]

The gyroscope and a 'velocity control' autopilot maintained the missile to a horizontal flight path, in the absence of guidance signals to change this. In the event of guidance failure, with a built-in gyroscope offset angle, Vigilant would gently climb to avoid hitting any friendly obstructions.

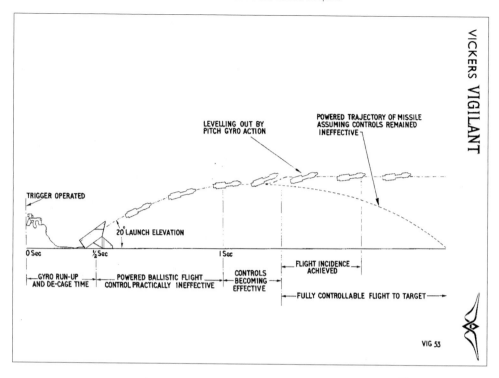

Fig.6.6 Flight elevation profile after launch, for initial level flight above the ground.[70]

The operator can select up to 20° left or right of the launcher-box firing direction, and again, in the absence of contrary guidance signals, the missile's velocity control autopilot is designed to fly a straight trajectory in the selected direction. The concept of guidance to the target is also depicted in graphic form for infantry training. Details of the technique will be covered later in this chapter. The transit times shown between active guidance periods allow the missile to settle onto a newly transmitted course in a smooth manner.

It was realised that provision for firing several missiles by one operator would be important in the operation of infantry against a formation of tanks. Besides the guidance controller and its battery pack with the 70 yards missile Separation Cable and its deployment drum (to permit at least 60 yards separation over uneven ground), Infantrymen were therefore also to be provided with a means of selecting successive missiles for firing. All this had to be provided with rock-solid safety arrangements including mechanical interlocks, to prevent premature rocket firing and to delay warhead arming until the missile had travelled to a safe distance ahead of the firing position.

For early aerodynamic and control trials purposes, the space normally occupied by the warhead (or dummy warhead in training) was available for radio telemetry of missile parameters. Using RAE trials facilities at Larhkill and Imber on Salisbury Plain, these telemetry signals would be recorded for later analysis in the same way as Vickers had already done with Blue Boar and Red Dean trials. Before embarking on a more detailed description of Vigilant's design and component parts, it is worth looking at the concept's overall design as used for flight trials.

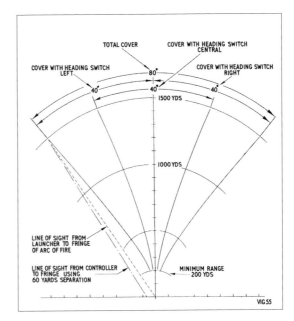

Fig.6.7 Azimuth profile available at launch.[70]

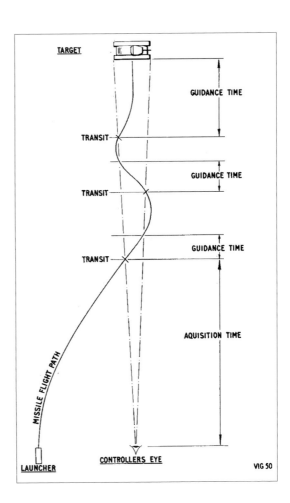

Fig.6.8 The phases of Vigilant guidance onto the target.[70]

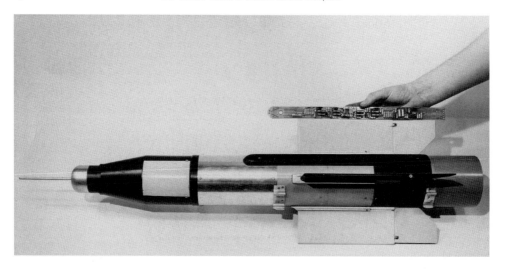

Fig.6.9 Vigilant trials missile, with Telemetry and antenna in place of the warhead.[71]

The above photograph shows the transistorised electronics 'potted' into one of the two fairings handling azimuth and elevation control and guidance information respectively. Thus, with the concept well established, Vigilant's detailed design could be commenced, and the first vital element was the rocket motor.

A small two-stage solid fuel rocket motor would at first glance appear to be a relatively minor design task. However, the project officer's report from the ICI Summerfield Research Station[72] shows otherwise. Following his early meeting with Dab and John Housego to discuss the specification, Hugh Nicols' November 2003 recollections mention his co-operative design work with Peter Rice, among others, and in the trials context, Henry Hunt and I are still remembered. With close design co-operation at Vickers, he recalls many static firings being necessary before a suitable design standard could be frozen and a proof series could be used for flight testing. The first flight trial resulted in a loop-the-loop and crash after a few seconds.

The motor body was effectively part of the missile structure, with a hot-gas tapping for powering the alternator and control actuators, and its blast pipe was to be surrounded by these powered items and the wire dispensing spool, which had to survive the high temperatures generated by the efflux gases.

The ideal asbestos-based body material, Durestos, for surviving internal gas temperature, proved to have insufficient strength in the thin-walled design required by the available space. A machined forging from high-strength Aluminium alloy to specification R77 became necessary, which initially had to be machined from solid bar for early trials. The aft enclosure was retained by a 'snap-ring' and embodied provisions to retain the blast tube and for the gas tapping to the actuators and alternator. Not only did the body strength have to be sufficient to contain the hot-gas pressure, the wing attachment channels to the body had to be so bonded on as to not be weakened by the 80°C external body temperature. A rubber lining was bonded inside the body tube for thermal insulation. Curing temperature of the adhesive had to be made low enough not to weaken the wing

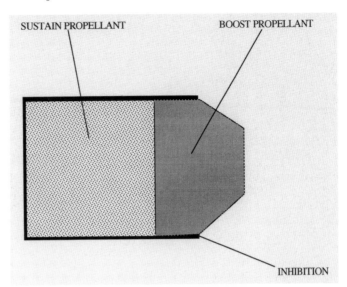

SUSTAIN PROPELLANT   BOOST PROPELLANT

INHIBITION

Fig.6.10 The 'cigar burning' nature of the propellant charge, with a high burning rate boost section followed by a slower burning section was simple enough in concept.[28]

attachment Redux bonding. Aerodynamic loads on the wings could cause problems with this attachment and ICI had to test fire rocket samples, with 90lb loads applied to each wing, as may occur during guidance manoeuvring.

The blast tube diameter had to be constrained to ¾in, to leave room for the surrounding components. An Aluminium tube with a 'Mintex' heat-resisting liner similar to brake-lining material appeared to be most suitable. But again, a thin wall was required, and to contain the high pressures in this effective extension of the rocket motor chamber and after burn-through occurring on some tests, a steel pressure tube became necessary. The method of retaining this blast tube in the aft end closure also underwent several changes before a suitable method was proved. The blast nozzle assembly at the very rear embodied the igniter and, finally, the tracking flare, for guidance visibility at long range. The Venturi nozzle assembly now included the 'Stand-Off Igniter' and had to be removable, in order to assemble the missile components around the blast tube.

This approximately 3in-long assembly itself posed many detailed design problems. A readily accessible connector to 'the outside world' of the launcher carry-box led directly to the electrically ignited 'match head' fuse, through a Radio Frequency filter to protect against spurious ignition by external radiations. In order to minimise the number of electrical initiators, the tracking flare was initially made from pure magnesium flame-sprayed onto an extension of the expansion cone. Later flight trials showed that in the brightest of tropical sunlight conditions, even this was barely adequate for visibility, and eventually a pyrotechnic flare had to be used. On firing the rocket motor, this was instantly ignited by the burning magnesium, thus avoiding the use of another initiator.

The motor ignition charge was required to blow a burning pellet forward, to impact the propellant. The initial placing of the igniter pellet in the apparently convenient tubular extension of the blast cone worked well enough at normal temperatures, but for reliability at low temperatures, the pellet was changed to 3.5 grams and of greater diameter and placed upstream of the nozzle throat, leaving the initiating charge and the match-head

Fig.6.11 Rig for Vigilant rocket motor test firing, with wings loaded to represent maximum manoeuvring. Thermocouples measured the maximum temperature reached, which remained within the 80°C specification.[72]

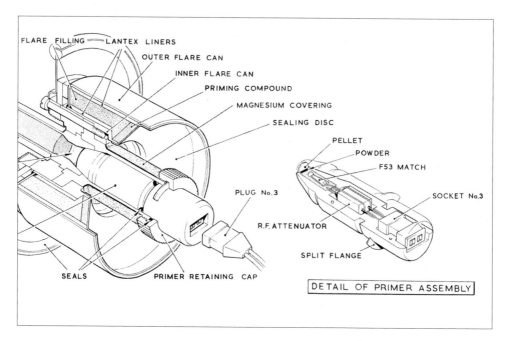

Fig.6.12 'Stand-off' Igniter and flare assembly, showing component parts.[73]

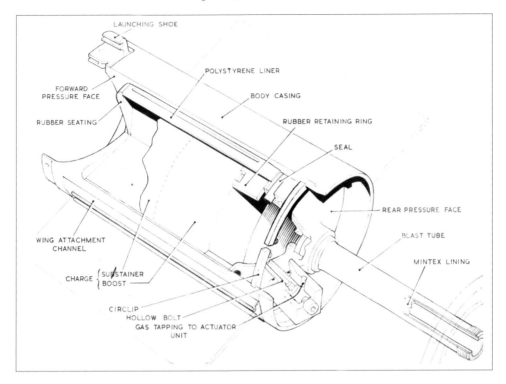

Fig.6.13 Rocket motor assembly detail, showing the two-stage charge within.[73]

on the downstream side. The pellet design and its method of retention were determined after a series of open firings with high-speed photography. This was all somewhat more complex than 'lighting the blue touch paper and retiring'!

The cigarette burning type CDB (Cast Double Base) propellant charge within the rocket motor body (see Fig.6.13) was inhibited on all faces except to rear face. That rear section for the boost phase was conical in shape, to provide the initial large surface area for high (180–200lb) thrust, and this regressed to the slow burning, smaller flat face for the sustain phase to maintain speed until impact with the target.

Besides the method of seating, cushioning, heat retaining and sealing of the rocket motor propellant, the drawing shows the rear pressure face retention by a circlip, the gas tapping for powering the alternator and the fin actuators. The thin-walled blast tube is shown, with its Mintex lining. Two of the wing attachment channels and outline wings can also be seen. The boost and sustain charge phases of the charge required different mixes of pyrotechnic powders and their blends. The sealing ring between the charge and the rear pressure face has cut-outs to allow the gas access to the forward end of the charge and so to equalise the pressure. Use of faulty ring (material) could cause movement of the charge and blocking of the blast tube inlet.

Manufacturing the rocket motor charge required as much attention as design. Charges were 'column cast' in vertical batches of six. A corset containing a cellulose acetate beaker was mounted on a base capable of serving a number of columns. The requisite quantities of powder for the boost and then the sustain sections were poured in from the top, followed by a small amount of 'dummy powder' to provide a separator between charges. Top and bottom connections were made after pouring the six charges in a column, and the casting liquid was then introduced. With connecting pipes clamped, the assembly was transported for curing and, after curing, the six individual charges could be sawn apart from each other. The aft face of each charge was then turned to the requisite conical profile in a lathe, and the forward face of dummy material was machined away, forming a small recess into which an inhibition disc (Plastic-Q) was bonded. Both visual and radiographic examinations were conducted on each charge, which received a unique identification number for the charge casting and its position in the charge column. Ballistic checks were performed on randomly chosen charges, with static firings at three proof temperatures. Such production and proof testing continued with Vigilant production into the late 1970s.

The rocket motor casing design, being also part of the missile body, was largely undertaken at Vickers, whose engineering team was closely involved in the choice of insulating materials and the mechanics of fixing the end closure and blast pipe. Some indication of the intricacies involved in arriving at a satisfactory rocket motor design may be deduced from the Progress Reports compiled by the project officer Mike Still, under the direction and approval of John Clemow. The process involved incremental design changes and proving trials on a continuing basis. The September 1957 report[74] recounts rocket motors being received for missile flight trials after six static proof tests, at temperatures ranging from -15°F to +125°F. As already described, these motors used steel blast tubes while awaiting development of the Aluminium alloy-tube design, and were locked into the motor end closure with a threaded ring. Only one Minex liner failure occurred in forty-two motors fired but, subsequently, all liners were visually and radiographically examined before use. When the first light-alloy tube was introduced for Phase 2 flight trials, the first firing resulted in failure after about 11 seconds of burning, due to overheating at the nozzle end requiring some detailed redesign. The March 1958 report[75] shows the adopted blast-tube design surviving tests where the nozzle was subjected to 400°F, and the missile's acceleration effect was simulated by loading the tube with a 1½lb weight during static firing. Further static firings with operating missile actuators placed around the blast tube proved that the extra load could be tolerated under trials level environmental temperatures. To meet the more stringent requirements of Phase 3 trials (under operational conditions), two further modifications were made to reduce the heating effect and for fitting of the new igniter for the later versions.

By September 1958, a special version of the motor was urgently required for a demonstration in the USA, where interest had been raised in Vigilant. This used a sustainer propellant with greatly superior storage life, but required temporarily reverting to steel blast tubes and firings of motors conditioned at up to 140°F. At this temperature, the flare body burned through and the upper limit was reduced to 125°F. The nozzle itself initially suffered from erosion by the blast gases, until Molybdenum was used in its manufacture. This material later suffered failures requiring detailed metallurgical examination of the molybdenum and, eventually, the manufacture of nozzles made from resin-integrated graphites, which were also cheaper.

Development of the little igniter/primer and flare unit was pursued during this period. The Phase 1 flare unit consisted of magnesium ribbon wrapped around the supersonic tailpipe, with stainless-steel gauze retaining container. Ignition of the ribbon by heat transferred through the tailpipe was sustained throughout the motor-burning period. Later, replacing the ribbon with flame-sprayed magnesium led to superior and constant light emission, without sputtering. A number of detailed design changes led to further improvements, providing extremely good flare visibility at a range of 1,600 yards under poor atmospheric visibility conditions. Nevertheless, the unusually bright conditions in the US trials at the Huntsville AL test range left visibility still requiring improvement. In fully functional guidance trials, the presence of the missile structure and the wire spool also led to an unwanted smoke trail, and this led to the provision of special vents in the rear cylinder of the Phase 1 missile, without entirely eliminating the smoke trail.

Other details related to the choice of insulation material for the motor charge, which changed from rubber to polythene. Manufacturing and assembly methods proved to be critical to developing a successful motor and proving it with trial firings. Anticipating later trials with the guidance wire dispensing around the rocket efflux required elaborate tests with the motor exhaust firing through an array of tungsten wires spaced at intervals from the nozzle. The forces exerted on the wires were measured with train gauges, while these trials also influenced the design of the carry-box launcher that would also be in the rocket motor efflux. The gas outlet connection to the missile actuators and the alternator were the subject of additional proving test. By September 1958, 340 rocket motors had been fired at Summerfield and thirty rocket motors for the USA trials were being assembled, a total of fifty-nine motors having been produced for flight trials. Into 1959, more detailed design changes relating to insulation, sealing and a motor body with an integral end closure and blast tube were made and tested. Among a variety of unusual safety-related possibilities investigated, the possibility of inadvertent motor firing without an igniter and choke (blast tube and nozzle) assembly during transportation was also explored by causing such ignition. The resultant thrust was only 100lb and died to zero in a few seconds.[76] A new pyrotechnic flare now also required development to overcome the visibility problem encountered in the extremely bright summer conditions experienced in the US trials. Initially, these flares affected the cotton-lapped guidance wires, requiring further changes, including the pyrotechnic powder composition.

The rocket motor gas-driven actuator and alternator combination, mounted between the motor and the wire-dispensing spool, required almost unbelievably intricate engineering. Squeezed between the 4½in-diameter missile body and the hot ¾in-diameter blast pipe, the assembly occupied the remaining 1.875in radial annulus. Until the use of rocket motor gas could be verified for powering units, early actuators were powered from a cordite (Mechanite 1) charge, emitting gases at 2,000°C to 2,400°C, which were described as 'fairly clean'. Filters of stainless-steel gauze in the breech head and the actuator cylinder heads were nevertheless required, to catch particles including molten metal parts from the igniter, that could easily clog or damage the actuator's tiny gas ports. A rocket motor static firing was required to verify actuator working with the additional heat emanating from the blast pipe. For the later rocket motor gas-powered units, the tapping is made by a junction block, secured to the motor's rear pressure face by hollow bolt. Inlet temperature to the actuator is reduced by a curved pipe acting as a heat sink, with seals and filters at the joints, and the equipment has to operate with input pressure of 2,600psi during the boost phase, and a much lower 465psi during the sustain phase.

Left: Fig.6.14 Actuator and Alternator engineered into its small space to operate Vigilant's controls.[77]

Below: Fig.6.15 Schematic functional diagram of Vigilant actuator.[78]

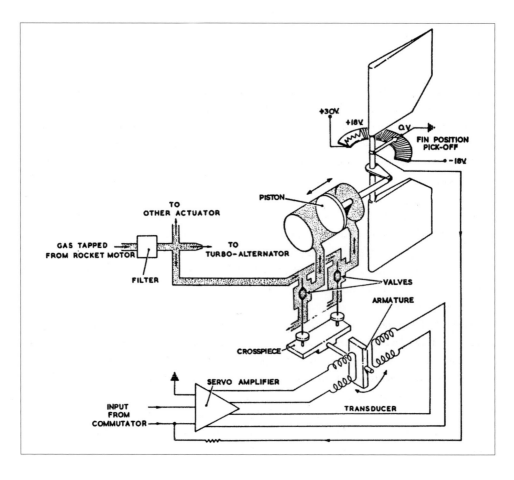

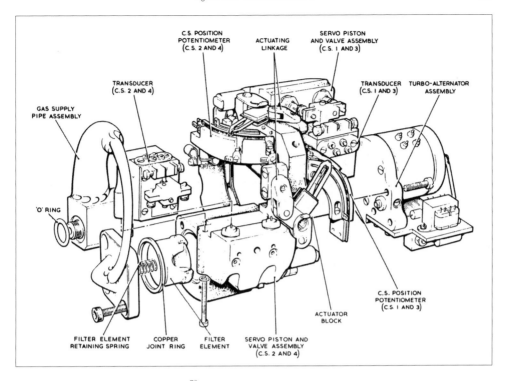

Fig.6.16 Actuator Assembly drawing.[78]

The basic functions of control within the actuator are more easily seen by studying the functional diagram, linking the actuator with the other missile components.

The basic simplicity of Bill Redstone's design as shown by the schematic does not make immediately obvious the delicacy of control to be exercised by the tiny spool valves on the motion of the piston that drives the control surfaces. Nor does it make obvious the potential effects of the hot gases tapped from the fiery rocket motor on the materials of the light-alloy casting and the little blocks into which the cavities, faces, surfaces and guides are machined, and the tight tolerances that have to be maintained at high temperature and pressure. The valves in the order of in-diameter work onto separate seating assemblies requiring the tightest of engineering tolerances and smoothest of finishes. Figs 6.17 and 6.18 give some indication of the scale on which the tiny parts were made, when the missile diameter of 4.5in is considered. The drawing of detailed parts below shows this scale in greater detail.

Driven by electronic input from mixing guidance signals with gyroscope stabilised autopilot signals, the tiny electromagnetic transducer moves the valves in appropriate directions to direct gas onto the piston for the required direction of control surface movement. The fin position pick-off signals when the control surface has moved to the demanded angle and cancels out the guidance demand of the moment. The assembly includes similar equipment for pitch and yaw controls, which are allocated their respective demands by a roll stabilised four-segment commutator (later eight-segment) as the missile rolls in flight. Fig.6.16 also shows the gas driven Turbo Alternator on the right of the drawing.

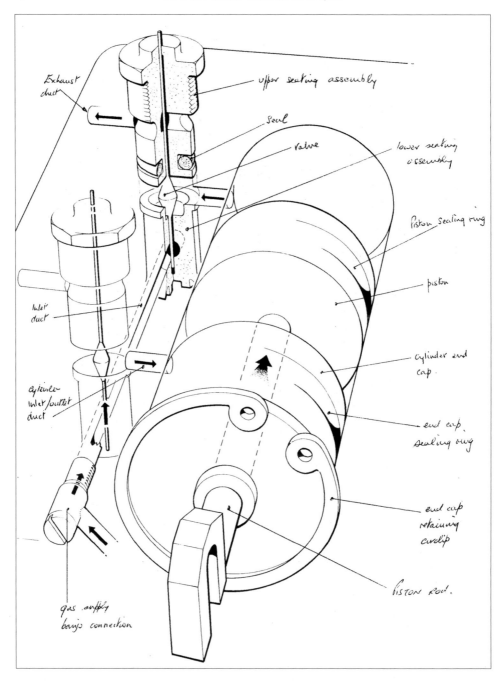

Fig.6.17 The Servo Assembly here shows individual part seals in even greater detail.[79]

Besides manufacturing to very tight tolerances, gas temperatures reducing in the heat sink to a still challenging 500°C to 600°C and 500psi operating pressure required allowances for the effects of differential expansions of the materials used in the assembly and the toleration of such heat by the numerous seals between parts.

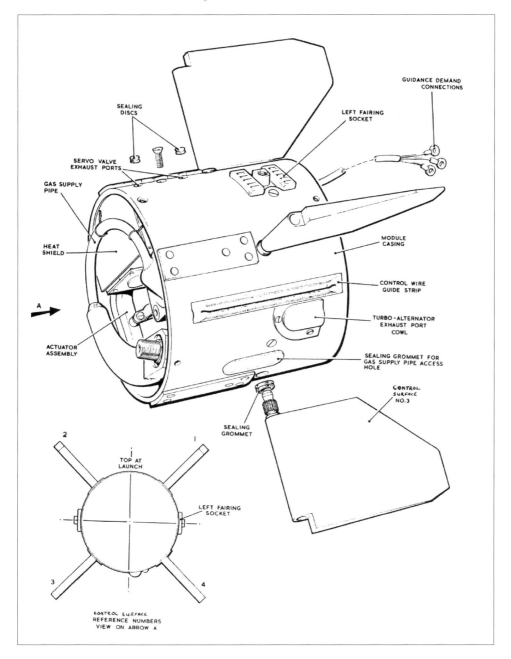

Fig.6.18 Drawing of the missile section containing the actuator and alternator assembly as fitted into the missile between the rocket motor and the wire dispensing spool. The wings which are immediately forward of the splined control surfaces are not shown.[79]

Much of the development effort was directed towards reliability, reducing weight and to ease of quantity manufacturing. Changing to a light–alloy casting with integral gas portings saved a very important ½lb in weight. By March 1959, the design of the Mk IIIB actuator system was completed and production of prototype units was well underway.

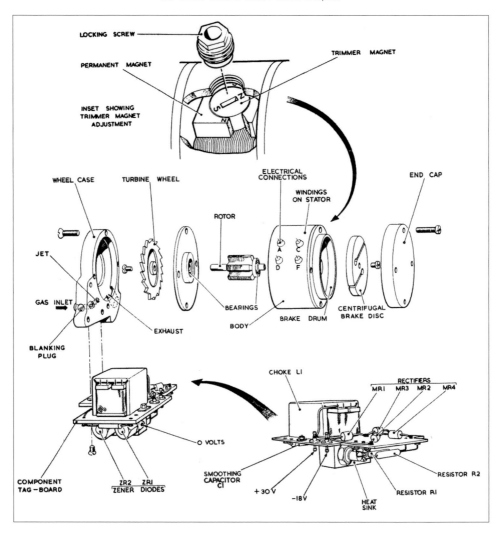

Fig.6.19 Turbo-alternator assembly, exploded view.

While the turbo-alternator design was proceeding, Vigilant trial missiles were powered by rechargeable batteries. Development of the turbo-alternator continued in parallel with the actuator development, again involving Bill Redstone under the overall direction of Mike Still. This rocket motor efflux gases-driven miniature power source required to be delivering its power to the electronic circuits of the autopilot and other items, within 0.5 second of motor ignition, before the missile will have flown very far. This requires running the alternator up to 50,000rpm within that time.

Gases tapped from the rocket motor impinge on the turbine wheel, to drive it up to speed and to sustain it over the efflux pressure range (nominally 500psi) during the boost and sustain phases of flight. The turbine speed therefore requires to be controlled using the eminently simple brake seen in the diagram. Operating by means of the centrifugal forces at this high rotational speed, parallel cuts in the centrifugal brake disc create cantilevered masses, which tend to fly outwards. At the design speed, they impinge on the brake drum, when the friction reduces the rotational speed to between the limits of 250rpm either side of the nominal speed. By September 1958, the basic concept of the turbo–alternator was proven, including run up to speed in 0.5 second and stable output throughout the flight period. Using nitrided materials in the disc brake material overcame wear problems, and the use of a magnetic shunt eventually overcame an initial need to select acceptable brakes in production. For long-running laboratory and other test purposes, the brake achieved a running life of up to five yours, without replacement. The diameter of the rotating parts was about 1in.

Two series-connected stator windings with pairs of poles linked by permanent magnets received magnetic flux from the six-pole rotor driven by the turbine. The flux changed direction six times per revolution, resulting in an alternating current output from the stator, at 5,000Hz. Using full-wave rectification with choke and capacitor smoothing, Direct Current outputs of +30 volts and –18 volts were regulated by Zener Diodes. The Zener Diodes were mounted on a heat sink, where the missile's 0-volts level was grounded on the body casing.

If possible, the design of the gyroscopes presented even more difficulties, for units subjected to Cordite-like discharge gases. The central importance of the gyroscopes in Vigilant are evident from the diagram below.

Pitch/Roll and Yaw/Roll gyroscopes are depicted, driven by a Cordite charge and showing the Roll Commutator on the Pitch/Roll gyroscope, for resolving the allocation of controls to elevator and rudder functions as the missile rolls in flight.

Besides the requirement for minimising drift rate during manoeuvring flight, perhaps the greatest difficulty was to meet a specification for the gyros to be run up to speed and

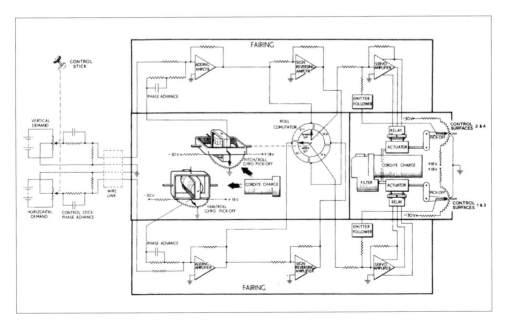

Fig.6.20 Diagram of Guidance and Control System.[80]

to be smoothly uncaged into the free condition by 0.45 second, when the 'uncaged' signal is used to fire the rocket motor. Next, the electrical angle pick-offs needed to output signals to the autopilot amplifiers, without excessive 'noise', despite the presence of hot dirty gases and the vibrations caused by the rocket motor and by flight manoeuvres. The small size of the gyroscope rotors led to the high rotational speed being required, in order to provide the stability of the spatial reference needed for accurate control and guidance. The drift of a gyroscope's axis is an obviously critical factor and in a small missile like Vigilant, difficult to minimise. Known as precession, drift is mainly caused by friction in the rotor bearings, which also causes the speed to run down during the missile's 12-second flight duration, reducing the gyro's inertial stabilising forces. It is also caused by friction in the gimbal bearings about which the missile moves during flight. Consequently, bearing lubrication is sufficiently difficult to achieve, that a single drop of lubricant can be enough to cause unacceptable drift, whereas no lubricant is also unacceptable. Experimentation with lubricants of different compositions and viscosities was necessary before acceptable performance became possible. For successful guidance of Vigilant, the drift rate was required to be within 1°/second in pitch and 0.5°/second in yaw.

Another problem was to achieve smooth uncaging, to free the gimbals on achieving run-up speed. Remembering that uncaging was also dependent on the mechanical operation of hot and dirty gas-driven components, the effects of high temperature and of differential temperatures between a piston and the (cordite cartridge) breech block within which it moved could also cause failure to uncage.

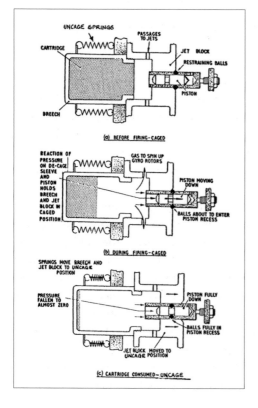

Fig.6.21 Gyroscope uncage mechanism.[83]

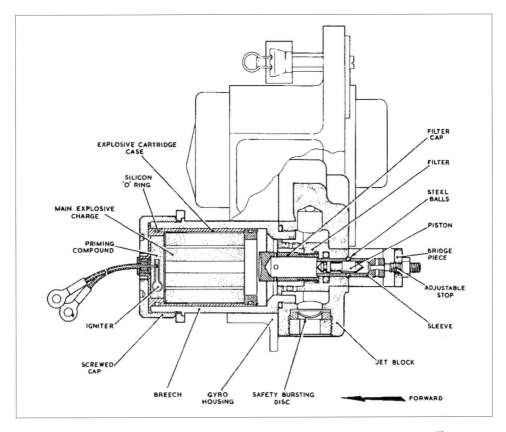

Fig.6.22 Exploded front view of Gyroscope assembly, showing commutator and slip rings.[83]

The uncaging action by spring tension (initially resisted by the gas pressure in the chamber) will be seen to depend on the movement of this piston, propelled by the cartridge gases that also accelerate the rotor to its running speed. The piston runs in a cylinder within the breech of the cartridge case and it is retained by steel balls, that latch into detents on completion of the uncaging action. Clearly, the heating of the mechanical parts and their relative dimensions and tolerances have a profound effect on the success of uncaging the gyroscopes.

Initially using brass rotors with Pelton buckets on which the gas jets impinged, the speed was designed to reach 96,000rpm. This proved to wear the rotor bearings too quickly and by March 1958 the design was changed to use a much heavier mass rotor employing GEC Heavy Alloy, running up to a maximum speed of 60,000rpm. The increased inertia of the Heavy Alloy provided better stability,even at the lower speed, and the lower-bearing friction helped to reduce precession. At the same time, lower electrical pick-off noise levels were achieved by changing the spring wiper design on the potentiometer. However, the cordite cartridge was producing sufficient contamination to cause electrical resistance breakdown, and it also adversely affected the commutator and the electrical connectors at the missile skin. These problems required the blocking of a pressure balance hole, changes to the commutator face contacts to eliminate resistance breakdown between segments and the use of WACO rubber to plug gaps around the skin connectors. At this time, successful missile firings were flown employing compressed air from the rocket launcher, to drive gyro rotors. However, cartridge-fired gyros still suffered delayed uncaging of up to 4 seconds in laboratory tests, until the cartridge breech diameter was fractionally decreased, to prevent it gripping the bore of the gyro case. The uncaging action remained an ongoing problem during the earlier flight trials and was finally cured by attention to such tiny details – differently for earlier compressed air-driven gyros, to operational type cartridge-operated units.

Developments of miniature high-revving devices for gyroscopes and the turbo-alternator running in parallel were not without their dangers. At such rotational speeds, rotors could 'run away' to excessive speeds beyond their design limits, leading to the rotors completely breaking up. Located on opposite sides of the same corridor in the Vickers GW building, Bill Redstone's actuator and alternator design lab and Chuck Fry's gyroscope lab both suffered rotor break-ups and, despite the reinforced test enclosures and strengthened laboratory walls, they occasionally projected hot rotor parts into each other's laboratories. Fortunately, nobody was killed in the process!

By March 1959, special rotor-bearing designs were employed, with miniature adjustable screwed-in bearing end caps and special lubricants employing two drops of carefully developed mixtures, comprising 5 per cent Aeroshell and 95 per cent Petroleum Ether. The locking of bearings and other parts into place was effected with Loctite sealant. Likewise, potentiometer wipers were improved using Beryllium Copper 0.003in in thickness, both for lower torque and for easier manufacture. Even thinner materials were

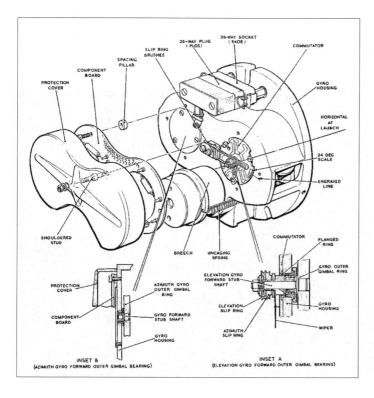

Fig.6.22 Exploded front view of Gyroscope assembly, showing commutator and slip rings.[83]

later used for yet lower noise levels, good for up to 30g acceleration. Extensive theoretical analyses were completed on minimising drift, when the gimbal angles were out of the orthonogal (mutually at right angles) by up to ± 50°. Remembering that the yaw gyro gimbals had to operate at large angles as the missile was guided in azimuth onto moving targets, drift rate could be exacerbated. The pitch gyro was also required to operate out of the orthogonal, but to a lesser (nominally 15°) angle – sufficient to allow for the 20° launch angle and the subsequent 5° incidence during level flight, plus or minus any missile manoeuvres in pitch. The roll commutator was therefore moved from the yaw gyro to the pitch gyro and using the best quality Barden bearings.

Meanwhile, much mathematical analysis by John Lattey appeared to prove that increasing the rotor size would not enable sufficient reduction in the drift rate. He had used the best looking of several highly complex solutions indicated in his mathematics literature, and chose the most likely one. However, further development continued, to increase the inertia of the gyro rotors, using enlarged split wheels of a spherical shape to increase inertia by a factor of more than 3, running at the much lower maximum speed of 24,000rpm. Lower friction and slower deceleration leading to more constant running speed curing the missile's 12-second flight would also factor into lower drift rate. The final rotor reverted to a cylindrical shape with two rows of Pelton buckets, running to a maximum of 28,000rpm[81] and, eventually, by 1960, flight trials showed that gyroscope drift was reduced to acceptable levels.

Before flight tests of the gyroscopes could be warranted, laboratory pre-flight testing of a complete missile system was necessary, to show that a rolling missile, autopilot controlled by gas actuators operating the control fins was likely to work as a completely connected system. This was part of my responsibility as head of the Test Group to which I was promoted in 1957, following service in the Trials Group. It was my concept of the 'Rolling Rig', that was built by my Test Gear Design Section under George Errington

Fig.6.23 Vigilant missile, cut away to show the gyroscope assembly in situ.[84]

Fig.6.24 Vickers Development
Test's Vigilant Rolling Test Rig.[83]

and operated by his Development Test Section under John Lewis. The rig performed complete missile systems test in the laboratory, before the Trials Group was allowed to flight test similarly complete Vigilant systems with live rocket firings. Using compressed air to run the gyroscopes, actuators and alternator, the Rolling Rig enabled realistic simulations of in-flight system operation to a high degree of confidence. As already indicated, flight tests also started with compressed air-driven units, until the cordite charge operated gyroscopes and rocket motor gas-driven actuators had been developed. Later, gyros and actuators were cartridge-fired.

The motor-driven rolling rig could also be moved in pitch and yaw, to simulate missile motions in flight. Using an aerodynamic simulator, open loop and closed loop tests were conducted, in which gyroscopes and actuators operated control surfaces via the autopilot, with voltages recordings via slip rings. Confidence in stability of control in flight was sufficient to allow flight trials. The tests led to a number of modifications, without which many expensive flight trials may otherwise have failed.

Environmental tests during 1958 in the Test Group's laboratory, under Peter Inglis, included temperature cycling and vibration tests exciting the missile structure's fundamental mode at 275Hz, by ±2.5g amplitude lateral vibration sweeps over the range 15Hz to 500Hz, and by longitudinal vibrations at ±5g over the same frequency range.

The Autopilot electronic circuits, seen diagrammatically in Fig.6.20 above, were embodied into two identical metal fairings containing the 'electronic packs', which were attached externally to join the forward gyroscope section of the missile to the rear-mounted actuator and alternator section. Transistorised electronic circuits were powered from the turbo-alternator's +30V and -18V DC outputs and consisted of an adding amplifier, a servo amplifier, a gyro demand phase advance network and an adding network, for the gyro demand and guidance demand signals. A well-known method for stabilising missile control systems, Phase Advance provided a measured degree of anticipation, to prevent instability due to overshooting of the control signals during flight.

Port and starboard electronic packs respectively controlled Azimuth and Elevation guidance channels, as identified by the roll commutator on the pitch/roll gyroscope. However, the servo amplifier controlling the actuator for control surfaces 1 and 3 was in the port electronic pack, and that for fins 2 and 4 was in the starboard pack. The electronic packs were resin-encapsulated to create 'solid' fairing units with connectors at the ends. Circuit parameters, once developed in the laboratory assisted by simulator studies and finally with guidance trials, became fixed in the design. No adjustment of the autopilot circuits could be made once the 'packs' had been 'potted'. Fig.6.9, shown earlier, includes a photograph of an electronic pack, with the transistors and other components visible, before potting.

Besides circuit development and the problems associated with 1950s level miniaturisation, the choice of early transistors and design for simplicity, reliability and greater economy dominated the engineering effort (though at this time, Texas Instruments expected Germanium Transistors would cost at least £2 15s each). An early simplification gained a reduction by forty components, when separated guidance signals over two pairs of wires took preference over a two-wire guidance spool, requiring demodulation of combined signals. Corresponding savings were obtained in the guidance controller on the ground. In the initial design, Germanium Transistors were soon replaced with Silicon transistors recently becoming available and more in tune with the requirement for operation of the required -40°C to +100°C. By September 1958, seven rocket-fired control flight trials had shown consistent success with the circuit pack fairings.

As so often in manufacture, the devil was in the details. All SCR OC470 transistors had to be selected by the manufacturers to a Vickers specification, following intermittent contacts due a faulty welding technique, and to meet tolerance requirements. The (as then) new technique of soldering onto printed wiring boards had to be perfected and the sixteen-way butt connectors at the ends of the fairings suffered early faults due to selection of contact material and to faulty heat treatment. Following more transistor problems in 1959, a mixture of PNP type and NPN type transistors were chosen from Texas Instruments and from Mullard. This was highly beneficial, obviating the need to select transistors in manufacture, and they also removed the need for Zener Diodes for temperature compensation. A new design of skin plug for the Phase 4 missiles in 1960 eliminated butt-type connectors in favour of fixed pins mating into sockets with floating spring contacts in the missile body, providing a wiping action.[81]

In February 1957, John Housego was lured into another position in the USA, when Mike Still took over continued design and development of Vigilant. In May, the highly experienced control engineer Charles Fricker also went to the USA, joining Booz Allen & Hamilton, when Mike also took up his Control Group responsibilities.

The Wire Link and its dispensing for guidance signals may be the choice, if any part of Vigilant's development could be considered to have been more problematical than even the gyroscope or the actuators. The choice of a four-wire system, that made for less complicated missile electronic circuits in the fairings, led to unknown strength and flexibility requirements, coupled with the essential insulation needed between conductors. A mile-length of preferably low-resistance wire would be dispensed from the rear of the missile around the rocket motor efflux. Wire guidance had been successfully achieved by the Germans in the Second World War, with very different configurations involving spools on missile wing tips, usually using techniques unsuitable for Vigilant. French missiles such as SS10 used 'enclosed' dispensing. We chose 'open' dispensing, where layers of wire lightly bonded with wax would be wound successively forward and rearward, to be pulled off the stationary spool at the tail end. First assumptions would indicate that the cable of four insulated strands should be flexible, yet as strong as possible to ensure against breaking during launch and the subsequent 12 seconds of manoeuvring missile flight. Meanwhile, after Trevor Wooderson developed an 'elephant's trunk' rig to dispense wire and, later, the 'pop gun' mentioned below, a high-flying Australian mathematician at Woomera 'proved' that wire dispensing would not be successful, even at 50 per cent of Vigilant's flight speed.

Initial laboratory tests using a compressed air gun to pull off the wire showed that low-resistance Cadmium Copper insulated wire with a nylon braid had insufficient strength. A new development with 4-strand 40 SWG Copper wire individually insulated with synthetic enamel, exhibited a breaking strain of 12lb and appeared to be promising. Flight trials were then attempted with steel wire, for which difficulties with poor adhesion of synthetic enamel insulation were well known. This wire exhibited over-dispensing during the first stage of boosted flight, and was also subject to the method of adhesion, which had to be strong enough to prevent blast dispensing, without exerting excessive load on the wire. One method considered using thin layers of shellac-coated paper inserted between each layer of wire, that would be melted by heat. The best method of attaching the wire to the missile launcher with minimised snatch loads also had to be determined. With wire tension being predominantly dependent on missile speed, further conflicting phenomena led to a lengthy programme of 'intelligent' trial and error, first in the laboratory and later in flight trials.

Records[13] show, including the above, seven specific variations of 4-core wire material and insulation techniques that were investigated during the development process. Indicating the extent of material and engineering technology applied, these included 0.0048in-diameter STA/4 with double Simgold insulation giving 30lb tensile strength, similar Copper with Formvar Insulation and woven Nylon with 12lb tensile strength, 0.0056in-diameter Stainless Steel with Formvar/Polybutyral insulation giving 32lb tensile strength, another Copper Formvar-insulated wire with a woven sheath giving 22lb and an enamel-insulated Aluminium wire of 0.07in diameter, before the final choice was made. The final choice that worked reliably employed Brass-plated Swedish Steel wires with Formvar/Polybutyral insulation, giving 30lb ultimate tensile strength.

An important and eventually successful development in 1958 was designed to give the spool a sloping flank at its trailing edge, to give a measure of support for the wire from the point at which it leaves the remaining turns and the point of departure from the missile at the flank. Known as the 'Wine-Glass' wire dispenser, kinks and any permanent set in the wire was avoided and the wax adhesive on the coils offered comparatively little resistance as the wire moves away. The wine-glass shape supported the rear face of the coil, allowing the use of a wider range of adhesives. A metal shroud was then also fitted around the spool, the wire then dispensing through an annular gap.

A further improvement was the use of an auxiliary spool at the launcher, which allowed the missile to clear the launcher and achieve speed before the wire began to dispense from the main spool. Without this, motor blast could throw wire over the launcher, causing damage as the tension built up during flight.

Besides the dramatic results of a wire break during guidance trials, high-speed observation of dispensing the thin cable during development brought its own problems. Ciné films were widely used as in all GW field trials, but in the early stages it was important to obtain a first view. A simple technique to enhance visibility against a contrasting background began to give useful results.

The connection 'carrot' embodies an anti-snatch guide, in which the wire is spirally would around a rubber cord secured at each end. This arrangement prevents the wire from breaking or pulling away from the plug if a sudden snatch occurs during launching of the missile.

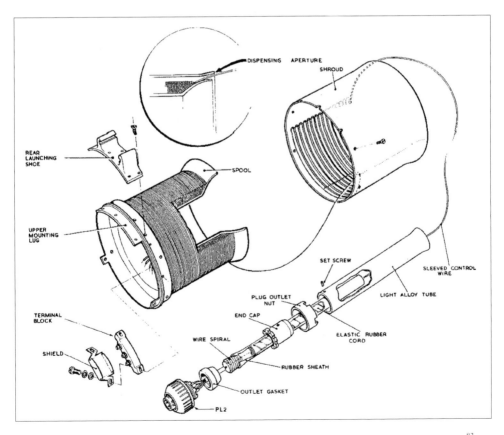

Fig.6.25 Exploded view of 'wine-glass' wire dispensing system with launcher attachment 'carrot'.[83]

Fig.6.26, Cut-away Vigilant missile from the Royal Army Museum, Chelsea, showing wire spool.[84]

Fig.6.27 Vigilant firing from a Ferret Scout Car, with dark background to show up the wire link.[86]

Fig.6.28 Vigilant firing from its carry-box launcher as used by the Infantry.[86]

By March 1959, thirty-five wire proving missiles had been fired in the UK, including controlled missiles, and a further twenty-six controlled rounds were fired in a somewhat prematurely forced US evaluation trial at the Redstone Arsenal in Alabama. At this stage, excessive snatch still occurred on some launches and occasional insulation breakdowns as well as wire breaks occurred under excessive missile manoeuvre conditions. The development had reached a stage of stable design with mostly successful firings, yet sufficient small detail improvements remained to be implemented as experience was gained.

In its final form, the Wire Dispenser carried a minimum of 1,730 yards of lap-wound cable on the wine-glass spool, now modified to a profile more resembling a brandy glass. The resistance of each strand was 28.5K, with the cable's diameter 0.02in, giving a minimum tensile strength of 23lb. Instead of carrying an auxiliary spool as earlier described, a 40ft second section of sleeved wire was arranged in zig-zag formation on the inside of the shroud. This was secured to the shroud by cotton stitches inserted through a series of holes drilled in the shroud, preventing excessive dispensing due to the rocket motor blast during the launching phase.[83]

The guidance controller used by Infantry soldiers and the Royal Armoured Corps on Ferret Scout Cars connected to the Wire Link, to constitute the remaining part of Vigilant's means of delivering a warhead to a target. After early designs incorporating binoculars, the controller became a lightweight, single-handed Sten Gun-like device, which enabled the operator to send guidance signals up the wire by movement of a thumb-controlled 'joystick'. The carpal thumb joints' mutually orthogonal natural axes of movement are singularly suitable for thumb operation of a joystick, to give separate azimuth and elevation demands, without the danger of pulling a missile into the ground due to cross-coupling. The controller therefore embodied suitably placed potentiometers, which delivered voltages proportional to the operator's thumb movements. Power for sending the guidance demands up the wire link was provided by a dry 4.5in x 2.5in x 1in battery pack of sufficient capacity for six missile firings, producing 33 and 67.5 on load volts for elevation and azimuth control respectively. A monocular telescopic sight was provided for use at ranges beyond 2,000ft for fine control and when the missile flare may not be sufficiently visible to the naked eye. The controller was housed in a waterproof haversack and the battery pack was carried on the soldier's body for warmth in winter conditions. The combination was specified to weigh 5.6lb, which together with a missile in its carry-box launcher and separation cable would keep the Infantryman's load to under 55lb. An optional six-way selector box enabled a single Infantryman to fire six missiles in rapid sequence.

Development commenced of the overall autopilot and guidance system design, along with the missile's guidance system design and development, from early 1957 onward. This had been led principally by Peter Fortescue, reporting to Dab, with sections under Warwick Syrett working on the theory, and Harry Fryer concerned with building a simulator and conducting the simulation. The Theory Section included a young engineer, Gill, who later became Peter Fortescue's wife. The design parameters were interwoven with the missile's aerodynamics, gyro-controlled autopilot and actuator system, together with the ergonomics of human control in a realistic military situation. The 2 to 3 second transfer time of an operator's attention from a the naked eye to a binocular sight led early on to the choice of a monocular sight instead, where one naked eye could remain on the target and the missile, while without appreciable transfer delay the other eye could concentrate on fine control during the latter stages of guidance at long range.

A simulator was built by 1958 and became key to the development, enabling the guidance formulae (or transfer functions) to be varied, along with variations in the field of view and the monocular's optical gain (magnification). A realistic scene was projected onto a curved screen, with targets of representative size for given distances, and a second projector created a spot of light representing the missile flare. A third projector could create moving targets on the screen. The missile (flare) position on the screen was controlled by operating the sight controller, whose effect on the simulated missile 'flight' was representative of the dynamics of missile flight, as see from the launch point. The size of the spot was also controlled, to represent the effect of increasing distance from the operator as the missile approached the target. With the ability to vary missile and controller parameters, it was possible to test the effect of different guidance techniques and the influence of operator skill on guidance accuracy. At the end of each simulated firing, it was possible to record accuracy and also how the controller made his guidance demands. Eventually, the simulator became an important training aid for the British and foreign armies that ordered Vigilant.

After the first design concept of the sight controller took shape in the 'Sten-Gun' format for use (initially) from the hip, and later from a prone position, the most important modification was a change from a 'joy-stick'-like control to a cradle or cup, for the thumb. Simulator studies showed that 50 per cent of operators applied reversed 'stick' control in its vertical plane, but the later thumb cup was correctly sensed by 95 per cent of operators.[92] The operator's thumb moved the thumb cup about spindles, providing the two axes of azimuth and elevation. Simulator work soon determined that an electronic shaping filter was needed, to give the operator's control demands Phase Advance. By this means it was possible to overcome the time delay while the missile built up the incidence required to respond to the manoeuvre demand. The filter was a simple resistor and capacitor network built into the controller handle, and its transfer function could be optimised as development proceeded. Similarly, the 'gain' or gearing of control could be optimised, a typical phase advanced gain providing a sensitivity of 17° of missile heading demand per inch of thumb-tip movement. The other hand operated a trigger to initiate firing of the gyroscope cartridge which automatically led to the rocket motor being initiated. The firing and arming mechanism with safety interlocks required no less than thirty-two parts designed into the controller, to ensure against firing until it was safe to do so, and if the next missile selected was not otherwise ready for launch.

For an apparently simple requirement to accommodate thumb control and the monocular sight, the sight controller became a complex mechanical device, with many

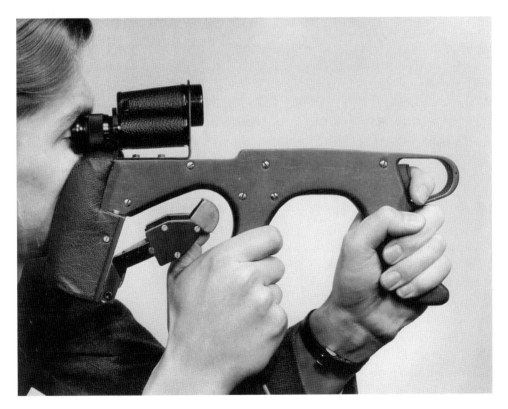

Fig.29 Sight controller and monocular
(a) In operation during guidance simulations by Guidance System Analyst Harry Fryer.[96]
Overleaf: (b) In Infantryman's carrying satchel.[87]

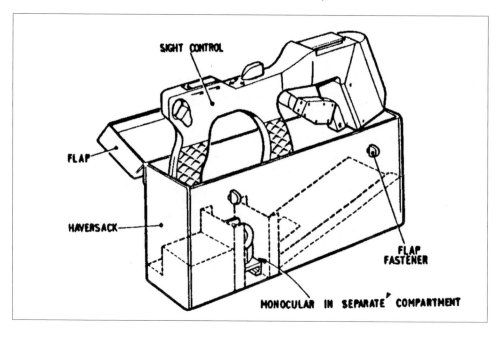

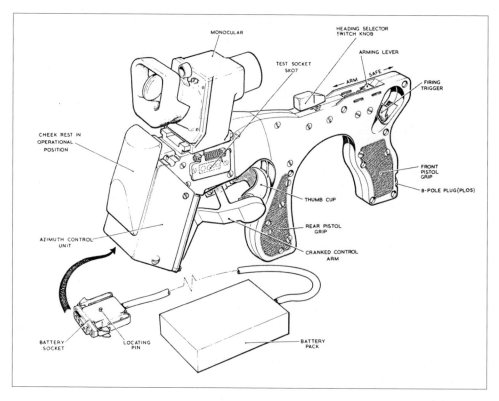

Fig.6.30 General view of sight controller, with battery and connection to the missile wire link.[87]

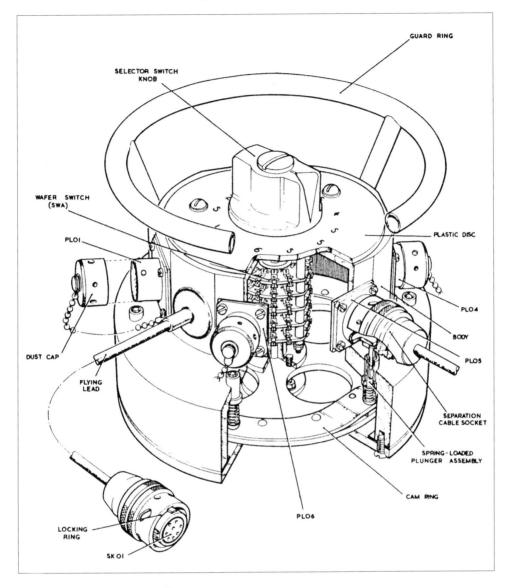

Fig.6.31a Missile Selector Box.[87]

components to provide for smooth control movements, spring restraints, the monocular viewer, battery power, shaping networks and the trigger mechanism and the mechanical arming interlocks with electrical circuitry for firing safety.

As indicated earlier in Fig.6.7, guidance trials on the simulator showed that for optimum control against targets offset from the direction of launch, a Heading Selector Switch enables the velocity control system to centre onto a sightline close to the target direction. Guidance demands can then be reduced to fine-tuning onto this sight line, without excessive movement of the thumb cap. The Heading Selector Switch is seen on top of the controller above, close to the Safe/Arm switch interlocking with the firing trigger. Much

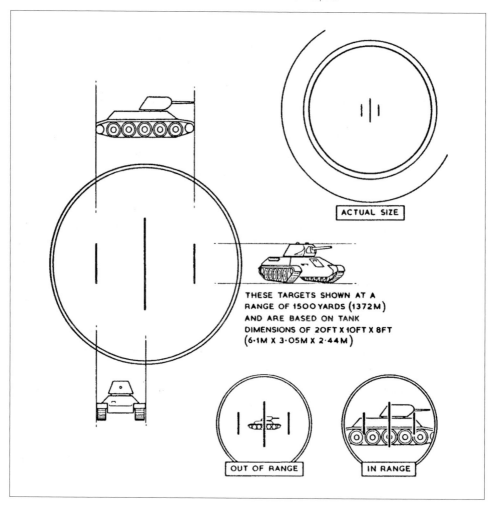

ACTUAL SIZE

THESE TARGETS SHOWN AT A
RANGE OF 1500 YARDS (1372M)
AND ARE BASED ON TANK
DIMENSIONS OF 20FT X 10FT X 8FT
(6·1M X 3·05M X 2·44M)

OUT OF RANGE

IN RANGE

Fig.6.31b Monocular Stadia Lines, showing a representative tank target, whose 10ft beam is encompassed by lines defining one side of the viewer. The tank length dimension of 20ft occupies the space between the pair of outer lines.[87]

of the controller body that is not used to house mechanical linkages is filled with electronic components for the two axes of control and for the firing/arming safety circuits.

Besides providing magnification for guidance at long range, the monocular sight was used as the means of estimating target range and generally ensuring that the Infantryman set up the attack in an optimal manner. After the first Avimo monocular sight was delivered in 1959 with 3.2 magnification and 15° field of view, this magnification and field of view gave the best compromise for sighting and for the transfer of the operator's concentration from the naked eye, to the magnified view. Stadia lines were etched onto the monocular sight to guide the operator's estimate of target range.

As the development of Vigilant began to approach its final phases in 1960, the sight controller had to be adapted for cold-weather operation with heavy gloves. Low thermal conductivity materials were utilised and the firing mechanism was re-engineered to meet all safety requirements. This was combined with a detailed review and re-engineering for reliability of wiring, potentiometer wipers for lowest noise levels and for the ruggedness of the thumb cup and control housing, as well as external connections for cables. With the cable links to the launcher – direct or via the selector switch and the launcher box itself – every aspect was engineered to withstand the most adverse handling by ordinary soldiers in battle conditions.

The carry-box launcher was a cardinal development as applied to Infantry use, an essential 'soldier proofing' feature being ruggedness against virtually anything a soldier might do to it (withstanding a 2ft drop onto a hard surface without the missile suffering more than 40g retardation). Other launch methods using a tripod were also developed, besides the separate requirement for mounting of Vigilant missiles to the Ferret Scout Car for Royal Armoured Corps use. Early carry-box launchers with wing-tip launching employing 'Hairlock' rubberised hair mouldings for shock absorbtion were tested by the Evironmental Test Section, with reasonable success. Live firings with wing-tip launching were also successful. Eventually, this method was abandoned, in favour of all metal missile suspension by launch rails and a removable light retaining ring at its forward end which also bore onto a nose pad in the forward box cover. Additional support was provided by the separation cable drum stowed in the rear, held on a spigot attached to the removable rear box cover. These supports on the two box lid ends helped to hold the missile firmly under conditions of transportation and rough handling. The two launch rails attached to a longitudinal member secured under the top surface of the box were mounted at 12in separation at different heights, and were arranged to ensure that the missile launch shoes left the rail together. Pre-deployment testing of the missile system and the safe fitting and preparation of igniters on deployment are covered later.

The launcher/box design provided holes in the side of the box, to equalise pressure caused by rocket motor blast at launch, avoiding effects on the departing missile. To provide for conditions such as long, wet grass, the holes in the lower face were covered with a screen while the box front end was closed. This dropped away from the box when the front end was hinged down and secured with telescopic rods, to act as the front support for the 20° launch angle. Once erected and when connections had been made to the missile separation cable, the launcher/box was secured to the ground with the aid of two lanyards pegged down into the ground.

For deployment by Paratroops, an alternative Polystyrene container with a lightweight tripod launcher were developed.

Details of Vigilant's installation inside the carry-box launcher, including its means of retention under operational and transportation rough handling, are shown, together with launching rails and the igniter connections for the gyroscope cartridge charge and the rocket motor. The rocket motor igniter is normally stowed in the 'plocket' at the base, but is also shown as installed at the end of the blast pipe. The soldier's carrying handle for the complete 50lb assembly can be seen at the top (Fig.6.35).

The gyro charge igniter is connected to the missile skin with a 'snatch plug' that pulls out as the missile leaves the launcher. The gyro 'uncaged' micro switch signal is passed along the cable to the rocket motor igniter. This is blasted away when the rocket motor fires, which in turn ignites the tracking flare. The cable drum will, of course, have been

Fig.6.32 Vigilant in erected carry-box launcher and sight controller, ready for final connections.[88]

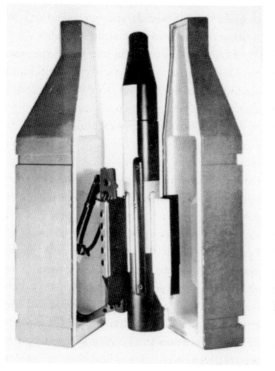

Above left: Fig.6.33 Expanded Polystyrene container with Vigilant for Paratroops, with lightweight Tripod Launcher.[88]

Above right: Fig.6.34 Paratrooper kitted out with EPS container, ready for dropping by parachute.[88]

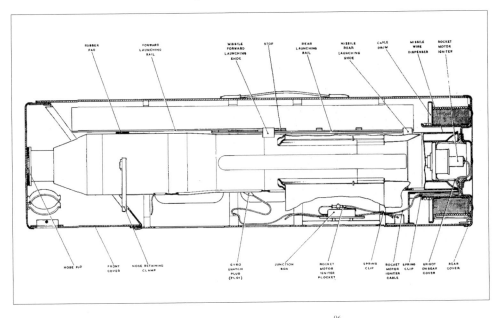

Fig.6.35 Drawing of Vigilant's installation in the carry-box launcher.[96]

removed when setting up for launch and the cable run out the distance up to 70 yards, to the selected location for firing and controlling the missile with the sight controller.

A further lightweight launcher with the missile in a lightweight carry bag was also developed for uses other than Paratroop's. This launcher was supported on a folding tripod and, similar to the early carry-box launching relying on the wing tips to stabilise the missile during launch, here the missile was supported only on its lower wing tips. Successful trial firings were carried out at Larkhill, enabling a wider range of military deployment options.

These items are depicted in the following photographs.

During this 1958–1959 period, besides development tests for system proving and the subsequent firings made possible, more environmental tests continued to explore the wider range of conditions under which Vigilant would be used. Some high temperature and humidity conditions were related to the USA demonstration trials in the Deep South.

Temperature cycling over a range from -46°C to + 70°C led to design changes in the actuator transducers, and wide temperature tests were conducted to establish the temperature coefficient of the wire link. The alternator's performance at high and low temperatures was also tested in the laboratory. After low reliability experienced in early human operator trials, two missiles underwent rigorous inspections and vibration tests at ±3g up to 500Hz, as well as further open loop tests on the Rolling Rig with pitch and yaw, when the gyroscope and actuator cartridges were fired. These tests revealed a substantial number of minor design or manufacturing faults, which were then rectified before subsequent firing trials.

Shock tests up to 65g for 10m/sec. and other extreme tests were conducted on Phase 2 and Phase 3B models. Relating to safety of the fuze, thermal shock and hermetic sealing

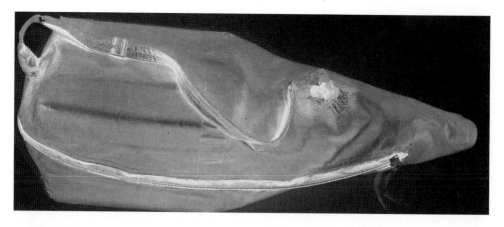

Above and below: Fig.6.36 Lightweight launcher and missile bag.[89]

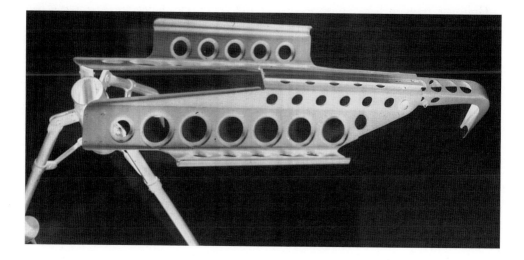

tests were necessary and excessive impact shocks of 7,000g were applied to verify that the fuze gear train components would not fracture.

In the aftermath of these extensive laboratory system and development tests and the improvements arising from them and from experience in the Environmental Test laboratory, only by flight trials using live operators controlling guided rounds was it possible to encounter the total environments in representative firings. As one would expect, these suffered a number of technical failures and the guidance technique used by simulator-trained operators required developing. Beyond the simulator exercises, operator suitability was an unknown, and the effect of practice in the field was yet to be determined. The original joystick control on the sight controller appeared to be a natural design, until it proved to cause reversed control movements with some operators, who instinctively moved the joystick in the opposite direction to the normal reaction with most operators. This led to the 'thumb cup' design already mentioned, where the natural joint movements of the thumb about the carpal joints corresponded exactly with the desired azimuth and elevation axes about which the thumb pad moved.

Fig.6.37 Vigilant lightweight launcher firing.[90]

Guidance trials in live firings became possible once the dispensing wire spool had reached sufficient reliability. The rounds of Phase 2, Phase 3 and Phase 3B carried telemetry or dummy warheads, giving the missile the required aerodynamic shape and centre of gravity. Remembering that development was still ongoing of the gyroscopes, actuators, the alternator and even the wire dispensing system with the choices relating to them, guidance trials starting in September 1958 were only a short two years into the project. Furthermore, notwithstanding the rolling/pitching/yawing tests on the Development Test rig, the survival of the control wire during missile manoeuvre could only be properly tested with live firings, while the effects of manoeuvre combined with vibrations and heat on gyroscope drift could not be fully examined.

Up to March 1959,[90] fifteen operator-controlled rounds had been fired in the UK, besides the highly premature 'now or never' demonstration for the US Army in that month. Over those six months, six of the fifteen rounds worked sufficiently well to provide useful operator experience, with the system designers Harry Fryer and Pip Piper at the sight controller. One was marred by excessive pitch gyro drift and another was aimed too far off the line of fire (31°) for the control 'stick' coverage then in use. Later, selection of the sight line was provided, enabling the missile to follow this direction with minimal operator azimuth guidance. Miss distances were measured as a flimsy range target was punctured with the five good rounds, and proximity to the target centre varied between 2ft up, 6.5ft right, where the operator had to contend with excessive pitch gyro drift, through distances mainly 6ft to 20ft, to the worst case when stick coverage was insufficient in yaw, which went 100ft wide.

On these firings at target ranges from 500 yards to 1,200 yards, analysis of operator stick movement records showed that on these otherwise working rounds, the stick movements for guidance demands were too coarse. The causes of the other rounds' malfunctions were successfully determined and this contributed to the process of detailed design improvements.

The missile's initial manoeuvre on launching posed separate problems, to be addressed with the aid of the guidance simulator and mathematical analysis. As earlier indicated in the section on the gyroscope, the gimbal configuration provided for a 15° pitch angle from the orthogonal, in order to bring the missile to horizontal flight at 5° incidence, from its 20° launch angle. Pitching down from the climb manoeuvre during the low-speed climbing phase after launch, coupled with roll phase errors from the relatively crude four-segment roll commutator, could lead to instability. Correcting this brought in the question of autopilot gain, advancing the missile's centre of gravity and further modifying the stick filter's characteristics. Furthermore, the effective roll measurement error could result in horizontal missile gathering commands causing a pitch error, with danger of flying the missile into the ground. Various solutions were tested to overcome these cross-coupling effects, including increasing the roll rate, making the downward pitching manoeuvre by controller demand instead from the gyroscope, and finally refining the roll measurement by using an angle resolver instead of the four-segment commutator. This made the difference, although it was later changed to an eight-segment commutator, to be less expensive and less susceptible to vibration noise. This provided sufficient improvement in roll-angle resolution to tolerate the slow roll rate and overcome the problem.[90]

Mathematical studies, simulator work and flight trials interacted in the gradual improvements in the guidance system. While differences between simulated behaviour and human operator-controlled flight trials were found and accounted for in the design, real flight conditions revealed another unexpected factor. Operator control of actual missiles revealed a livelier response than experienced with the simulator, and this was found to result from the operator being able to see the changes in missile body attitude as it pitched or yawed in response to commands. Aerodynamic incidence lags were evidently less than predicted in wind tunnel tests and, once this was recognised, operators were trained to concentrate only on the missile flare and to ignore the body attitude. Another improvement to increase short-range coverage was achieved by increasing the range of control stick demands to cover ±70° in azimuth and ±35° in the vertical plane.

At about this time, funding for Vigilant underwent a marked reduction, resulting in staff cuts and further delays in the development programme. This incidentally caused considerable pain for me. As head of the Test Group, I had been authorised to build up the Environmental Test and other areas in my group by hiring engineers in a company-wide grand recruiting drive, with interviews at a London hotel. The resulting hire of almost a dozen excellent engineers filled out my departments in the necessary slots – for not more than a week. A bland notice came down from top management notifying me of newly required staff cuts, with instructions to declare most of the new hires redundant. To avoid such a travesty, I suggested offering testing services to outside entities as a business proposition, but this got nowhere. When the authors of the instruction refused to take personal responsibility by coming to my department and explaining their decision face-to-face with engineers who had just given up their jobs elsewhere, incensed, I personally interviewed each angry engineer and made the best of a very bad job. It was my first experience of losing sleep over a management problem.

At a time when the US Army was considering its next procurement following not entirely satisfactory experience with the French acceleration controlled missile, the Clevite Corporation in Ohio, on a partnership basis with Vickers, persuaded the US to offer a technical evaluation at Redstone Arsenal near Huntsville, AL. The lack of controller experience at the currently early stage of guidance trials, coupled with remaining reliability problems with incompletely developed system components, strongly indicated that we were not ready for such an important technical evaluation. However, the US Army made it clear that unless Vickers brought Vigilant for evaluation before its intended procurement decision in early 1959, the opportunity would be lost for good. It was a big risk, but the decision was taken to make the attempt and, after special design modifications to cope with the humidity and high temperature environment that would have come later with the final service weapon design, manufacture was put in hand for a quantity of 'Clevite rounds'. This level of design was to be used for much of the coming year's flight trials programme.

By then the assistant chief designer, Mike Still visited Clevite in advance to agree design details for these rounds and for setting up the evaluation. The playfully ebullient Don Kerbo, Clivite's Programme Manager for Vigilant, made trips to Weybridge, and with a good spirit of partnership, the evaluation was set for 9–20 March to fire twenty rounds, with expectations of five further demonstration firings at Fort Benning in Georgia. Chief trials engineer Frank Bond led the team, with Harry Fryer and others who were the most experienced, by developing the system on the simulator and in controlling the early guidance rounds. Les Vine, earlier of the Red Dean project management team, acted as general liaison and organising coordinator. A simulator was shipped to Huntsville for the selection and training of US operators. The evaluation was intended to verify Vickers' claims for the control system in respect of accuracy with our velocity (heading) control using a gyroscope controlled autopilot, ease of learning and operation – and to compare the learning performance of operators with and without previous experience with the less responsive, French acceleration controlled SS10 system. Unfortunately, the Redstone Arsenal's range instrumentation was designed more for gun firing tests than for missile guidance trials, producing less than the desired amount of useful information, and as the firings of Vigilant proceeded, it became apparent that insufficient information would be gathered with the twenty rounds to be fired. As a consequence, the Fort Benning trial was cancelled and a total of twenty-seven rounds were all fired at Redstone Arsenal.[90]

Eleven of these missiles malfunctioned in various ways, including four wire failures, three motor misfires, a possible actuator failure and three more (in the absence of range telemetry reception facilities) unknown causes. Of the sixteen good firings, there were two direct hits, five near misses and nine misses that were clearly due to operator error. A contributing factor was that the brightness of the tracking flare proved to be inadequate at long range, in the extremely bright conditions pertaining at Redstone Arsenal. While these results demonstrated our claims for the basic control system employing velocity control as opposed to acceleration control used in SS10, we had underestimated the difficulties for operators in the transition from simulator to live firings. One fall out from the US experience was the first serious simulator training scheme. In attempting to research the needs for an 'average' operator, it was found that after eleven half-hour simulator sessions and two lectures, the best four from an original group of sixteen trainees reached an acceptable standard. There was much more to learn and to accomplish in regard to consistent reliability of a missile at a competitive price, but not with any short-term likelihood in the USA.

Shortly after returning to the UK in April, four more guidance rounds were fired against targets at 1,500 yards, two of which made direct hits with miss distances from target centre of only 6.5ft right and 2ft low in one case, and only 1ft high and 2ft left of centre in the second case. The other two rounds suffered gyro drift, causing them to miss. However, performance was improving and demonstrations were mounted for the Army School of Infantry, the Army Air Corps, NATO Headquarters and the Royal Military College of Science. The Americans appeared to remain interested. A total of 250 Clevite type missiles were in manufacture and production planning was in hand for the first 150 Vigilant Mk.1 service missiles, as then intended for military use by 1959-60. Nevertheless, despite Vickers' highly visible activity and interaction with all the relevant government departments, incredibly, the British Army Council Secretariat in Whitehall, in its 1958 War Office Policy Statement No.81 First Revision[91] still afforded no official recognition, that any requirement existed for a light anti-tank guided missile, for Infantry or the Royal Armoured Corp. By 1959, this was showing up in discussions and position papers, but little more.

Development continued with a further fifty-five operator-controlled firings over the next half year, to optimise the electronic 'stick' filter in the sight controller, to confirm a final missile centre of gravity and stick filter with an experienced operator, and to train new operators including one from the Army. It was also important to test the limits of the system in respect of target range and target offsets from the launching direction. Of the first thirteen firings to optimise stick filter and C.G. position, discounting three wire failures, all remaining ten rounds worked satisfactorily. The next five firings to confirm the above parameters resulted in good shots, with two at 1,500 yards, a first hit on a real tank target at 1,000 yards and a good shot against a short-range target at 500 yards. The next thirty-seven rounds enabled Vickers systems engineer operators, Clarke, Pip Piper and Trevor Wooderson, as well as an Army operator, to be trained. Ten of Piper's eleven rounds worked well and the eleventh also worked for 9 seconds – long enough to obtain information. Two of these launched on the line of fire were very accurate hits at long range, including a round that had been parachute dropped for good measure. Of his six short-range shots, the first two went low, three were very accurate and the sixth missed due to a bad launch. Two more medium-range shots with 15° offset from the line of fire (LOF) confirmed that offset is possible, but one suffered a bad launch and the second one was a near miss after a failure at 9 seconds. His medium-range shot with 24° offset missed, due to insufficient stick controller coverage. Wooderson started with three unlucky wire failures, due to flare interaction – one only after 1,400 yards. His fourth round suffered a rocket motor choke failure, causing it to blow up. The remaining ten good rounds achieved six hits out of seven at long range (the first two after only simulator training); three at medium range produced one hit, a near miss and one bad launch. Four of Clarke's six rounds suffered failures due to various malfunctions, but he hit two medium-range targets with his first truly satisfactory missiles. The British Army operator had not performed ideally on the simulator, but was chosen before receiving more training. He achieved one hit and one near miss at medium range.

Albeit with a few warts, this encouraging series of firings produced a statistically significant number of well-guided missiles achieving hits and near misses, with operators with little or no previous experience. Much useful information was gained and a new technique of recording operator commands during guidance and feeding these into the simulator enabled improvements in the training method.

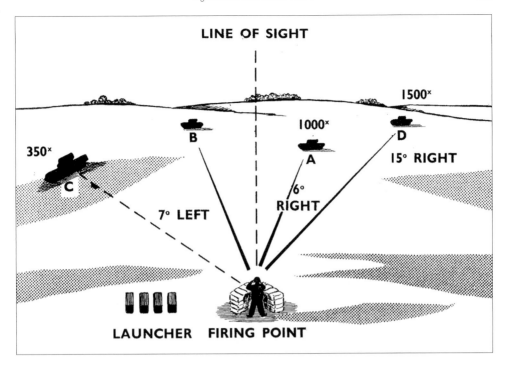

Fig.6.38a Disposition of targets for Vigilant Presentation at Larkhill, on Salisbury Plain, September 1959.[90]

The Vickers team was now gearing up to an all-important Vigilant Presentation to the Army, which was finally beginning to take notice. A field presentation was made on 26 September 1959 on the School of Artillery ranges at Larkhill on Salisbury Plain, to more than 200 observers from the War Office, Ministry of Supply and NATO, as well as other countries.

The presentation commenced with a Tactical Exercise, to show the advantages of a man-pack anti-tank guided weapon in the hands of troops. At a time when official War Office records still indicated considerable Army's scepticism in the absence of any experience of Guided Weapons in the hands of troops, this was as important as the following firings to demonstrate guidance against representative targets. A platoon from the 2nd Battalion Scots Guards, advised by The School of Infantry, provided a Rifle Company support platoon to show how such a force might be equipped, to supplement an anti-tank gun detachment.

For the firings, a procedure based on normal range practice and safety requirements was adopted, employing a battery of four inert warhead-equipped Vigilants in carry-box launchers, to ensure an acceptable firing rate. Three groups of four missiles were fired against Comet tanks and a Centurion Tank silhouette at varying ranges and offset angles, as seen above.

Eleven rounds were fired, eight of which performed satisfactorily, scoring seven hits. Two of the defective missiles were sufficiently accurate to hit medium-range targets and since every target was hit, the presentation demonstrated the breadth of field conditions

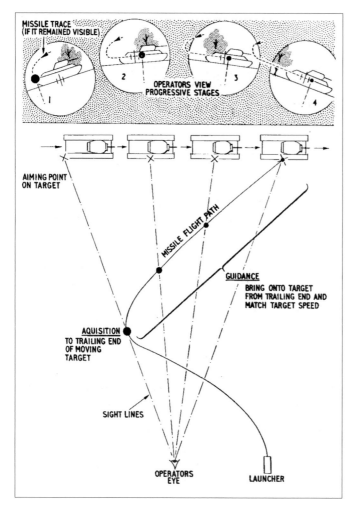

Fig.6.38b Following a
moving target.[70]

within Vigilant's capability. The proportion of hits and technical failures were as were
expected at the current stage of Vigilant development. The table of results opposite gives
interesting detail.

This performance was the best sign of real progress towards an operational weapon
and its potential use by ordinary soldiers, according to John Housego's original concept.
Achieving fifty-seven firings with only one break indicated that one of the most intractable
problems was virtually solved. The War Office and the Ministry of Aviation could not help
but take notice, and six months later on 16 March 1960, Sir Stuart Mitchell, Controller
of GW and Electronics (CGWL) at MOA, wrote to General Sir John Cowley, Master
General of the Ordnance at the War Office, 'We consider that the recent performance of
Vigilant in the firm's trials are impressive and that it warrants further examination'.

The improvements over the six months to March 1960 to which CGWL referred
were the result of more painstaking design improvements of missile components for both
performance and reliability – a task undertaken under conditions of continued funding and
staff shortages. A number of fundamental changes that had been 'in the works' were flight

PRESENTATION RESULTS SUMMARY

Firing No.	Round No.	Target		Broad Result	Remarks
		Range (nominal) yards	Bearing (sight-line rel. to LOF)		
1	546	1,000	6° R	Near miss	Hit ground just short of target.
2	547	1,000	6° R	HIT	Rear of turret
3	548	1,500	7° L	Near miss	Barrel-rolled, which worried operator, but kept close to sight line.
4	549	1,500	7° L	Near miss (missile failure)	Heavy yaw drift. Lost control just before target. Wire damaged at 1440 yds.
5	550	350	3° L	HIT	Approx. 4' L, 0' U/D rel. to aiming point
✗ 6	551	350	3° L	Missile failure	Wire broke at 50 ft. Not known yet whether wire was primary or secondary failure.
7	552	350	3° L	HIT	Approx. $11\frac{1}{2}$'R, $4\frac{1}{2}$'D rel. to aiming point. Ricocheted off ground.
8	553	350	3° L	HIT	Approx, 3'R, 5'D rel. to aiming point.
9	556	1,000	$\frac{1}{2}$° L	HIT	Root of gun barrel.
10	557	1,500	9° R	HIT	Turret hatch.
11	554	1,500	$1\frac{1}{2}$° R	HIT	Middle of turret.

✗ Round 551 is exceptional in having a wire break – the first
for 57 rounds – and it is felt that this may have been
induced by some other failure at launch.

Fig.6.39 Details of firing results at a presentation to military officials, September 1959.[90]

tested and proved their worth. These mainly related to improved controllability during the early phase of trajectories, mainly by means of changing to an eight-segment roll commutator for more accurate roll resolution during gathering, doubling of the autopilot gain, coupled with a change in the missile centre of gravity position and further optimising the stick filter characteristics. These changes were incorporated and proved in the Phase IIIB rounds, which also newly employed rocket motor gas powered turbo-alternators and fin control actuators. The latter items were accompanied by component failures that required further detailed design changes, as typical development problems were ironed out.

Reliability of wire dispensing was also further improved from 12 per cent failures to 4 per cent, by doing away with the external subsidiary spool, in favour of winding enough double cotton-lapped wire inside the dispenser shroud, to prevent motor blast dispensing during the first 100 yards of flight. Besides this, for increased lethality, a Mk.II (inert) warhead with 5in maximum diameter was carried, producing a change in the aerodynamic profile and, along with the changed c.g. and control characteristics, this was proved to permit stable control and guidance.

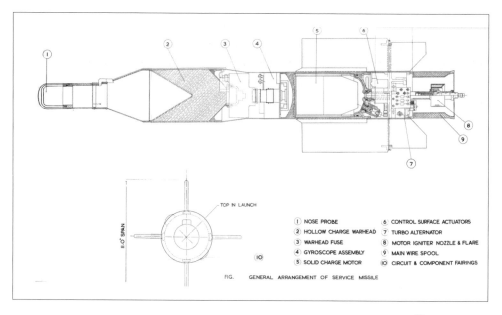

Fig.6.40 General arrangement of the Service Missile (Phase 4) with enlarged warhead.[88]

The net result was that trained operators could achieve hits with an accuracy of 1ft from the point of aim, and that the most demanding minimum target range was reduced to 200 yards. Control against targets offset by up to 30° became much easier, by the introduction of an operator set 'offset' azimuth bias switch, that altered the heading automatically taken by the missile, in the absence of azimuth guidance demands. Crossing targets at 15mph were successfully hit at 950 yards range. For maximum range, the flare was redesigned for extremely bright background conditions such as experienced in the USA, employing a specialist pyrotechnics contractor. The missile weight was held to 31lb, and length allowing for a retracted warhead nose contact piece allowed for carriage within the length of the original carry-box launcher. To assist with training, an automatic performance measuring device was developed, to ease the instructors' task in training large numbers of trainees. Using a photoelectric target, recordings of time taken to achieve the line of sight were made possible, together with checks on the operator's ability to keep his errors within a prescribed angular tolerance.

Phase 4 rounds began their development, representing the Service Missile design. These were essentially similar to the Phase IIIB missiles, with changes in electronic components to give improved performance at the extremes of temperature and to reduce manufacturing costs. At the same time, sight controllers were modified for winter conditions and for use by operators wearing gloves, and demonstrated to be satisfactory in successful trials.

However, the funding and staff shortages took their toll on the originally scheduled late 1959 completion of a service missile. Nevertheless, interest in Vigilant at home and overseas continued to grow, stimulated by its ability to carry a larger, more lethal warhead with a 6lb hollow charge.

Combined with increased accuracy, the overall lethality was greatly increased. Development of the warhead and the fuze became significantly complicated by the politics of the government ministries and their general inhibitions about supporting a private venture missile project. That interesting political saga is described in the following chapter.

6.2

VIGILANT ANTI-TANK MISSILE PART 2

Initial design of the hollow charge warhead led by Peter Rice started in 1957, with the original 4.2in-diameter body diameter and in consultation with ARDE at Fort Halstead, whose armament experts gave the Vickers team valuable advice leading to the scheme with a radiused nose contact button as used on other rockets. At this time, the Royal Armoured Corp. told Vickers that only a 60lb HESH (High Explosive Squash Head) would penetrate a tank. So much for the 'experts' – as will be seen later. Design of the fuze proceeded in parallel, attention being focused on safety aspects, such as initiation being dependent on prior ignition of the rocket motor and the missile having physically travelled some 120 yards from the launch point, before arming could occur. A further safety element was the dependence of the arming process on the availability of power from the rocket motor gas-driven alternator. The initial RDX/TNT explosive charge weight was a little over 2lb, detonating around the hollow copper cone to provide the characteristics for penetration of armour by a jet of molten copper. The efficacy of penetration being dependent on the 'stand-off distance' between the cone and the target armour plate, this was provided by a retractable nose button.

Within the Vickers Group, the Vickers range at Swanley in Kent was available for explosive trials and Vickers Thames Ammunition Works was used for filling warheads with the explosive charge, after initial fillings executed by ARDE at Woolwich. By March 1958, 18in penetration of mild steel plate had been achieved with the first two trials.

The basic explosive chain design started from an igniter operating through a mechanical fuze shutter that masked the main initiator and warhead explosive elements, through a secondary detonator booster pellet to the main booster pellet, to the shaped charge. Details of the fuze are described later.

By September 1958, forty-six warheads had been fired in the six-month period at the Vickers Swanley range, and of the eighteen filled at Thames Ammunition Works, twelve were fired at the 90° normal to the test plate, achieving penetrations between 17.75in to 21.25in, where no nose contact assembly was fitted. The presence of the nose cone assembly reduced these penetrations by about 3in full stop Penetration depths with

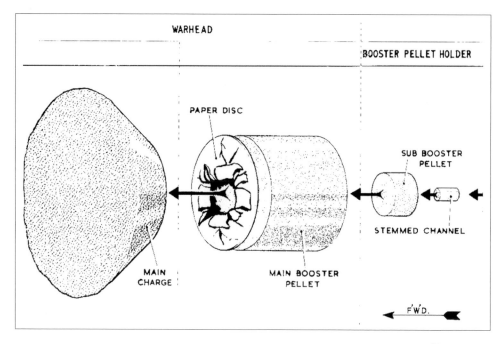

Fig.6.41 Diagrammatic representation of the explosive sequence for the Vigilant warhead.[79]

an attack angle of 60° to normal achieved similar penetrations, when measured in the direction of attack – that is, along the effective plate thickness in that direction. The stand-off distance was kept to 1.8 times the 4in effective diameter of the charge. These tests led to changing from the retractable nose unit in favour of a fixed unit with reduced stand off. Further development continued into March 1959, to establish reliability of charge filling, for preliminary testing of the initiation system and to improve lethality. Fifty-three rounds static fired at Swanley verified that the Thames Ammunition Works filled warhead gave consistent penetrations with acceptable scatter. In probing for optimum performance, nine hollow charges were fired with varying charge diameters, cone liner angles, materials and stand-offs.

Over the following year to March 1960, in a preliminary design of the Mk.II warhead, development for increased penetration and lethality continued, increasing the charge to 5in-diameter and weighing 6lb. The effect of the increased warhead size on the missile aerodynamics and, consequently, on the cg position required for stable control and guidance, has been discussed and proved acceptable. The nose contact section that proved to reduce penetration of the copper jet now became a separate retractable nose probe unit with optimised stand-off and was attached by a simple rapid-acting joint. Missile weight was now 31lb and its length, allowing for nose probe retraction, still permitted carriage in the carry-box launcher. Penetration and lethality of this Mk.II warhead was then expected to be considerably increased – one hardened armour plate test piece being penetrated to 24in depth, leaving a small open exit hole.

The critical elements of the warhead design were the copper cone and, behind it, the 6lb, 60/40 mix RDX/TNT charge of 5in-diameter. Behind this, the fuze was attached

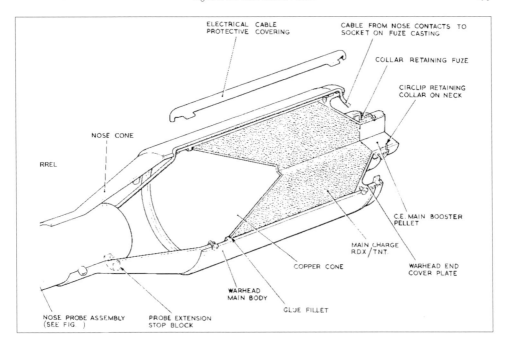

Fig.6.42 warhead Mk.II section, showing design detail.[79]

by a collar. The rear end also formed the spigoted joint for the gyroscope assembly casing. Fitting to the main warhead body with rivets and the glue fillet were important details. The Main Booster Pellet of the igition chain is seen at the rear.

Ahead of the main warhead lay the retractable nose cone and Contact Assembly, with its readily crushed brass Radio Frequency screen, to ensure against any possible detonation by external radiations.

The retractable nose probe assembly was made of light alloy, forming the crush contact assembly, housing two brass electrical contacts for completing the firing circuit. Forward movement on extension before a firing and the rearward movement into the body for stowage are mechanically limited by machined surfaces and a stop-lock dowel engages in a machined groove, to prevent rotation of the tube assembly. Two spring-retained lock buttons engaging in the nose cone neck through holes locked the sub-assembly in the extended position, and these had to be simultaneously depressed before extending the sub-assembly. A nose protection cap was provided for storage and transportation purposes and this was only removed when the missile was being prepared for firing. The assembly was retained in a secure retracted condition by the carry-box launcher's forward end, exerting restraint against the nose probe's extension spring.

The design and proving of the crush contact operation over a range of glancing impact angles up to 70° away from the normal represented a considerable part of the development effort. This included determining the time delay from first impact until electrical triggering of the charge by the fuze when the crush contacts on the warhead closed. In cooperation with ARDE, who provided a 100,000 frames per second camera, Vickers Environmental Test Dept. under Peter Inglis, with John Stroud, fired 6lb slugs

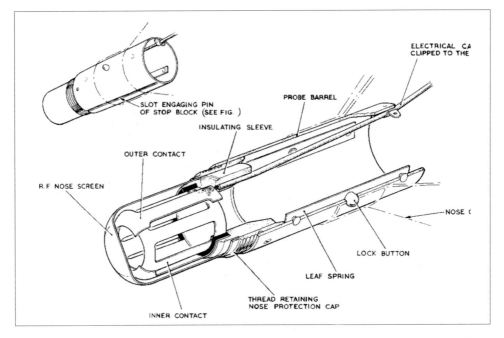

Fig.6.43 Nose probe assembly with the crush contacts, making the detonation circuit on impact.[79]

at the nose contact of a model warhead assembly, to simulate the forces of a missile impacting its target. The time taken from the instant of impact to the firing circuit was completed, determined the effective stand-off distance and the consequent lethality of the warhead. These tests resulted in ARDE's report stating that no significant distortion of the hollow charge occurred, and that the time delay until firing would not reduce the 'stand-off' distance sufficiently to cause significant reduction of the warhead's lethality.[101] At the same time, detailed design of the whole mechanical assembly and the electrical connections had to be proof against fouling of the cable and the moving parts.

Fuze development proceeded in parallel with the warhead development and the means of initiating the explosion. An important part of the design was the addition of a secondary detonator for speedy initiation during missile impact, before the nose contact deformed to the point of reducing the stand-off distance.

The technology of Safety and Arming applied to weapon fuzes had been established over many years. It primarily depended on the physical separation of the igniter from the explosive train leading to the warhead. This separation was by means of a steel shutter that would not pass any energy from an igniter, should it be prematurely activated. The shutter contained the primary detonator, which was positioned to be physically out of line with the warhead components it would eventually ignite, until it was rotated into line by a series of events, without which it could be guaranteed that the explosive train remained inert.

Before any electrical initiation can occur, the alternator has to be running on rocket motor gas pressure and, therefore, the missile must be in flight. Once sufficient current is being generated, it is applied to two capacitors and to an explosive motor, which

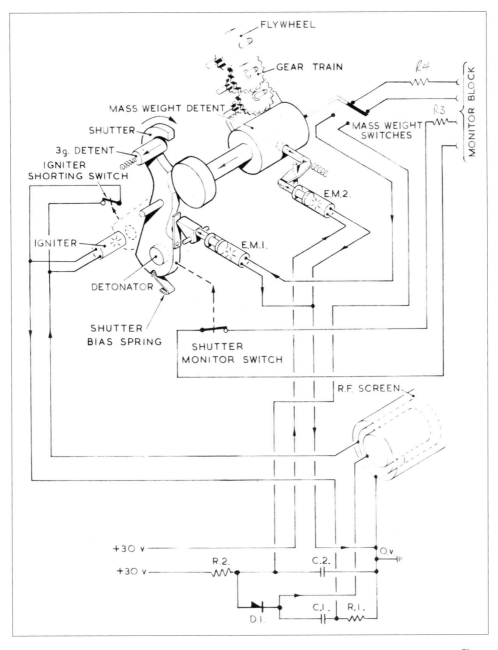

Fig.6.44 Diagram of fuze operation principle and the main safety features in the arming process.[79]

withdraws a plunger from a mass weight. The arming sequence then needs to rotate the shutter, in order to move the igniter into alignment. This is physically prevented by a 3g detent that obstructs the hook-shaped shutter, which is then further prevented from moving, until the missile has flown 100 yards +60 yards –0 yards. The delay is determined by the missile's acceleration acting upon the released inertia mass for a sufficient time to ensure that the missile has travelled the required distance. Under sustained acceleration of the missile, the mass drives a flywheel through a gear train to achieve the distance measurement, when a contact carried by the mass weight breaks a monitor circuit used for safety testing. In the safe condition, the igniter is also short circuited, to obviate any possibility of firing. With the shutter hook otherwise unobstructed, when the mass weight reaches the position corresponding to 100 yards of missile flight, its electrical contact powered from the alternator operates a second explosive motor and this now moves a cam, to rotate the shutter and align the igniter with the explosive train to the warhead. At this point, the fuze is armed and crushing of the warhead's forward nose assembly on impact with the target fires the igniter and the detonator carried by the shutter.

As indicated in Fig.6.44, once all the items are armed into the aligned position, the detonator fires a sub-booster pellet through the stemmed channel into the main booster pellet, to ensure reliable and consistent firing of the main explosive charge with minimal time delay.

The complications described and indicated in Fig.6.45 are necessary to ensure safety from detonation, except in the case of impact with the target – and to provide for reliable detonation when the arming conditions have all been met.

Involving a great deal of choice and proving of many detailed materials, finishes and critical tolerances, the fuze mechanical design and its operation were developed in the laboratory. Through 1959 and 1960, samples were environmentally tested, to verify resistance to enormous (6,000g) shocks and the case sealing was subjected to thermal shocks over a over a temperature range from -46°C to + 77°C without deterioration. The overall geometry and means of installing the fuze to the warhead and initiator took on a deceptively simple form.

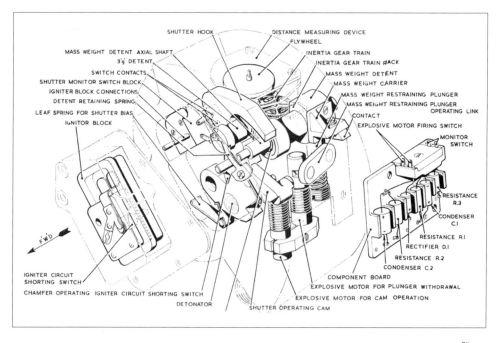

Fig.6.45 Arrangement of fuze components, for safety and arming after 100 yards of missile travel.[79]

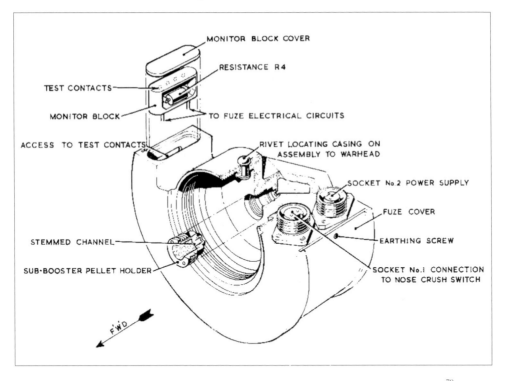

Fig.6.46 Assembly of main fuze body and peripheral components into the detonation chain.[79]

Flight trials of the warhead and fuze combination were scheduled in 1960, while in 1961, a series of overseas demonstration firings were added to the UK guidance trials and demonstrations of the nearly completed prototype Vigilant. By this time, largely at the behest of the Government, Vickers had merged with English Electric Co. and the Bristol Aircraft Co., to form the British Aircraft Corporation, with the odds being strong that Vickers Guided Weapons, including Vigilant, would be transferred to the English Electric GW operation at Stevenage. The Vickers team from Weybridge mounted demonstrations to the military authorities in Australia, India and Italy, employing regular Army soldiers to fire and control the missiles. The Indian demonstration was the subject of a colour video in which Vigilant performance was summarised as:

Location of Demonstration	Correctly functioning missiles	Hits
UK	13	12
India	12	6
Italy	13	11
Totals	38	29

These indicated a reliability level of 90 per cent and a target direct hit rate averaging of 85 per cent.[93]

Meanwhile, the warhead and fuze development in which Vickers had had some assistance from ARDE became the subject of significant correspondence and activity at the Ministry of Aviation (previously Ministry of Supply), the War Office and ARDE.

Recording the politics within the ministries and its effects on the Vickers private venture development of Vigilant relies upon correspondence files researched by the Author at the Public Records Office of the National Archives at Kew. They seem to paint an overall picture of disregard, disbelief and agonising over Vickers' role and whether the Government should recognise it for its value – particularly since it did not pay for this weapon project, as had always been the norm. The choice of warhead and fuze was a significant factor among Civil Servants wishing to exercise the maximum possible amount of control and wanting to make their particular contribution to posterity.

A good start is to look at the Army Council Secretariat of the War Office and its Weapons Policy Committee. On 6 April 1956 when Vickers was starting its Vigilant design, the committee issued its War Office Policy Statement (WOPS) No.81 as Paper No.W.P.C./P(56)8 for consideration by the committee in a future meeting. In its Part II on General War Office Policy, this comprehensive document was drafted with paragraph 16 entitled Guided Missiles. This reads as follows:

> With the quest for high destructive capacity, in conjunction with lightness and mobility, thought must be given to the design and development of a simple and light type of guided missile, effective from as close to the launching site as possible, up to a range of 2,000 yards. Wire control is acceptable. The same destructive capability as outlined in paragraph 12★ is required with a weight of about 35 to 40lb. A policy statement has been drawn up to guide the development of a light pilot model, trials of which should give the War Office an opportunity to assess the usefulness of such a weapon and to decide both its method of employment and desirable characteristics...

(★Refers to defeat of 150mm or 6in of homogeneous armour at all angles of obliquity up to 60° from the vertical or the equivalent by weight of spaced or sandwiched armour.)

Incredibly, this whole paragraph 16 was struck out by hand and did not reappear in later versions of WOPS No.81 for several years.

The first General Staff Operational Requirement (No.1011) I was able to find entitled 'LIGHT MEDIUM RANGE ANTI-TANK GW SYSTEM' was issued some time in 1959 as a 'Discreet but cleared for Canada' document. Requiring an in-service date of 1962, this referred to WOPS No.4 sponsored by director, Royal Armoured Corps (RAC 2), with director general of Armaments (A6) as Technical Sponsor, director general of GW (GW(Mil)1) as Approving Authority and the Developing Authority being ARDE and the Fighting Vehicles Research & Development Establishment (FVRDE). In this document, Requirement 11 stated:

> There is a requirement for a light and simple anti-tank guided weapon system to be mounted on the turret of a reconnaissance vehicle i.e. FERRET Mk.2 Scout Car. It is desirable that this weapon is the same as that adopted by the Infantry...

In the Appendix, the requirement called for 95 per cent reliability, without testing between the time it leaves the factory and firing, a three-year shelf life, the missile to be delivered to the launcher from the factory completely assembled and to be capable of functioning after parachute delivery in a suitable container. Range of targets was specified between 300 and 1,500m, with desirability of engaging targets between 100 and 2,500m. Together with remote control and azimuth coverage requirements, this sounds to be very much like Vigilant, with greater range as was later specified for the English Electric (Stevenage) Swingfire, then commencing its early research phase.

At a time when Vigilant development was well advanced (25 June 1959), the PS to the Ministry of Aviation permanent Secretary, G.W. Clark, wrote a memorandum to Deputy Secretary (C) Denis Haviland, and referred to the Secretary's visit to Vickers on 17 June when he discussed Guided Weapons with Sir George Edwards. Sir George evidently took the position:

> that Vickers had no GW project from the MOA since the cancellation of Red Dean and could see no future project emerging. He was therefore disposed to cut his losses and disband the team and brushed aside the suggestion that Vickers might make headway with the War Office in the requirement for a short range surface to air missile and that they had been considering some form of merger with Short's GW interests.

The Secretary at MOA then requested a note to be prepared in consultation with the Controller, Guided Weapons & Electronics (CGWL), on the extent to which MOA was using Vickers in the GW field and, 'what use we see for the team in the short- and long-term future.'

The note by W.E.D. Bruton, LGW1(a), in July, summarised the position following the cancellation of Blue Boar and Red Dean, with somewhat patronising phrases such as:

> The Ministry sympathised with the representations which the firm then made at Minister and Permanent Secretary level against being put out of the GW field, and Vickers were given a monthly 'retainer' of £20,000 for five months so that they could keep a nucleus of their team together in case any new work came along...

> ... Despite the cancellation of their government contracts, Vickers decided that, as a leading armaments firm, they should continue to work on Guided Weapons at their own expense. They hoped that, if they retained the nucleus of a team, they would be in a strong position to secure any new government orders, if any emerged. To this end, they recruited a former MOS director of Guided Weapons, (Brigadier Clemow) and began work on a number. The one on which they had done the most work is a lightweight anti-tank weapon known as Vigilant. This project has been virtually completed, but, despite a vigorous sales campaign, the firm have not succeeded in selling it either to the British Army or to foreign countries...

> ... The Ministry has given Vickers a certain amount of technical guidance... the rocket motor...

... The firm is unlikely to receive, in the near future any significant amount of GW work from the Ministry... a design study for a lightweight Army surface to air weapon.... Contracts would be worth about £10,000 and last about a year.... At least two other firms will be asked to undertake similar studies... although Vickers have done some private venture work on a system which might be suitable...

...The size of the Guided Weapons programme is now governed largely by the amount of money available.

The memo went on to discuss other projects and GW firms likely to decline, adding, 'This is therefore not the time to contemplate building up a new team at Vickers'. And finally, in the conclusion, 'We should not wish to intervene if the firm decided to close their GW Department'.

Among a long series of memos, George T. Rogers AS/LGW, in Minute 5 on 8 July, indicates that, 'Vickers are being difficult... the insistence about a design study contract', then, DGW R. Burne in his Minute 6 on 14 July, writes, ' ... no other conclusion is possible... nothing in the wind for which we could use Vickers... I have a slight feeling however, that pressure may develop for lighter and cheaper weapons and that we might find ourselves regretting the disappearance of Vickers from this field if that were to happen'... and with further dismissiveness, 'there was nothing in this which would justify us saying anything to Vickers, that might be quoted later as misleading encouragement'.

On 21 August, this is followed by DG/GW J.E. Serby, who refers in his Minute 11 to discussion, 'whether our placing a contract on Vickers to do a design study of a low altitude SAGW is consistent with the policy endorsed by the Minister'. Then,

... in seeking design studies from Industry to assist ARDE in their thinking about this particular GW system for the Army, I could not have refrained from inviting Vickers (among three other firms) from doing this since they had in fact done more work on such a system than any other firm in the country and to have excluded them would have been unwarrantable.

Rogers follows on 21 August in Minute 12, to Haviland, the Dep. Sec. (C), with some portentous words:

A contract has already been issued to Vickers Armstrongs (Aircraft) Ltd for a feasibility study of a Field Army Low Level Surface-to-Air Guided Weapon System [this was to become Rapier]. No contract has yet been issued for a design study of an anti-tank weapon; but the Contracts Division have been negotiating the precise terms of the contract with Vickers Armstrongs for some time and in their view, we are morally committed to placing the contract with Vickers unless the design study requirement is cancelled.

Then:

I would myself draw much the same distinction, as DG/GW has done in Minute 11 above, between, on the one hand encouraging Vickers to stay in the guided weapon business against their commercial judgement and, on the other, making use of their expertise for getting valuable work done at a modest cost.

This is followed by:

> It is plain, also, that Vickers Armstrongs (Aircraft) Ltd have decided not to withdraw from the Guided Weapons field until they have made at least one more attempt to find a market for their Vigilant anti-tank weapon. They have arranged a large (and no doubt expensive) demonstration for September 26th... The indications are that if this demonstration is successful, the War Office may well make the same abrupt change of policy towards Vigilant as they have already done towards MALKARA. Over and above the production order, this would probably entail giving Vickers some fairly substantial financial support for the completion of the weapon's development.

Minute 12 to the Permanent Secretary of MOA reinforces the Government's policy with, 'In the light of this and of a conversation with CGWL, you advised the Minister in a Minute 8 that, 'we would not be justified in encouraging the company to maintain their Guided Weapons design capacity. The Minister approved this.'

This led to the draft of a letter to Admiral Sir Colin Jarratt, who seemed to have been batting for Vickers, in view of Vickers' ship-building work. The draft included the cynical clause, '... his view is that the two small contracts represent a cheap way of picking the brains of the Vickers' team which, though inadequate, happens to be led by a man of outstanding brilliance'. This was somewhat toned down later, with the statement:

> In agreement with CGWL I recommend that we should allow the second study contract to a value of about £10,000 to be placed with Vickers with the object of picking their brains; that we should make it plain once more to Vickers as soon as possible after the election that we shall be unable to place any contract to develop a new weapon with them and that their GW future should be found in association with some other company.

A further draft again modified this language to:

> ... since the rump of the company's organisation still possesses a small number of men of ideas and brilliance, we have seen fit in the last few weeks to place with the company two small study contracts to a value of about £10,000 each as an inexpensive way of making use of their brains.

CGWL Denis Haviland's letter of 29 September 1959, to Sir Colin Jarrett at the Admiralty, followed these drafts, adding a qualification that the private venture Vigilant was an exception,, and that, 'we have done our best to help them exploit'.

Whether looking from the perspective of the time, or from that in 2006, this does not strike me very much like the Ministry was exactly playing 'cricket'! Clearly, Vickers were applying all the pressures possible and, as seen earlier, the demonstration to 200 military observers on 26 September was relatively successful.

Further stirring the pot on 11 January 1960, Lt-Col. J. Proudman, for the Ministry of Aviation's director of Guided Weapons (Military) – DGW(M), wrote to LGW1 (presumably Mr Silver's superior) in the same ministry, 'The War Office interest in an infantry anti-tank weapon is obviously increasing and I anticipate that before long we shall be asked to advise or participate in firing trials at the School of Infantry'. He referred essentially to tactical trials requiring twelve rounds, of which eight would be for investigations of circuits, explosives, power supplies and so on, and four would be fired against targets at various ranges and angles of launch. He went on to refer interest in other WEU nation's interest in Infantry Guided Weapons and to demonstrations of ENTAC. He seemed compelled also to say, 'It would be a pity if Vigilant were left out of this competition'. He also strongly advised that a further twelve rounds, making a total of twenty-four rounds, be ordered, 'so that we can give the weapon a proper assessment'.

By mid-January 1960, this led to Minute 21 addressed to C.L. Silver, LGW(1)d, regarding the possible purchase of twenty-four Vigilants. This included the statement, '… even if the War Office decided to adopt an Operational Requirement for a light anti-tank weapon, the choice might fall on a foreign weapon in preference to the Vigilant.' Then it referred to three points: 'In GW(M)'s opinion, the Vigilant has been much improved since the presentation given in September, which was not entirely successful...'; 'DWD had decided that the War Office should be evolving a tactical doctrine for the use of a light anti-tank guided weapon, with a view to introducing a weapon at a future date. They would like to use the Vigilant for this purpose; failing the Vigilant, they will use a foreign weapon...'; '... Meanwhile, various foreign missiles have been or will be presented for earlier adoption and GW(M) consider that the Vigilant should be entered in this competition.'

One might have said, 'very generous indeed'!

The price for Vigilant was estimated at £900 each and availability was 'off the shelf'. The minute went on to list the main rivals to Vigilant and made some comparisons:

COBRA (German)	with range of 1,600m
SS10 (French)	with range of 1,600m
ENTAC (French)	with range of 1,800m
SS11 (French)	with range of 3,500m but too large and heavy for Infantry
Vigilant	with range of 1,500 yards (could be extended to 2,000 yards)

C.L. Silver's Minute 22 of 22 January side steps back to 'CGWL's ruling that purchase of rounds for investigation was purely a matter for the War Office' and, after a red herring from Brig.C.W. Dennison D/GW(M) to the Ordnance Board, indicating his preference for Fairey Aviation's Orange William (which was shortly after cancelled), C.L. Silver returned by minuting (No.24) to AS/LGW1, following a call from Col. Lacy of Vickers. This now referred to the merger of Vickers with English Electric Aviation being under consideration, leading to Vickers' expected decision latest by 31 March, as to what should be done about the Vickers Guided Weapons team. 'However, the future of Vigilant might decide to a considerable extent whether the present Weybridge group would remain intact either at Weybridge or at Stevenage or whether it would be dispersed'. Then after noting that, 'the War Office were considering a possible order for 100 for user trials and that the Ministry of

Aviation were considering a possible smaller order for technical assessment', he finished by saying, 'There would appear to be a danger that unless we act quickly the Vigilant group will be dispersed before we can place any contract. You may wish to consider whether it might not be wise to give a firmer statement of intent to Vickers subject, of course, to Treasury agreement' – another bow in the quiver of governmental caution (and prevarication?).

In his 15 March Minute 25, C.L. Silver returns once more to the problem they all see in giving Vickers any hint of encouragement by writing:

> … approval of Dep. Sec.(C) and possibly the Secretary would be required in view of the fact that at Minute 8, the Secretary ruled, with the agreement of the Minister, that no action should be taken which would encourage Vickers to maintain their guided weapon design capacity. It has become clear that the Guided Weapons' activities of Vickers are now to be taken over completely by the new combined Vickers-English Electric-Bristol Group. Under these circumstances our proposed action would not seem to be in conflict with the policy of the Secretary and the Minister.

This was, of course, a reference to what became British Aircraft Corporation. While the Weybridge team was generally aware of the new corporation and its possible implications, the question of the Weybridge team being disbanded or moved to Stevenage was not enough to the fore to affect the continuing enthusiasm towards completing the Vigilant project as a service weapon.

The next day, the Controller of Guided Weapons and Electronics (CGWL), Sir Steuart Mitchell himself wrote to the Master General of Ordnance, Lt-Gen. Sir John G. Cowley, on the subject of Vigilant. After writing that 'the recent performance of Vigilant in the firm's trials is impressive...', he reverts to bringing the cheaper French 'ENTAC' missile into competition, 'although it is probably inferior to Vigilant in performance', and to support 'interdependence' with other European countries.

Proposals for trials to compare Vigilant with the best foreign equipment followed, intimating that while ENTAC was already being brought into service in the French Army, in a year the German COBRA missile might be better – but too late. It was clearly indicated that 'Vigilant was almost certainly more accurate and easier to train on than the ENTAC' and the objective of the trial was to determine whether the extra cost of Vigilant could be justified by the extra performance and less costly training expected. Because of the easier training possible with Vigilant's velocity-controlled guidance, the number of rounds required for ENTAC would be 111 against only 76 for Vigilant. Costing the Vigilant at £750 against ENTAC at £300, after allowing for the difference in numbers required for training, the cost of training an Instructor in France and the expensive ground equipment required for ENTAC, its price advantage was almost totally eroded. Thus, the total cost of testing the two missiles was estimated at between £100,000 and £150,000.

Yet one more minute on 22 April, now from George Rogers (AS/LGW1), repeated the mantra that:

> This faces us with the problem of our future relations with Vickers Armstrong in the guided weapon field. In July of last year (Minute 8) the Minister agreed that 'We would

not be justified in encouraging the Company to maintain their guided weapon design capacity'. Later he added: 'I suggest that it would now be opportune to take a decision on Vickers, at any rate. If the Department's policy is to oblige the newly formed British Aircraft Corporation to amalgamate the small Guided Weapons team at Weybridge with its bigger teams (i.e. at Stevenage or Bristol), it would be best to do so at this stage rather than to try to enforce a change later on'.

However, Rogers also reported that in the view of DGW(P), 'taken in isolation, it would be to the Department's advantage to have these requirements for Vigilant missiles manufactured by Vickers themselves. Not only have they done the development work but, also, Vickers Armstrongs Aircraft Ltd have a better reputation for economical and efficient production'. To this, the undersecretary (LGW) Robert Burne replied, asking, 'Would it impose an unacceptable delay if we insisted that the work should be done elsewhere than at Vickers?', and in suggesting that if the order were made conditional on the work being done other than at Vickers, this would be 'likely to land us in fresh difficulties vis-à-vis the War Office who are interested in getting the weapons and not in the structure of the Aircraft Industry'.

Soon, on 28 April, the Treasury's D. McKean found 'some difficulty in this proposal' on the grounds that, 'The War Office have not yet established whether the infantry can handle weapons of this type'. He asked, 'But need you go as far as purchasing models of private venture developments for the purpose of evaluating them before the Service Department concerned has decided whether it even has a requirement for any weapon of this type?' He then continued on about developments by the Germans.

And so it continued to go – round and round. At this point in the story, it would be worth recounting an episode at Vickers, where the prospect of Stevenage taking over its GW project was becoming more and more apparent, particularly to one of our most professional and brilliant of leaders, chief designer Howard Surtees. Occasionally of an acerbic tongue, if this was deserved, he would semi-jokingly refer to the much larger and less efficient GW team at Stevenage as, 'The 5,000 Amateurs'. Howard was conducting a large and intensive technical meeting in his office, when his secretary Mrs Fox knocked on the door to say that an executive from Stevenage wanted to see him. 'No, he does not have an appointment', Mrs. Fox confirmed, so Howard asked her to tell him to wait until the meeting ended. A minute after she went out with the meeting resuming, the executive pompously burst in, declaring, 'I am _____ and want to speak with you'. At this, Howard looked up from his notes and, fixing the intruder with a hard glare, asked, 'And which of the 5,000 Amateurs are you?'! He sent the executive away with a big flea in his ear, not to be seen again.

Deputy Controller of Electronics (DCL) G.P. Chamberlain was the next one on 19 May to refer back to the policy of discouraging Vickers GW activity in a memo to the Denis Haviland, Dep. Sec (C). However, he warned:

Fulfilling the initial order elsewhere (Luton/Stevenage or Filton/Cardiff) implies transferring some personnel from Weybridge and setting up some new facilities; the delay might be of the order of six to eighteen months and might cause the War Office to eliminate Vigilant as a source of learning what the Army needs to know.

Fig.6.47. Howard Surtees, chief designer, Vickers
Guided Weapons, wearing his Vigilant tie.[103]

He concluded by reference to Haviland's upcoming meeting with the British Aircraft
Corporation's (BAC's English Electric originating) executive director, Guided Weapons
Lord Caldecote on 30 May, when the urgency of making a decision 'will be precipitated
any day now by the arrival of War Office requisitions'.

This cardinally important meeting took place, with Howard Surtees in attendance,
along with a clutch of the senior Ministry of Aviation directors already featured in this
account of the saga, where they discussed whether to recognise Vigilant's place in the
UK's defences – or to bury it. Meeting minutes indicated that Lord Caldecote could see
no alternative to manufacturing the 160 missiles urgently requested for evaluation (against
ENTAC), and while the facilities at Weybridge were not suitable for mass production, its
technical team would be required to give Stevenage technical support for its production,
should quantities warrant setting up there. This would apply to at least 1,000 more missiles
he expected to be ordered.

With some delay, tools could be made for the manufacture of about 300 missiles and
these could, if necessary, be duplicated for further manufacturing at Stevenage. In order
to provide initial missiles for the Army as quickly as possible, Weybridge could make
these by existing model shop methods, after which production still using 'hand-made'
methods would be possible at a rate of sixty per month starting in January 1961. At least
some of the missiles should be made from production tools, in order to prove the tooling,
production and inspection facilities.

Lord Caldecote answered Dep. Sec. (C) Denis Haviland's question as to Vigilant's
advantages over French series of Guided Weapons, by pointing out its greater accuracy due
to ease of control and the greater simplicity of training. He now also pointed to the interest
being shown by Sweden and still, the Americans – emphasising that foreign purchasers
would be heavily influenced by the decisions of the War Office. He confirmed:

that it was the long-term policy of the British Aircraft Corporation to keep a small Guided Weapons unit at Weybridge. The present team consisted of about 160 people of whom about half were employed on the TSR2 and about half on various Guided Weapons projects of a simple character of which Vigilant was one. The Vigilant group itself at present numbered 22. .. (BAC) would continue to use the expertise of this team in connection with Post Design Services (PDS) work on Vigilant, assuming it went into service, and on the development of a Mk.2 version. Lord Caldecote considered that this was the most economical approach in that a transfer of this work to Stevenage would mean that it would have to be dealt with there by people who had a perfectionist philosophy and were used to thinking in terms of highly sophisticated weapons.

Transferring the Weybridge team to Stevenage with key people accepting to move was not considered to be practicable by Lord Caldecote, nor the improved overhead the Ministry hoped would pertain in the large Stevenage organisation. Howard Surtees confirmed that Vickers had borne in mind the possible service use of Vigilant during its development, and that a great deal of supporting work normally required in a development contract had already been done, including catalogues, spares schedules, instruction manuals and so on. Finally, Surtees would provide quotations for 100 missiles to be made quickly by hand methods followed by 100 made from production tools, with costs for the tools and for production quantities. These figures would be requested, 'for policy guidance rather than as a tender'.

A Ministry that had apparently been in denial since 1956 at last seemed to be taking the first very cautious steps. And the Vickers GW team at Weybridge appeared to have won a stay of execution! However, C.L. Silver's 7 June Minute remained at best sanguine, if not openly sceptical, with:

> To avoid complication, we should not ask the firm to attempt any 'production tooling for the order for 100 which would inevitably be made at Weybridge... we are bound to buy as a proprietary article and we will have to rely on the commercial acumen of the British Aircraft Corporation as an assurance that the weapons we buy will be good ones'.

Director general (production) R.E. Sainsbury's formal request for quotation from Vickers encapsulated the decisions of the 30 May meeting, adding the hire of a simulator, and removed the original prospect of partial tooling (at Weybridge). Poignantly, he asked, 'How and where and at what approximate cost (or rise in composition of the team) would you develop a Mk.II missile...'

The perennially paranoid question kept coming up. When the Vigilant quotation came in on 14 July, J. Steen LGW(1)d warned his superior, Mr Silver, '...You may wish to see the return of Vigilant tender by Vickers instead of BAC .... may be a move to secure further recognition of the continued existence of GW team at Weybridge...' To this, the Assistant Secretary LGW1 G. Rogers replied in Minute 35, 'Dep. Sec. (C) said that he did not regard the Vickers problem as one of policy but of the best way of securing value for money'. The U.S. LGW agreed on the 19th, assuring the troops of BAC's, 'intention was to deal with all new work on a Corporation basis but that old projects would be dealt with by the individual companies and for the purpose of this initial order they regarded Vigilant as old work'. A couple of days later, without clear plans for a competitive evaluation against French and German missiles, AS/LG1 G. Rogers was:

> alarmed... that we are now in danger of falling into the very trap that our proposals... were designed to avoid – and that we may in the end find ourselves accused (i) by the War Office and Treasury of not being able to give the advice for which we are responsible, and (ii) by the French and the Germans of having acted with what they regard as normal British perfidy'.

Silver now authorised the placing of a contract with BAC for execution by the Weybridge team.

On 26 July in Minute 39, Silver agreed to be alarmed and lamented MOA accepting the Treasury's rejection of an international comparative trial and proposed that US/LGW should again approach the Treasury to include trials of the German COBRA, which would require six months delay, but he thought might have the advantage over both Vigilant and ENTAC. In Minute 40 of 27 July, Rogers noted that the, 'change of attitude, within the Controllerate, stems from CGWL personally'. He went on to ask the undersecretary for his instructions regarding pressing the for Treasury's authority for these internationally extended trials, so that he could 'put clearly on the record, both with the Treasury and the War Office, the limitations under which we shall be operating if, in the event they come to the conclusion that they want to arm the Infantry with this type of weapon, within the next two or three years'. True to form, Civil Servants watching their back!

Burne then fought a rearguard action, by his 'off the file' letter to Sir Steuart Mitchell, CGWL, on 2 August, noting that, 'the Army was now authorised to purchase a number of Vigilants... we have been refused authority for a similar purchase for technical evaluation'. Notwithstanding the long ongoing, if not yet complete, warhead and fuze developments at Vickers detailed above, he also wrote 'No warhead or fuze has yet been developed for Vigilant'. He further emphasised, 'The French ENTAC is in service, the German COBRA under development and there may be other candidates'. Finally, in an epitome of Civil Servant desire never to be on record as being in the wrong:

> If the War Office are satisfied with the handling qualities of Vigilant there is bound to be immediate pressure for the development to be completed and the weapon adopted for service. Are we right to let this happen without our having done a comparative evaluation and in the knowledge that we shall once again have put ourselves in the position of being unable to adopt a common NATO weapon unless the other countries can be bullied into taking Vigilant – which is highly improbable?

On 4 August, Rogers conceded that, 'this was too late to prevent the Contracts Division from issuing an acceptance of the tender from Vickers Armstrongs (Aircraft) Ltd. Minute 41 records that Lord Caldecote is content for the contract to be placed with Vickers Armstrongs (Aircraft) Ltd. on this occasion'. On being consulted about possible pressure to be put on the Treasury for competitive trials, Brig. D.C. Denison, D/GW(M) replied to U.S.(LGW) Russell Burne, indicating that, 'it is now too late to do any comparative trials. A potential delay may be considered acceptable by the Treasury'. To delay spending money is always acceptable – whatever the military need!

The newspapers published news of the War Office order on 26 August, noting, among other details, that Vickers had spent nearly £1 million on developing Vigilant, which they reported would cost 'as much as £500 each'. *The Times* article, picturing an Infantryman aiming the sight controller next to a ready-to-launch Vigilant, like the *Financial Times* article, was brief; *The Daily Telegraph* gave a fuller account, mentioning Brig. J. Clemow, chief engineer (Weapons) and Howard Surtees, chief designer (Weapons) and the Vigilant team. Before giving a good account of Vigilant's main design features and performance, it wrote, 'Unfortunately, it is now almost certainly too late to sell the weapon in large quantity to NATO or the United States since France has been first in the field in this respect with the Government subsidised SS10 and SS11'.

Vigilant's continuing troubles with officialdom next rose with G. Burne's Minute 46 on 12 October, following a call from W.T. Horsley AS/ES1 at the War Office, relating that the requirement for a light anti-tank weapon to be fitted to the Ferret scout car was now urgent. But the WO:

> would be content to await the outcome of comparative trials of Vigilant and whichever foreign weapon we thought promising before deciding which weapon to adopt for the Infantry. The War Office agreed that it would be politically highly undesirable to adopt Vigilant without first giving its competitors proper evaluation... and they had been impressed by the reported decision of the American Army to adopt ENTAC.

In consequence, first G.T. Rogers of the MOA, on 7 November (indicating the desire to add French ENTAC missiles to the already proposed trials), then Horsley at the War Office, wrote to D. McKean of the Treasury, revealing a 'more positive development' since his rejection of the joint Vigilant and French trials in April, and pending the as yet uncompleted trials of Vigilant for its suitability for the Infantry. This was the 'firm and urgent requirement' of fitting a light anti-tank missile to the Ferret scout car to counter medium and heavy tanks. He asked for authority to spend £52,000 for an additional seventy missiles and associated control equipment, with another £5,000 for the installation on a Ferret scout car. The expenditure would fall in the 1961/62 period, since the trials could not be mounted until the coming spring.

On 11 November in his Minute 49, C.L. Silver once more repeated MOA's responsibility to test and to advise the War Office concerning the safety and suitability of a weapon they wish to purchase, and of course the question of comparative trials with foreign weapon designs. In his final paragraph came the statement that today looks like it was responsible for his and the Ministry's continuing 'run around' the problem: 'The purchase of a British private venture guided weapon is unprecedented. It is also difficult to find precedents in other areas'. Then, on the 14th, Assistant Secretary AS/LGW1 T.M. Wilson, referring to the Treasury's April rejection of comparative trials, made the interesting remark,'... it is the timing that stuck in their narrow gullet'.

There followed on 18 November a meeting 'to discuss a further War Office requirement for Vigilant missiles for trial'. Chaired by D.L. Skidmore of the Treasury, with the Treasury's

Mr Hancock reporting, besides C.L. Silver, Horsley and others from the War Office, a Mr D.E. Locke of the Ministry of Defence participated. Ranging over the Ferret-related application for funding:

> The proposed Ferret trials were, if anything more important than the infantry trials already agreed. The highest priority was to equip one car of each troop of the air-portable squadron in the strategic reserve with anti-tank weapons. This squadron had to operate miles out of range of the main anti-tank weapons of the main limited war force and the might well meet tanks... a plan for forming one air-portable squadron (i.e. consisting entirely of Ferrets) in each armoured car regiment was under discussion... the requirement for the air-portable squadron in the strategic reserve was firm and urgent. A tentative proposal for equipping 220 Ferrets with the launching equipment had been drawn up... only £165,000 (i.e. 220 x £750). If the Infantry had the same missile, it should not be necessary to hold a large stock of the missiles to cover both roles. (Note, a reduced Vigilant price.)

After further discussion about quantities and technical questions, the War Office contingent made what was so far their most favourable statement, that they:

> did not think they would want the French ENTAC in this role because their firm view was that a velocity control missile, like Vigilant, was preferable to an acceleration control missile like ENTAC: the former was more accurate, simpler to control and needed fewer missiles to train the operators to the same standard.

Furthermore, if Vigilant were chosen, it could be substituted for the WOMBATS in the Army's programme.

In the Infantry role, it should have been staring them in the face for at least two years, yet Horsley indicated (admittedly in the Ferret context) that, 'The reason why the requirement had not been stated before was that it was not known that there was any way of meeting it'. However, he denied the Treasury being told that the Germans were to take the lead in development of this sort '... the Anglo German Committee had made it clear that the Germans expected the UK to lead'.

Shortly reporting to his boss McKean, Skidmore recommended agreement of the proposed further buy for £55,000, making the point that, 'Until the advent of light anti-tank missiles such as Vigilant there was no possibility of giving Scout Cars this capability'. Not quite satisfied, McKean handwrote back to Skidmore:

> Are you and Mr Marshall both satisfied that it is missiles to deal with this proposal in isolation from the MOA proposal for comparative trials of Vigilant and ENTAC? Could I see the record of the meeting of the Anglo German letter referred to in the last page of Mr Hancock's note of the meeting of 18/11?

Meanwhile, still looking at ENTAC, G. Wheeler, another undersecretary wrote to the French authorities requesting information about the US ENTAC trials. Attempts to obtain this information from the US authorities foundered on a condition of confidentiality placed on them by the French. This finally led to F.A. Kendrick's letter from the Ministry of Defence on 19 January, confirming that the French Technical Services had offered to provide the requested information about ENTAC trials in the USA, as well as offering ENTAC to fulfil the requirements of foreign countries – and to mount a demonstration either in France or in Great Britain. After long haul for a modest step forward, the following day, D.L. Skidmore's letter to Horsley at the War Office finally approved the funds for the additional Vigilants required in trials with the Ferret scout car.

A meeting of top brass at the War Office on 13 February was graced by one lieutenant-general (Sir John Cowley, master general of the Ordnance or MGO) in the chair, five major generals, a brigadier and two colonels and others on the 'home side', together with Ministry of Aviation representatives headed by Sir Steuart Mitchell (CGWL), the dep. sec. D.G.W.L. Haviland, air vice marshall Shirley DCL and directors general J.E. Serby and Dr McPetrie, responsible for GW and Electronics R&D respectively. For the War Office, one undersecretary, W.C. Downey LGW, and Brigadier A.T. Abate, representing the director general/BM, completed the assembly, aided by two more Lieutenant Colonels as a Secretariat.

The Minutes of this widely ranging meeting appear to show the first direct references I was able to find relating to the Light Ground-to-Air missile designated PT428, which was the subject of Vickers' second small £10,000 study contract and which later became the Rapier missile system finally developed at Stevenage. This saw service around the world – including in the Falklands. Discussion also covered requirements for 'a weapon similar to' Swingfire, for which a General Services Operational Requirement (GSOR) had been issued. (In later documents Swingfire is referred to as the primary light anti-tank weapon for the British Army, to which Vigilant became the 'interim weapon'). The next main area of discussion of interest in the Vickers story concerns the warhead and fuze for Vigilant.

After noting that Infantry trials with Vigilant were proceeding and that the Treasury had approved purchases for trials with the Ferret, the purpose of trials with the Infantry was, 'to establish whether there is requirement for such a weapon'. More caution than ever, just in case the Infantry could not make proper use of Vigilant after all the experience already gained! Next came the statement, 'Vigilant has, as yet no adequate warhead and fuze and we were in danger of reaching a situation later this year, when the user would confirm his requirement but we should be held up for lack of a warhead and fuze'. Perhaps it was implied, but the Minutes make no mention whatsoever of the well-advanced development of both warhead and fuze at Vickers, with co-operation from ARDE! The Minutes continued:

> There might be justification to proceed with the development of the warhead as it is probable that this could be used for other Guided Weapons; the fuze was however peculiar to Vigilant and could not be used with other Guided Weapons... CGWL considered that it was most important to pursue the development of the fuze... Dep. Sec (C) suggested that a development contract be placed for the warhead and the fuze, the former at least being financed from Government funds.

A new saga now ensued, concerning the development of these items and the ministries' control over them. MOA's Assistant Secretary, LGW1 T.M. Wilson, wrote to the Treasury on 7 March about 'Research and Development on Hollow Charge Warheads and Fuzes', including the following phrase:

> ... the object of getting the highest possible lethality from a hollow charge warhead of a given weight and size, ARDE are at present engaged actively on a research basis towards this end. Their research programme includes the firing of hollow charge warheads of about the size and weight suitable for Vigilant but only at establishing the minimum size and weight of hollow charge warhead to give the lethality that will be required in the long term for this class of weapon.

The letter continued:

> The status of Vigilant as a private venture presents some problems... To await the conclusion of the infantry trials (with Vigilant in May or June) and the subsequent formulation of a firm requirement before starting the development of a suitable warhead and fuze would impose an unacceptable delay. An alternative is to accept a warhead and fuze combination designed and developed by Vickers.

Without qualification as to the results Vickers were already obtaining, he states: 'This would certainly mean that the warhead lethality would not be as high as it could be'. This statement was given as Gospel, even though a Vickers warhead had penetrated 24in of armour (originally specified minimum penetration of 20.5in) and the ARDE research was far from complete, let alone conclusive.

Further:

> The position on the fuze if somewhat different. Fuzes usually have to be designed to meet the specific requirements of a particular missile... therefore unlikely that a fuze designed for Vigilant will have an application in any other weapon system... for service use. Our interest... stems only from the possibility that Vigilant will be required as a Service weapon.

Then, finally:

> The War Office and the MOA jointly ask your authority, therefore for:
> Initiating a general R&D programme on hollow charge warheads expected... £50,000
> ... development of a warhead for Vigilant at a cost of £35,000 in terms of extramural contracts and a further £30,000 in terms of intramural work;
> Offering Vickers the help of ARDE in the completion for their development of the Vigilant fuze... Acceptable to the Army.

On 5 April 1961, The Treasury's D. McKean repeated these basic points in a letter to T.W. Wilson of the MOA, also rubbing in the unusual nature of authorising development in advance of a formal requirement from the War Office, but acknowledging the unacceptability of a year's delay. Then:

on the other hand we have heard the War Office views the balance of opinion appears to favour Vigilant rather than ENTAC... we are prepared to agree <u>in principle</u> [McKean's emphasis] to your financing some of the work associated with Vigilant subject to... What exactly do you mean by 'interim' in relation to Vigilant? If the in-service life of the weapon is to be very short we may have serious doubts about whether it is worth buying at all.

In a further paragraph, he writes:

... I realise you must have a stake in the Vickers work... indeed, in view of this might we not go further and try to obtain from Vickers some support for the work to be done by ARDE both on the warhead and the fuze?... provision of a satisfactory warhead for *their* weapon (... sales prospects) appear to be very great. Clearly we must take as much advantage of this fact as we can.

In short, one could paraphrase the Treasury's attitude as: Vickers need our help to complete their development to our satisfaction, so make them pay!

In the Treasury-chaired meeting on 26 April, Mr Wilson:

confirmed that it was not proposed to seek any contribution from Vickers in respect of this work, the estimate of £35,000 being the full cost of the extramural part of it. He pointed out that... 'the firm had already invested about £1 million in the development of the weapon itself'.

For the first time, an official had actually given recognition and credit for Vickers' consistent progress on private funds, rather than sweep it all under the Ministry carpet!

The Minutes show the Treasury fighting a protracted rearguard action, which went back and forth. The War Office argued that the Vickers warhead would be more effective if ARDE were brought in; it would have general application, possibly to Swingfire; if Vickers met some of the costs, they would want to share in the Design Rights, which would be embarrassing for HMG of they wished to use it on a different weapon; negotiating a settlement with Vickers could easily be vastly more expensive than the cost of the development proposed. McKean finally backed down and agreed that he could approve the proposal.

Now, on 1 May, J.F. Ezechiel ES(1)a of the War Office, in a letter to C.L. Silver of the MOA, waded in with another missive, promoting consideration of comparative tests of the French ENTAC missile. Comments on Silver's behalf concluded favourably for Vigilant, since, 'Efforts are now in progress by MOA – to ensure that a warhead and fuze for Vigilant will be developed to marry up with the possible in-service dates for both the Infantry and the RAC during 1962... ' and, '1) It could be in service by the latter part of 1962; 2) MOA advice to WO comparing ENTAC with Vigilant could not be available till late 1961 at the earliest; 3) Information about ENTAC is not now available'.

In his 2 June letter, LGW(1)a once more explained in great detail to Skidmore of the Treasury, the technical reasons why Vigilant's autopilot-based velocity control gave superior guidance and training advantages over ENTAC's acceleration control. The message, now slowly getting through at the MOA, was being passed up to the Treasury.

On 14 June, the Army Council Secretariat Weapons and Equipment Policy Committee produced a paper, 'Interim Light Anti-Tank Guided Weapons' for consideration at a future meeting. This finally confirmed that:

> ... 3. 100 Vigilants were ordered in June 1960 to determine whether there was a place for such a weapon in the infantry battalion... Trials begun in March 1961 have now been completed and have shown that:- (a) there is a firm requirement for a man portable anti-tank guided weapon in the infantry;... (c) ....A guided weapon system should be introduced into service as soon as possible, even if it des not fully meet the suggested operational requirement... this must not however, prejudice the later fulfilment of the full requirement probably by Swingfire.

The paper continued, confirming that:

> 4. The Royal Armoured Corps (RAC) has a requirement for... fitted to the Ferret scout car... Trials of Vigilant missiles are due to take place in September, when missiles are received from Vickers... 5.Under present plans the infantry will have until 1966/7 nothing capable of engaging frontally a tank standing back from our position and using its machine gun... 6... Ideally the medium anti-tank weapon's maximum range should be increased and the light anti-tank weapons minimum range should be reduced until there is substantial range overlap... it should be possible to eliminate the heavy anti-tank weapon from the infantry battalion... 7. Meanwhile, until Swingfire can be produced, the anti-tank defence of the infantry is seriously lacking... 8. It follows that to meet both the training and operational requirement, we need an interim weapon... 9. The cost of an issue to all battalions with an operational role would be formidable and in view of the intention to introduce Swingfire clearly cannot be justified... As a compromise we propose to equip units... at the School of Infantry... an initial training requirement of 750 missiles, together with 220 warheads...

Similar arguments were put for Vigilants to the RAC:

> 11... with each Ferret equipped with four operational missiles (+ 20 reserves) and one controller... Two Ferrets in each troop of the air portable squadrons, giving a total of 98 and possible one Ferret in each troop of an armoured car squadron giving a total of 60 Ferrets. 12... for both roles an initial requirement of 1,770 missiles with an annual training requirement of 1,120 missiles thereafter, together with 750 warheads...

The combined requirement given in section 12 of the paper for the RAAC and Infantry indicated about 7,500 missiles up to the end of 1966. This was no longer 'small potatoes'!

In section 15, the paper discussed Vigilant v ENTAC and the Swiss Mosquito and in section 16 it went on to say about Vigilant:

… Its principal deficiency was in range, 1,500 yards as against 2,500 yards and in minimum range, 300 yards as against 150 yards… its lethality will probably be just adequate for the infantry role when fitted with the 5in warhead now being developed. (By Vickers, as described earlier.)

The paper went to recount its views that Mosquito's lethality was doubtful and that ENTAC was extensively tested in the USA who are adopting an interim weapon. The paper also reiterated the major military advantages of Vigilant's shorter (300 yards) minimum range compared with ENTAC (500 yards) and quoted the training requirement for ENTAC to be 50 per cent to 100 per cent greater than for Vigilant. Furthermore, since Swingfire will also have a velocity control system, Vigilant would be a better lead in than ENTAC. Analysis of costs and quantities of Vigilant against the cheaper ENTAC, gave Vigilant the cost advantage, even if its cost was £700 per missile against only £350.

With regard to Exports, the paper was clear:

BAC have been conducting a vigorous but hitherto unsuccessful sales campaign… They have also made great play of British Army interest and there is no doubt that if we do not order further Vigilants in the near future, (and especially if we order ENTAC instead), Vigilant will be as good as dead… What is certain is that if HMG does not buy Vigilant, we shall, rightly or wrongly, be assailed publicly for having ruined the firm's prospects.

The paper's recommendations were: (a) to approve in principle the need for an interim anti-tank GW for the infantry and to be mounted on the Ferret; (b) to approve the scale of equipment proposed; (c) agree that Vigilant should be the weapon chosen, provided: (i) it can be bought for a reasonable price; (ii) in the case of the RAC, user trials prove satisfactory. Accordingly, (d) MGO should invite the MOA to obtain written quotations of delivery and cost for initial orders of 3,000 Vigilants and ENTACS; (d) provided the Vickers price is satisfactory, Treasury authority should be sought for procurement of Vigilant.

It was a clear Army statement at last, with specific and favourable recommendations.

On 15 June 1961, after a conversation with Air Vice Marshall Shirley of MOA, things were beginning to move and a letter went out to J.M. Sowry of BAC's Guided Weapons English Electric arm, in Stevenage. Still based on no firm decision to adopt Vigilant, MOA requested close estimates (short of a formal quotation) for the supply of 5,000 and 7,500 Vigilant missiles for completion of 2,500 within one-and-a-half years and the remainder within three years of a firm contract, possibly to be placed by 31 December 1961. This was to assume 50 per cent of missiles would be equipped with live warheads and fuzes and 50 per cent with inert warheads. Launcher/carry-boxes, Ground Control Equipment and Field Test equipment, the classroom simulator and Field Training equipment were to be included along with full Service Packs, transit packaging etc. While this invitation followed the policies of BAC undertaking production at Stevenage as opposed to Weybridge, at last it appeared that outcome of the Vickers private venture was for Vigilant to be 'getting down to business'.

The top Army and MOA brass met again the following day under the chairmanship of Lt. Gen. Sir John Anderson, deputy chief of the Imperial General Staff, to consider the Weapons and Equipment Policy Committee paper. The paper's arguments were thoroughly discussed and the additional opinion was recorded, that:

> work had already started on the development of the warhead which should prove a comparatively simple project... the MOA representatives confirmed that the proposed warhead would achieve the required lethality;... should be possible to begin producing it in the first half of 1962 and that the development of the fuze would keep to the same timetable.

Phew! At last!

Another point emerging in favour of Vigilant related to equipping the air portable Ferret squadrons. The RAC director Maj. Gen. G.C. Hopkinson was, 'not sure that Swingfire would prove practicable in this role. Vigilant appeared to be satisfactory and, if so, might meet the long-term requirement. In particular it had a satisfactorily low minimum range'. The only negative views were expressed by the chief scientist, Dr Cawood, who questioned the price of Vigilant and finally, the committee endorsed the recommendations of the paper, invited the MOA to report as soon as possible authoritative prices and invited the chairman to submit a short paper for approval by the Army Council.

6.3

VIGILANT ANTI-TANK MISSILE
PART 3

Before looking at the Army Council's response to the committee's paper, it may be appropriate to mention that in early 1961, the Author had moved from heading the Test Group to conducting design project studies, reporting directly to Howard Surtees. Howard asked me to produce a design proposal to compete with Swingfire, employing better control over the length of its grater range. Thrust Vector Control (or TVC) in Swingfire was achieved with a swivelling rocket motor nozzle, giving the missile greater manoeuvre in the early low speed stages after launching, thereby reducing the gathering problem and the minimum range at which targets could be hit.

Our proposal would also use TVC, but retain aerodynamic control surfaces similar to those used on Vigilant, with each carrying its own rocket motor nozzle at its outer tip. Thus, four TVC nozzles would be vectored by the control surface movements, providing both aerodynamic and vectored thrust control of the missile. In the early stages of guidance, the missile would provide the manoeuvre capability of Swingfire; in later stages, particularly at the extremes of the missile's range, guidance could be from the aerodynamic fin controls without dependence on the rocket motor, in the event that its thrust expired. We believed we could overcome the engineering problems associated with diverting the rocket thrust to four fin-carried fixed nozzles, with lesser penalty than the difficulties we could foresee with the swivelling nozzle in the Swingfire design. Another advantage we could see related to wire dispensing, which would no longer be endangered by a swivelling rocket motor efflux possibly burning the wire, since the wide spacing of fin-tip mounted rocket nozzles would keep effluxes well clear of the wire as it dispensed. This design could save development effort, cost and the time Swingfire would require at its relatively earlier stage of development than Vigilant, by taking advantage of the already developed Vigilant fin actuators and the other components for control and guidance, modified for the greater maximum range and other differences in specification. We put this proposal to the Ministry of Aviation, but perhaps the position of the Stevenage operation within the new BAC and any 'not invented here' inclinations at BAC's final GW centre of gravity prevailed.

Following the Army Council's approving position, things began to happen at MOA, not without further confusing initiatives. A meeting on 26 June chaired by C.L. Silver reopened the question of the cheap Swiss Contraves missile, Mosquito. Any consideration was surprising, when its merely 2lb charge warhead's lethality was clearly going to be unsatisfactory – when even Vigilant's 6lb warhead charge for some reason seemed to leave MOA sceptical. A greater head wind to the Contraves prospects was their agreement for UK production under license by Plessey. This would mean one more player in the UK GW Industry, which MOA was busily trying to reduce.

Now Vickers mounted its first public Vigilant firings for a large audience including military attachés and journalists. *The Guardian*'s 5 July article reported that twelve hits were scored from thirteen Vigilants fired against Centurion tanks by two British Infantry soldiers: '… rockets settled on to their course with certainty and steered against their targets at distances varying from 800 to 1,400 yards'. And, 'One possible situation was demonstrated today when two men jumped out of a helicopter, each with a Vigilant slung over his shoulder. It took them 68 seconds to prepare to fire'. And:

> Vickers… statement… The hollow charge warhead of Vigilant is more than adequate to penetrate the most heavily armoured tank… Vickers is remarkably frank on the question of costs. The firm says that a Vigilant costs more than comparable missiles. It claims, however, that this is more than justified by an autopilot and control system which avoids radical corrections during flight. It has been found that men can do 90% of their training on a simulator, hit a tank on their first live shot, and keep up to standard in their training by firing only one or two rounds a year.

The Ministry of Aviation's 14 July Request for Contracts Action Form was nevertheless sent to the French authorities and to Contraves, as well as to BAC, in whose case the Enquiry specifically excluded the motor and igniter and the warhead, which the MOA would separately provision. Contraves was asked to state, whether deliveries would be from production in Switzerland or in the UK – and were Contraves, 'are they inescapably committed to any UK licence?… which company will be concerned?' One wonders whether manufacture outside the UK would have gained the Swiss the requisite brownie points!

The equipment schedule clearly details the range of quantities and the items on which Vickers – and the foreign competitors – were asked to offer their prices and delivery dates.

In 19 July Parliamentary questions, in the light of British Army deficiencies in Kuwait, the exchange when Mr Mayhew asked the Secretary of State for War whether he proposes to place orders for Vigilant, Mr Profumo was, 'considering the question', then reverted to saying, 'we have to assess this weapon against other light anti-tank weapons ….', undoubtedly as his Civil Servants kept advising him. He did, however, concede, 'So far, the Vickers Vigilant has cost us nothing, because it was a private venture by the company…'

Lord Caldecote clearly became exasperated and having visited him a couple of times in Stevenage after leaving Vickers a year or two later, to relay Litton Industries' interest in purchasing his Precision Products Group, I can imagine his irritability. He dashed off a handwritten letter from his home to the junior Minister Geoffrey Rippon. This was addressed as all the correspondence of the time, 'Dear Rippon'. He complained of hearing about a 'scheme afoot to ask for competitive tenders from the Swiss for MOSQUITO and

APPENDIX 'A'

Schedule of Quantities

ITEM	EQUIPMENT	SEPARATE QUOTATIONS REQUIRED FOR					REMARKS
		(a)	(b)	(c)	(d)	(e)	
1.	MISSILES (With Inert filled Warhead and Fuse Section)	1,000	2,500	5,000	7,500	10,000	
	Delivery } Start Period }	As soon as possible					
	} Finish	18 Mths	18 Mths	3 Yrs.	3 Yrs.	3 Yrs.	
1.1.	FULL STANDARD PACKAGES	320	900	1,800	2,500	3,500	) For use with Item 1.
1.2.	TRADE EXPORT PACKAGE (Transit Packages)	250	700	1,400	2,000	3,000	) See Notes Below
1.3.	FUZE (LIVE), with Full Standard Packages	200	400	660	960	1,500	
	Delivery } Start	As soon as possible.					
	Period } Finish	18 Mths	18 Mths	3 Yrs.	3 Yrs.	3 Yrs.	
1.4.	WARHEAD (LIVE), with Full Standard Packages	Quantities and Delivery as for Item 1.3.					
2.	LAUNCHER	400	1,000	2,000	2,500	3,500	
	Delivery } Start	As soon as possible.					
	Period } Finish	18 Mths	18 Mths	3 Yrs.	3 Yrs.	3 Yrs.	
3.	VEHICLE INSTALLATION EQUIPMENTS (Including Sight, Controller, Selector Boxes (Vehicle role) Wiring, etc.)	25	70	135	220	270	Delivery as soon as possible.
4.	SELECTOR BOXES (Ground Role)	10	25	45	45	75	- do -
5.	SIGHT CONTROLLERS (Ground Role)	32	100	180	265	350	- do -
6.	FIELD TEST EQUIPMENT (Sets)	2	6	10	15	20	- do - For use in the Field.

Fig.6.48 Appendix A to Request for Contract Action, Equipment Schedule.[10]

Continuation Sheet No. 5 of 5

REQUEST FOR CONTRACT ACTION FOR:
Dated 14/7/61.   Reference DQ/391/01

EQUIPMENT SCHEDULE

Item	Vocab. Ref.	Specification No.	Drawing No.		Description				Quantity	Est'd Value each/total

APPENDIX 'A'

Item	Vocab. Ref.	Specification No.	Drawing No.						Quantity	Est'd Value
7.	OVERALL FUNCTIONAL TEST EQUIPMENT	1	2	2	3	4				Delivery as soon as possible. (For Workshop use)
8.	CLASS ROOM TRAINER	2	4	4	4	6				Delivery to be given PRIORITY
9.	FIELD TRAINER	4	12	22	35	45				- do -

the French for ENTAC' and besides once more covering the ground repeatedly discussed in the papers and the meetings that led to the tender invitation, expressed concern at the delay this would cause, '... from the Army's point of view but even more serious will be its effect on export sales'. He continued to enumerate enquiries from the Dutch for 5,000 to 10,000 missiles and over thirty other countries such as Norway, Sweden, Austria, as well as India and Australia. He continued strongly:

> In addition the Americans are not happy about their interim buy of ENTAC and it is certainly not impossible that they still buy some or manufacture under licence. In all I am very optimistic that we could sell 12,000–15,000 abroad (excluding America)... But no one will order until the British Army has announced its decision to adopt Vigilant. If because of administrative delays the decision cannot be made and announced for several months I am afraid that many of the interested countries will look elsewhere and a substantial part of the export market will be lost. As I don't believe there is any doubt of the Army's wish to have Vigilant in (view) of its technical merit it seems that the present problems are largely political and I am writing to ask for your help...

With unexpunged pique, he added in a P.S., 'There is also the point that if a foreign weapon were to be ordered it would be poor encouragement to the British industry to risk their own money in this field'.

This created a flurry of correspondence between C.L. Silver at the MOA and other high officials, resulting in a typical 'politician's reply' – obscure and somewhat patronising. Rippon was:

> grateful for your exposition of the Vigilant situation *as you see it*... No decision has yet been taken... I am sorry if this procedure appears to you to worsen the export prospects... I should have thought myself that should purchase of Vigilant for the Army be made eventually, it would strengthen you in your export efforts if it is known that your orders were secured against competitive tenders submitted in respect of foreign equipment.

Nice for politicians who do not have to fight technology, a time-dependent market and disappearing customers – and if you don't ever have to 'make payroll'!

While Contraves were falling over themselves to offer ever more attractive prices and support, the MOA continued to debate the foreign missiles and warhead lethality. As already highlighted, the Contraves Warhead's 2lb charge would not compare with Vigilant's 6lb charge and it took a letter from the Master General of the Ordnance Sir John Cowley to Sir Steuart Mitchell to confirm the Army's rejection of MOSQUITO, while CGWL replied acknowledging the urgency of getting 'a good A/T weapon into the hands of the Infantry and the RAC as soon as possible'.

Right up to the time when the Weybridge team was disbanded, Vickers sales efforts included exhibition at the Farnborough Air Shows presented by the Society of British Aircraft Constructors (SBAC). The booths were manned by a mixture of Sales, Technical and Administrative executives, who were soliciting export business as much as trying to bring the British Army order home.

Fig.6.49 Vickers SBAC Farnborough stand manned by, from left to right: Bill Murdoch, Frank Gregory, guidance marksmen 'Pip' Piper and Harry Fryer, and assistant chief designer Mike Still.[96]

Following a BAC Board meeting, Lord Caldecote drew a line in the sand, with his 18 August letter to Sir Steuart Mitchell, CGWL at the MOA. Conceding that work remained to be done on the warhead, for which BAC had been promised a contract and on the fuze, for which no contract appeared to be on offer, BAC had decided to maintain a small team in being and to continue this development work at a reduced rate. The company could still deliver missiles fourteen months after receipt of instruction to proceed, provided this arrived at latest by 31 October. He took MOA to task for continuing to pursue ENTAC and MOSQUITO, since they would clearly not meet the conditions specified in the tender with regard to minimum range or for installations on the Ferret, on which only Vickers had done any work. If MOA insisted on further firing trials delaying a decision well into 1962, deliveries will in fact be postponed until mid-summer 1963 and this will delay the Army being trained and operational until 1964.

The punch line then came:

> Having invested some £1.3 million in developing Vigilant, which so clearly meets the Army's requirements, the BAC Board do not consider that the Corporation should risk more of its own money (beyond the small expenditure referred to above) in developing or in setting up a production line in advance of production orders.

Eric Beverley of the original Vickers headquarters staff followed on 21 August with a letter listing the foreign countries which had expressed interest in Vigilant. Besides the Netherlands, Rhodesia, Ecuador, Chile, Kuwait and Greece which had requested quotations, eleven more countries had expressed interest in Vigilant.

Soon, on 22 August, CGWL briefly assured Lord Caldecote in 'Personal and Confidential' letter that tried to maintain the ministries' dignity (or self importance?) before the assurances:

I think I can fairly say that all the points you make are well known to both the War Office and myself though we do not necessarily agree with your viewpoint on each of them... Prior to your letter I had some discussion with John Cowley on this very point and between us we have already taken steps to enable the decision to be taken as quickly as is practicable. The matter, of course lies primarily with the War Office and the Treasury, but I am sure you will find that it will be pushed on with quickly.

The nay Sayers at MOA were still blowing smoke screens and over the next three days, AS/LGW1 T.M. Wilson, U.S.LGW W.G.Cowley and subordinates created more letters disagreeing with drafts of CGWL's letter, arguing whether the War Office was or was not, 'determined to buy Vigilant despite the price'; discussing warhead weights – now using total instead of charge weights, at which level the differences between Vigilant at 10lb and ENTAC at 9lb and MOSQUITO at 8lb were less marked, in the context of uncertain effectiveness before final tests; regarding export prospects, among which D.G. Purnell LGW4(b) would disregard Finland, Austria, South Africa, Portugal and Indonesia on security or political grounds; denying any question of 'being willing parties to a course of action which will enable an order to be placed for Vigilant without facing up to the consequences of strict competitive tendering'; differentiating between the term 'quotations' as being too strong, with 'estimates' being 'more apt'. And so the arguments to water down their boss CGWL's response. Presumably, these people had not seen his pre-emptive Personal and Confidential letter to Lord Caldecote.

Comparative paper estimates continued to be produced into mid–September. Among the unfavourable price comparisons quoted (using 'artificial prices per missile' after adding ancillary equipment) showing Vigilant to be three times the cost of the foreign weapons in quantities of 2,500 and twice the cost in quantities of 7,500 – without allowing for the extra training quantities required for the foreign weapons, the logistical advantages of using the same missile for the Infantry as for Ferrets were conceded. As seen in the following table, it was not difficult to conclude that 'Vigilant is technically superior to the foreign weapons in terms of warhead weight, minimum range, speed of flight, ease of training and ease of installation on the Ferret. Only the maximum range of 2,000 yards gave the foreign weapons any operational advantage'. These operational performance comparisons stand out starkly in the Ministry's Appendix 'B'.

For BAC, Eric Beverley rammed the performance of Vigilant home in a letter of 14 September to Dep. Sec.(C) D. Havilland, following a request relayed by L.C. Silver. Under the heading 'Initial Training', Beverley summarised:

the results achieved by the six Army operators who carried out the initial firings for the School of Infantry... operators who were all SC.4's or SG.5's (this meaning a fairly low IQ as far as Army ratings go), had an average of between 4 and 5 hours simulator training each, the highest figure of any man being 6 hours. Scott in fact, only received 2.5 hours. They were then put straight out on the range to fire, the first two missiles being fired against net targets, third at a static tank target and the fourth at a moving tank... we would claim that no more than three initial training rounds are necessary for normal proposed, although understandably for the most difficult shots, i.e. those of a crossing target at a minimum of 200 yards, further

APPENDIX "B"

	VIGILANT	ENTAC	MOSQUITO
A.U.W. lbs.	30.5	26.7	26
Length ins.	42"	33"	44"
Wing span ins.	11"	15.5"	23.6"
Warhead A.U.W.	10	8.7	7.7
Explosive weight	6	–	4
Cone dia.	5"	4.7"	4.6"
Max. Range (yds.	1,500	2,200	2,200
Min. "	350	450	450
Sustained speed	370 – 510	200 f/s	300 f/s
Lateral acceleration	4–5 g	1.5 g	2 g
Roll Stabilisation	No	Yes	Yes
A.U.W. in carry box.	41 lbs.	80 lbs.	44 lbs.
Control Unit weight	6.5 lbs.	29 lbs.	16 lbs.
Power supplies	(Turbo-alternator ((Battery for (ignition	(Missile battery (activated at (launch. (Accumulator (3 lbs.) in (control unit.	Ni/Cd batteries.

Fig.6.50 MOA performance comparison table for Vigilant, ENTAC and MOSQUITO.[94]

training might be necessary... This sort of minimum range is quite beyond achievement with acceleration control weapons, whose minimum range is 400 yards or more.... the War Office reckon they need 6 Vigilant missiles for initial training of a soldier as compared with 13 acceleration control missiles, but from Appendix 'A' we would feel... 3 Vigilants as compared with 13 acceleration control missies.

Under the heading 'Sustained Training', Beverly adds:

To keep an operator up to the required state of efficiency, we feel that the ratio is at least 2½: 1 in favour of Vigilant... cost of equipping and training an infantry battalion with Vigilant and with a typical acceleration control missile over a period of five years. Using our own assumptions on the costing comes out significantly in favour of Vigilant... even feeding in the much more pessimistic assumptions at present being used by the War Office and your own Ministry the cost with Vigilant is only 10–15% higher than with the acceleration control missile.

Haviland's Minute 66 the same day made the point:

The Company take a more optimistic view of exports... and the are prepared to back their view with their money; they have quoted to us on the basis of selling 2,500 weapons to export customers. Incidentally it is only the US Army who have bought ENTAC. The US Marine Corps have asked for quotations for a trial batch of 100 Vigilant.

On the next day, the MOA's director of GW(P), R.E. Sainsbury, injected more political negatives:

... the outstanding fact that the Guided Weapon Industry needs the stimulus of effective competition and that if Britain succeeds in joining the Common Market such competition could be avoided only by exceptional measures of protection which the Government would be reluctant to take. No more favourable opportunity is likely to occur for the Government to make it clear that the economic situation necessitates a new approach to the supply of armaments.

He continued on the subject of 'Interdependence on America', noting Sir Solly Zuckerman's discussions based on British claimed leadership in the anti-tank field. To follow the American lead by buying ENTAC would weaken that claim, and would probably create an unfavourable impression in all NATO countries, except France.

Under the heading 'Practical Effect on BAC', Sainsbury writes, 'on the other hand it will not be easy to make the firm effectively tackle the problems of keeping down the price of Swingfire, if they obtain an order for Vigilant against such severe competition in terms of price, such success must foster *a belief that they enjoy complete protection*'. Then in a sting in its tail, the Sainsbury memo concludes:

> In view of the above facts, this is a favourable opportunity to make it clear to British Industry that the economic situation does not allow the Government to give complete protection to the industry; to do so would be incompatible with Britain's application to join the Common Market. *The political factors on balance reinforce the advantages of the foreign weapons, particularly MOSQUITO/ Of this can be satisfactorily fitted to the Ferret, we recommend that this weapon system should be adopted.*

This attempted a body blow against Vigilant that was developed without government funding was happily negated by MOSQUITO's large (23.6in) wing span that precluded it from installation on Ferrets, its speed of only half that of Vigilant, reducing its rate of fire by the same amount, besides all the other disadvantages already enumerated. Russell Burne, U.S./LGW pushed somewhat in the Vigilant-favourable direction on 19 September, saying:

> two main considerations:- (i) effect on the morale of the UK Guided Weapons industry which could be caused by decision adverse to Vigilant, (ii) the effect of a UK Government decision to order one of the foreign weapons on price grounds on the cost consciousness of the UK industry in general and particularly in relation to the development and production of Swingfire.

Then, in Burne's conclusion:

> The War Office concludes with a recommendation in favour of Vigilant and I understand that P.U.S. (permanent undersecretary) is being briefed to support this with the rider that Ministry of Aviation be invited seek to negotiate a rebate in respect of subsequent export orders... a lower price was necessary to tilt the balance in favour of the UK product, was to invite us to seek revised tenders; the War Office are not however prepared to face up to the resultant delay.

Fig.6.51 MOA summary of Vigilant
prices.[10]

Dep. Sec. (C) Haviland now getting to the end of the line – perhaps of his tether hand wrote onto the above letter, 'We greatly need work for BAC and indeed for the Aircraft Industry & GW Industry on the whole at present. A W.O. decision in favour of Vigilant should therefore be welcomed... If W.O. propose Vigilant please put up a short memorandum to Minister requesting his approval'.

C.L. Silver sent the draft request for Ministerial approval on 27 September. Reinforcing the principle of obtaining a rebate on BAC's price based on its export sales was one way of Government trying to obtain the best possible deal on behalf of the taxpayer and this featured strongly in the ministerial recommendation, to the point of stating: 'It is considered important that BAC should not know the Army Council's decision until we have had an opportunity of obtaining some firm assurance from the contractor on this point'.

After all the agonising in all departments including the real customer and user – the War Office – which finally made a decision, the rest of the government machine was evidently dragged kicking and screaming into supporting the adoption of this 'unprecedented' British private venture missile.

Eric Beverley's finally telephoned BAC prices for Vigilant were summarised by C.E. Silver in his handwritten Minute 64 of 29 September.

These prices are significantly lower than the Ministry's estimates referred to earlier. The exports related price abatement was concurrently taken up by the Army Council and the Treasury, with G. Leitch of the War Office now warning (or conceding?), that, 'the weapon which we now adopt may not turn out to be a short term weapon and will be with the Army for a number of years'.

Now the serious negotiations really began. MOA's LGW, W.G. Downey, on 5 October wrote to Leitch at the War Office, after meeting with Lord Caldecote following BAC's 'final' prices letter. On asking Caldecote whether these price were 'the last word', the reply he reported was, 'The company could not estimate either the total volume of orders for Vigilant or the prices at which those sales would be made; they could not therefore say at what point they would be prepared to make a rebate to the Department – and in particular, they were not prepared to gamble'. At the same time, the Ministry was torn between ordering as many missiles in one batch as possible, for the best price – and reducing its commitment to the minimum expenditure for as long as possible.

Now on 9 October as the decision to disband the Weybridge GW team and to transfer the work to Stevenage was made, Brig. John Clemow (whom the MOA correspondence labelled as being of 'outstanding brilliance') left the company.

The Vickers Vigilant Joint MOA/WO Development Evaluation and Development Trials were ongoing at this time and the 18 October working party met, consisting of seventeen officials and a lonely Frank Bond, Vickers' chief trials engineer. Referring to the total of sixty-seven evaluation missiles producing twenty-eight hits, twenty-seven misses and twelve apparent failures, the chairman opened by saying that 'the trial had run into certain difficulties'. The Army's separately reported notes of a discussion without BAC being present and did not mince its words:

> on the evidence available it was obvious that Vigilant would not meet the military charac-
> teristics which had been issued… There might be divergence of opinion on which missiles
> failed in flight and which missed the target due to operator errors or other cases, but the fact
> remained that of 67 missiles fired only 28 hit a large target 7ft. 6in. square compared with the
> requirement that the chance of a hit on a smaller target 5ft. x 3ft. should not be less that 70%
> and 80% in most cases… THE RELIABILITY OF THE WEAPON IS SUSPECT.

Many details meticulously discussed, including the operator's changeover from using naked eye, to the monocular on the sight controller and the since corrected simulator set-up, where the missile launch could represent an offset position. Indications of poor trial results due to worsening reliability in these firings (implying increased numbers of missiles that may be required for training) darkened the mood, with Frank fending off criticisms and undertaking remedial actions. The research status of mounting Vigilant on the Ferret was to, 'become a development project aimed at having a weapon in service by February 1963. The only weapon that could meet this date was Vigilant'. But darkly, the Minutes added, '… but a properly developed vehicle was essential. If Vigilant should prove to be unacceptable the possibilities open were to investigate other weapon systems or postpone the requirement'.

The concurrent Army Council Paper agreeing to seek Treasury support for procuring Vigilant, succinctly listed the operational inferiority of British tank numbers compared with:

> BAOR. The Russian and East German armed forces facing the 1 (Br.) Corps Sector are
> estimated to contain 5,000 tanks. 1 (Br.) Corps contains only about 500 tanks. .
> NEARBLF. Egypt has 450+ tanks, Syria 375+, Jordan 172 and Israel 500. We have no tanks in the
> Mediterranean and it would take two–three weeks to ship them from England or Germany.
> MELF… estimated that Iraq could deploy up to 78 tanks against Kuwait… In the Middle East
> Command we could deploy rapidly about 33 tanks, but it would take several weeks before
> any more could arrive by sea.

The Army Council paper went on to cover the contribution of Vigilant and Swingfire towards meeting these deficiencies, including the effect of employing air transportable Ferret scout cars equipped with Vigilant. It continued, pointing out that 'Vigilant's potential successor Swingfire in not expected to be in service before 1966 and the Infantry version may be later than...' In conclusion, the paper invited the Army Council to authorise the purchase of 6,000 missiles (1,000 equipped with warheads), at the same time to invite options at the most favourable prices possible on 2,000 and 4,000.

As reported by his private secretary on 19 October, the Minister himself met with Lord Caldecote, where the latter stressed the urgency of making an announcement as soon as possible, in view of the overseas interest in Vigilant. The minister had another go, pressing for reduced costs if Vickers/BAC succeeded to sell abroad. Lord Caldecote replied that BAC had already allowed a margin for exports in their existing quotation. Even when the Army order had been met, BAC would still be writing off outstanding expenditure of £700,000. When all was said and done, 'Lord Caldecote... doubted whether on examining the case, BAC would be able to advance much beyond what they had already said'.

The following day, Vickers (now BAC) director Geoffrey Knight confirmed the position with more figures and examples to D. Haviland at the MOA, showing that the BAC investment standing at £1, 350,000 expected to rise to £1,750,000 was expected to recover £370,000 on sales of 5,000 missiles to the Army. Now the offer of rebates was made at £10 per missile after the first 12,000 missile exports up to the 18,000th missile. Then £25 per missile after the first 18,000 exported missiles. However BAC would limit the total rebate to no more than £150,000. These figures could be altered if the Army purchased more than 5,000 missiles.

On 1 November, Lord Caldecote ratcheted up the negotiation in a letter the Permanent Secretary of the MOA, Henry Hardman. He reminded Hardman of BAC's hope for a firm decision by 31 October in order to maximise the export opportunities. He continued:

> In view of the uncertainty of the situation and our difficulty in assessing the risk involved, the Board have decided not to authorise any further expenditure until a decision is taken by HMG or at least a clearer indication of the present situation can be given. This means that as from today, the date on which we can offer missiles for evaluation purposes to overseas customers will go back until further expenditure is authorised... May I ask for your help in persuading the Treasury to accelerate a decision on this matter?

No doubt with the excuse of the recent trials difficulties, Hardman's aide scrawled a handwritten note to the AS/LGW1, 'The Secretary has seen your note on the newly emerged technical weaknesses of Vigilant and had told the Treasury that a financial decision on the W.O. order is now less urgent'. Back to 'square one'?

Dep. Controller Weapons J.E. Serby of the MOA, chaired a meeting on 9 November, 'to consider what could be done jointly to satisfy the War Office that Vigilant... meet their requirements fully'. He was accompanied by Sainsbury, Silver and Brigadier Abate DGW(M) from his own Ministry and the War Office was represented by Maj.-Gen. Lindsay Dir. Gen of Armaments as well as AS/ES1 W.T. Horsley and Col. F. Grant, DD or Armaments. BAC fielded a powerful team including Eric Beverley, Col. Lacy and Frank Bond from the original Vickers team, with Lord Caldecote's most senior executive G.R. Jefferson and others from Stevenage.

After the DG of A noted that the Army Council wish to have Vigilant provided that (i) The military characteristics and specification must be guaranteed, (ii) The dates quoted in the tenders must be met and (iii) The prices must not be greater than those quoted, the discussion turned to the military characteristics. These, 'did not ask for anything more than Vigilant was capable of doing... essentially the characteristics against which the firm had tendered with a number of relaxations – e.g. 1,500 yards maximum range, not 2,500 yards'. Newly added additional requirements for flares to be removable for night firings and for the warhead to be interchangeable with any other warhead on any missile were acceptable to BAC. So far, the points were relatively benign.

Horsley then made an additional requirement as a condition of purchase:

> The War Office would adopt Vigilant as an interim weapon. Should any work… to make the weapon suitable... delay the commencement of deliveries, the Government must be in a position to accept only those missiles delivered within the stated period... the price of the missile must not rise in consequence.

BAC stated that the time schedule was very tight – but would be acceptable provided that no modifications were introduced by the user on the production line. Three classes of changes were being introduced, to improve reliability, to make Vigilant a 'good production job' and any changes which might be required as a result of the current series of evaluation trials.

Besides noting that this would be a fixed-price contract, which would provide an extremely powerful incentive 'to provide a satisfactory article', D.G.W. (M) would draw up a schedule with the company for a series of acceptance trials using the first fifty production models. Maintaining the hard-nosed stance, 'While these trials were going on the firm would continue production and in that respect would be taking a calculated risk. On the other hand the Department would have to accept the risk that if their trials were not completed in time, they must continue to accept production missiles'. BAC accepted that this should be written into the contract, however, while they would accept a small number from each production batch be subjected to proof firings, they were not prepared production to be constrained to fits and starts.

While this main contract for 6,000 Vigilants including 1,000 with live warheads along with associated equipments was in negotiation, the promised contract for development of the warhead had still not been received. BAC made clear it would not go ahead with their private development of the fuze until this contract was received and Mr Silver now undertook to hasten it. Not too soon, since DG of A made clear, 'the 50 to be supplied as the first off production for acceptance trials must be complete with warhead and fuze'. But rejecting all BAC's pleas, 'there was not yet a Government decision to equip the Army with Vigilant and until there was – no announcement could be made'. Perhaps it was too much to expect for the Government to jump this gun!

Horsley's ensuing War Office letter to Silver at MOA summarised the outcome of this meeting and ended, 'Even so, we shall have great difficulty in carrying the Treasury with us on our proposals. As the result of our meeting with BAC we hope that they are under no illusions about the fine balance in our assessment'.

The Minister's PS sent a tetchily chastising memo to the L.G.W. Russell Burne on the 17th, saying:

> The Minister agrees to a press release stating that subject to satisfactory contract negotiations, the weapon will be bought. The Minister says that the Minutes give him little confidence in security arrangements. Why are the firm told that the War Office wish to buy Vigilant? Why should they know the moment Treasury authority is given? Who tells them?

On 20 November, Russell Burne, MOA's AS/L GW1, in taking up the question of 'Publicity on War Office Vigilant Order', added an interesting twist. They would:

> ... advise the Minister that a Ministry of Aviation announcement would hardly be appropriate in what is essentially a private venture and a Government announcement was to be deprecated as it could not help and might hinder contract negotiations, which may be particularly difficult in this case. Hence we should let the company make the running, subject to our agreement of the text.

Four days later, things somehow seemed to come to a head. CGWL D. Haviland handwrote to the minister's personal secretary,

> Treasury authority to buy this weapon is expected later tonight or on Monday. To enable the company to sign a contract on Monday to sell the weapon to the Indonesians, we shall have to tell them at once – in terms which safeguard our contractual position. May I please have authority to do so?

At long last, a draft of the War Office Policy Statement No.81 that had hitherto ignored light anti-tank Guided Weapons altogether came out in its second revision, in a paper for consideration to replace the three years old 1958 policy,. Besides covering the ground of previous issues, it somewhat belatedly conceded: 'Recent evaluation trials of an A.T.G.W. system have confirmed that there is an urgent need to introduce such a system into the service as soon as possible'. Without naming Vigilant, for the time frame 1961-1965 it continued '.. It has been agreed that to met this requirement that the infantry should be equipped with a limited quantity of an interim weapon'. In the time frame 1966-1970, 'the successor to the interim GW ... will be introduced'. This referred to Swingfire.

BAC now issued the long desired press release, headed, 'BRITISH ARMY CHOOSES VIGILANT ANTI-TANK MISSILE'. Still subject to negotiations for a contract for a substantial quantity in progress, Lord Caldecote was quoted, 'This is the first time that a guided missile developed entirely with private capital and at no cost to the taxpayer has been bought by the British forces'. The sale was hailed as 'A TRIUMPH' and the text gave details of Vigilant's man portability for the Infantry, its high speed enabling rapid firing against multiple targets, the warhead 'capable of penetrating the armour of any known tank, which could be safe and easy to handle under the roughest field conditions and able to remain safely ready to fire. The press release finished with reference to the Royal Armoured Corps use on the Ferret Scout Car, from which successful firings had already take place and finally the strategic significance of air portability by Royal Air Force Britannias, which could carry 705 Vigilant missiles, or 184 missiles with 100 troops and other combinations.

After the drafting of a press release in MOA despite intimations that BAC should do this, on 6 December after D. Haviland had told Israel's General Ayalon, 'of our recent decision to buy Vigilant and of our reasons for doing so. This stimulated his interest in the weapon and he asked… let him have calculations particularly on the question of costs of equipping and training a given force'. The Ministry's draft note in response to this stated, 'Vigilant is clearly a better buy than ENTAC'. The Government and BAC seemed, at last, to be on the same page!

Ironically, while the Vigilant concept initiated by John Housego at Vickers – back in 1956 – was essentially for an Infantry weapon, for the first time enabling a 'simple soldier' to kill tanks, the application which largely motivated its adoption was for the RAC's Ferret Scout Car. This installation and its proving followed well after Infantry trials were well advanced, but the RAC's realisation of the possibility and its perceived urgency may have been the key to breaking the log jam of governmental disbelief, inertia and reluctance to countenance a private venture weapon which was not developed entirely under its control.

Into 1962, the correspondence mainly moved on to matters of standardisation, training, post development services (PDS) and deployments to BAOR and various army units. The Vickers GW team at Weybridge was effectively disbanded in the first quarter of 1962, with Sam Hastings and very few others agreeing to make the move to Stevenage. A number of people remained and provided continuity and advice to Stevenage, from Weybridge. The BAC team at Stevenage continued the remaining tasks and production engineering for making the Army orders, also taking up the marketing of Vigilant to the many interested overseas armies. Remaining development still requiring design work was for completion of the fuze. The MOA regarded the original Vickers design as 'complex and unreliable' and, after considering developing another fuze at the Royal Ordnance Factory (ROF) at Blackburn, under supervision by (now with the 'Royal' added to its name) RARDE – which did not have the available effort – it was decided to give BAC a contract to sub-contract the fuze to the Swiss firm CML in Geneva, with some consulting assistance from RARDE.

In May, the MOA was already looking at an improved Vigilant, to compensate for the cancellation of the 'medium-range Swingfire'. Partly due to fuze uncertainties, but very much due to the lengthy contract negotiations still dragging on, Treasury authority was confirmed by D.L. Skidmore to J.F. Ezechiel of the War Office only on 14 June 1962 – half a year after basic agreement and announcements had been made. This was for a total of £5.66 million, reduced from the originally agreed £5.9 million by £240,000 due to 'savings' related to using the CML fuze.

Besides a total eventually of 12,000 missiles to the British Army, Vigilant was subsequently sold to a number of countries, including 3,000 missiles to Kuwait, Saudi Arabia and Abu Dhabi, to a total value of £4.5 million[97] A number were also sold to Libya and twenty Ferret

Fig.6.52 Tank Museum at Bovington, Dorset exhibit of Vigilants mounted on Ferret Scout Car.[95]

Scout Cars to U.A.E. and similarly to.Yemen.[98] The total number of Vigilants sold was in the region of 18,000 and, according to Charles Gardner, gave the BAC Stevenage Guided Weapons operation the introduction to the anti-tank business.[98] The result was Swingfire, which went into service in 1969, leaving the 'interim weapon Vigilant a clear field for some years, with continuing rocket motor production well into the 1970s'.[72]

Vigilant in service with diverse military users

Fig.6.53 Infantry on a beach head.[96]

Fig.6.54 Dropped by parachute.[96]

Fig.6.55 Paratrooper readying for action.[96]

Fig.6.56 Helicopter Infantry.[96]

Fig.6.57 Vigilant waiting to launch.[96]

Fig.6.58 Infantryman with controller and Vigilant ready.[96]

Fig.6.59 Twin missile launcher.[96]

warhead penetration of tank armour was the final factor for Vigilant's lethality and while the ultimate warhead design overseen by RARDE was thought to be the most effective, the Swiss-made CML warhead tested by Vickers as part of the original Private Venture offer already proved excellent penetration. Defeating the strongest current (Soviet) armour required the penetration of offset Nickel-Chromium-Molybendum 300mm-thick armour plate, with an ultimate strength of 90-110kg.mm^{2}.

The hollow charge warhead, as already described, created a metal slug travelling at 700-1,000m per second, followed by the molten copper jet from the hollow cone, travelling at 3.000-10,000m per second.

Against armour plate as that protecting the hull of a tank sloped at an angle of 60°, the resulting penetration distance of 424mm was proven, creating exit holes of 20mm diameter. With various combinations of plate with cemented sides, also 50mm and 100mm plates, separated by 150mm the armour was again defeated, with more than enough power to obtain a 'kill'. This was achieved by the molten jet itself, the violent projection of a metal slug from around the exit hole and the vast overpressure created within the tank. Against semi-infinite thickness of armour plate, the warhead penetration was shown to be a 585mm (23in).

Above: Fig.6.60 Entry hole inside 300mm, 60° sloped armour inside a tank.[104]

Opposite above: Fig.6.61 Exit hole at impact point on 300mm, 60° sloped armour plate.

Oppostie below: Fig.6.62 Sectioned 'Semi-infinite' armour plate sample, penetrated to a depth of 576mm (22.7in).

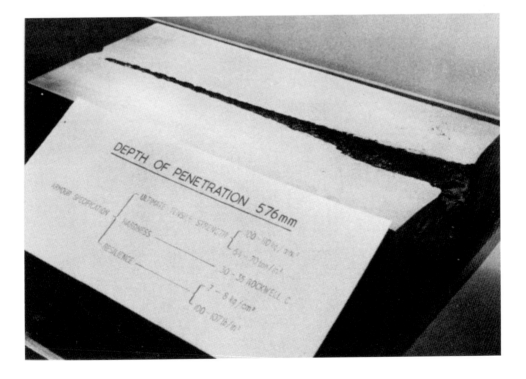

Fig.6.63 Vigilant's warhead strikes. The end of a tank!

Fig.6.64 Triumphant Vigilant top team. From left to right: 'Dab' (just visible), Frank Bond and Howard Surtees.[86]

EPILOGUE

In the chapters relating to Vigilant, the influence of British Aircraft Corporation's formation already showed with some clarity. Likewise, the details I have recorded from Public Records Office archives show how seemingly capricious and even subversive attitudes were set in the concrete of Government's desire to reduce capacity in the Guided Weapons industry. These attitudes were evidently related to the even bigger picture of governmental pressure to bring about amalgamations, relating equally to aircraft as to Guided Weapons activity. Thus, the recorded accounts of War Office, Ministry of Aviation and Treasury correspondence from 1959, about Vickers Guided Weapons and Vigilant reflect the wider Government policy, that the TSR2 contract must go to a merged Vickers/English Electric combination. As I have recorded in the companion volume on the TSR2 Navigation & Attack System, this 1 January 1959 TSR2 contract was effectively the midwife to the birth of BAC. By the time that BAC was formally incorporated on 1 July 1961, Vigilant development was close to completion and pressures were being applied from the Ministry, for Vigilant manufacturing to be at Stevenage. And all this, notwithstanding BAC's policy on formation, that Vigilant be listed as an 'old account' project, keeping its finances with the Vickers shareholders as opposed to the BAC's 'new account' projects. Such 'old account' projects were also slated to continue at their existing locations.[107]

Besides the Vigilant, the TSR2 Navigation & Attack system developments and work described in a chapter 'Missiles & Systems for the Future' (of a following book) were proceeding throughout this corporate turmoil. Though we knew about the overall plan, engineers below the top management level such as myself saw little day-to-day evidence of the turmoil. Nevertheless, even the acknowledged leading expert Brig. John Clemow, who had been specifically recruited from the Ministry of Supply by Sir George Edwards in 1957 to head Guided Weapons was evidently not privy to the Ministry correspondence and shenanigans I have recorded. This seemed to be going on behind John Clemow's back and when the final decision was being made to close Weybridge down and move GW to Stevenage, John first heard about it by a chance comment, while he was attending the 1961 Paris Air Show. Back in Weybridge, he tackled Sir George, who confirmed the intention and asked John to move with the team to head up the Stevenage operation.

In the early summer of 1961, Sir George called a meeting of all the more senior GW team members, to promulgate the Stevenage move policy, undoubtedly to gauge reaction and to see the extent to which we were willing to make the move. Sir Geoffrey Tuttle, lately an RAF Air Marshall, and other Vickers Board members attended this large gathering and in anticipation, I got together with some of my contemporaries. A few levels down the organisation, we were senior enough to be invited and I wanted to prepare our best shot at a defence of Weybridge. We were also conscious that since the end of Red Rapier, Sir George Edwards had taken little interest in the GW work. John Lattey, Arthur Carter and I sat down to discuss tactics, around a summary of the main points I had listed, as the anticipated reasons for making the 'split' – with our possible counter arguments.[108]

To streamlining the organisation, I argued that a separate operation at Stevenage effectively duplicating Weybridge would not amount to streamlining. Against quantity production having to be at Stevenage, I countered that liaison with a Weybridge technical team would be equally feasible as was already occurring with Supermarine at Hurn. Against arguments for projects requiring the employment of large facilities and staff numbers at Stevenage, we would counter that extra staff at Stevenage would increase problems and require extra housing – and that Weybridge facilities were largely adequate. Numbers would need to be reduced at some time anyway. To any suggestions that the Weybridge buildings would be required for other purposes, we would cite the multiplying buildings and floor space over the past ten years – and the small amount of area GW would now need. Regarding Government policy directives, our answer was the benefit of utilising available GW talent at decentralised facilities – and contended that BAC was sufficiently powerful to decide for itself, how to arrange its facilities around the UK, without bowing to Ministry influence.

After we heard the directors' statements, I started our responses by pointing out the success of Vigilant, the work on (Howard Surtees') Long Range Project and other extended studies resulting in all the anti-tank work now going to BAC. I contended that the team which achieved this must be kept together. John Lattey followed by pointing out that the factor of the Navigation & Attack System part of TSR2 being handled by the GW Department was as significant, as the design of the aircraft itself. For this reason, the prospect of obtaining a military aircraft contract such as Swallow (originated by Barnes Wallis) would be greatly increased, if a team with GW's exceptional leadership remained in being. The same argument if properly pressed at high Government levels would also apply to a Supersonic Airliner (Concorde).

I continued – the team had had its back to the wall for five years and in the face of severe setbacks and redundancies remained loyal and enthusiastic. John Lattey continued – the team lived in Surrey and was not inspired by the prospect of moving to Stevenage. Weybridge was much closer to ARDE, the RAE, Larkhill and the London ministries. I resumed, indicating our fear that we would all lose two or three years of seniority vis-à-vis our opposite numbers at Stevenage until we could be accepted, then John Lattey chimed in to say that the numbers at Stevenage would have to be reduced in the next year or so; adding to numbers there would only make this more difficult – and anyway, who would be the first to be laid off in any redundancy?

Sir George took the view that we should be glad to 'get into the main stream'. However, John Lattey eruditely quoted in his best Latin – *'Maximum in udam ite, et immergiti'* – and for everybody's benefit translated it to, 'Get into the main stream and drown!'. To which Sir George's sardonic response was, 'You don't only stick the pin in, you twist it round!'.

Arthur Carter continued the attack, contending that the weapon systems concept of military aircraft such as TSR2 represents a major part of any (Weybridge) aircraft contract. Its efficient execution depended largely on coordination of the whole by one company and the prospect of gaining further contracts of this type would be greatly enhanced by the presently constituted Weybridge facility. John Lattey continued, arguing that the techniques available in a GW team are those, which apply to aircraft navigation, scheduled automatic landing, airborne communications and the air traffic control of modern subsonic and supersonic transports. The future of BAC Civil Aircraft may well depend on those skills. I continued the arguments further, contending that besides aircraft systems, the weapons to be carried must have their effect on the design of a military aircraft. In the project stage, these effects can only be properly allowed for by close cooperation between the Military Projects Office and a well informed and up to date Guided Weapons team – as was the case with TSR2 and with the projected supersonic fighters on which I was working. Arthur then continued by referring to Lord Caldecote's recent discussion paper to the Institution of Electrical Engineers citing the advantages of close integration between GW facilities and an aircraft design organisation.

Arthur and John had further questions affecting any engineers who were asked to remain at Weybridge to work on TSR2. How reliable career opportunities would electronic engineers, control engineers and physicists have in the Weybridge aircraft organisation? And – how would the TSR2 Navigation and Attack system team be used after TSR2 was completed – or if it were cancelled? I concluded with questions concerning any of us who might elect to stay in Weybridge, to be absorbed into the aircraft team – would all including the more senior members be able to find sufficiently interesting work offering an adequate degree of responsibility and status, with continuing prospects? To what extent would GW team members be accepted on equal terms with aircraft staff at management and other levels?

Perhaps unsurprisingly, we did not receive too many direct answers to this raft of questions and assertions. George Edwards concluded by saying, 'Well, I am going home', and we dispersed without much expectation of any reprieve. On 31 July, I sent a memorandum to John Clemow on behalf of the Guided Weapons Department, with copies to my two colleagues asking for answers to the many questions that would influence our decisions as to moving to Stevenage. What compensation might we expect for the many and varied costs associated with moving house and children's schools? What would happen to our Vickers Pension Fund? Would the company agree to a three-years' contract for those uprooting to Stevenage? Under what working conditions would we live and what kind of organisation and work prospects could we expect within the English Electric part of BAC?

No copy of the reply survives in my archives, but in the end, very few of the team were willing to make the move to Stevenage – I only remember Sam Hastings and in the event, Mike Still, John Lambie, Arthur Carter, John Lattey, John Goodwin, Jim Cole,

Fig.6.62 Brig. John Clemow (Ret'd).[3]

Les Vine, Bob Taylor, John Doyle, Bob Elen, Pete Inglis, John Stroud, Charles Reeves, Colin New, Teddy Pearce, Sid Horwood, Don Streatfield, Tony Parsons, Peter Mobsby, John Teague, John Garrett, and a number of others remained with the aircraft Systems/ E organisation. John Clemow quite openly told us that had he been, say, sixty years old, he might have thought of his continuity in employment – but he was only fifty and would therefore look to newer pastures. It was 9 October, before we received a memorandum from top management, setting out the responsibilities relating to the TSR2 Navigation and Attack System. This quoted a press report of the Guided Weapons work at Weybridge having now been transferred to the English Electric Guided Weapons Division – and that, 'further to this, Mr J. Clemow has left the Company'.

To ensure continuity for TSR2, the aircraft division's chief of electrical design Harry Zeffert was appointed chief systems engineer/E at Weybridge, responsible 'for the co-ordination and progress of the TSR2 Navigation/Attack System and its associated equipment'. Mike Still was appointed Deputy Chief Systems engineer/E – effectively running the day-to-day TSR2 work. John Lambie would continue his existing responsibilities as chief project officer on TSR2 weapon systems.

Chief designer (weapons) Howard Surtees started the new Elliott Automation Space and Missile Systems company ('EASAMS'), joined by Dab and Frank Bond – with an offer for me also to join.

As the year unfolded, I was already considering my future career. I had spent ten years in engineering, caught a whiff of the business side with Vigilant – and, especially now, could not see a clear path towards management at BAC. From my starting in early 1952 as a novice under Barry MacGowan's earnest and friendly tutelage when I was launched into serious trials in Canberra jets, through the 'Hen Coop's' late 1954 visit of to our home – each bearing a knitted garment for our imminently due firstborn, the sympathy and friendship shown by my colleagues after my mother died in a motor accident in 1956, Paul Leyton's rumbustious leadership and Frank Bond's humorous if sharp edged leadership till I was promoted to head the Test Group in 1957, the innovative period with Vigilant in that group where I had my first taste of managing three laboratories full of engineers – all the way through my latest two or three years project engineer period under a brilliant Howard Surtees, I could hardly have had a happier work experience. John Clemow had already reinforced his style of leadership, when he gave me free reign to take whatever reasonable time off I may need, while my wife Mary was unwell during the later stages of her fifth pregnancy. Only later, elsewhere, in a company that suffered that corrosive problem was I to realise bliss of working at Vickers in a team without serious 'company politics' to overshadow the worthwhile challenges. Now I was hankering toward getting into marketing and to experiencing the world of business.

Judiciously attending interviews, by the time of the October memo, I had obtained job offers from Peter Hurn at the highly divisionalised and entrepreneurial Elliott Automation to market avionics, from Dick Haines at Decca Radar to market ground Radar data handling systems – and from Howard Surtees, as he was starting up EASAMS. They all offered promising careers and starting salaries around the still desirable level of £2,000p.a. – a modest if not insignificant improvement on my current £1,650p.a. With our family well on the way to producing a fifth child, any good career prospect was worth pursuing and every penny would count.

Then, suddenly, I was asked to accompany Dab and Les Vine for a two weeks stint with Honeywell in Minneapolis, to help them with their proposal for the tube-launched TOW anti-tank missile. Ever since the Vigilant team had been travelling to America while I remained in my Weybridge labs, I had felt some envy for those able to sample the America one otherwise only saw through Hollywood and the media. And here was an opportunity I could hardly miss. But now my conscience pricked, since the new baby was due towards the end of the American project – should I leave Mary at such a time? On unburdening myself, Mary was emphatic. 'I have had four babies and I know exactly what to do, so you don't have to worry. In any case, you may never have the chance to go to America again'. Not only did I have her permission, I had marching orders!

Dab and I flew out together, with a stop in New York just too short to get further into Manhattan than a few minutes walk from the East Side Terminal. We finally arrived in Minneapolis around 1 a.m. London time, to be met by an ebullient crowd from Honeywell – who promptly took us to a smart night club. For several hours, bemused in such unfamiliar surroundings, we sat in low armchairs drinking large whiskies on the rocks served by long-legged, short-skirted waitresses. After this unexpected introduction to American hospitality, we got to bed in our overheated hotel at around 6 a.m. London time, with a few hours to go before we were picked up and taken to meet Clyde Parton, vice president in charge of Honeywell's Ordnance Division. Before long, we were on chummy terms with Clyde and his group of engineers, who took nightly turns after work, to drive us in one of their pair of gynormous cars to even more gynormous homes, fitted throughout with unfamiliarly deep pile white carpets. At each place we were treated as family – 'home from home', to our great surprise among people who not only failed to ram America down our throats as I had expected – but who actually asked how we did things in England. They had super kids, responsible teenagers who worked to earn their own money while at school and college. At work, it was a matter of getting down to it and getting an urgent job done. Even on Thanksgiving Day, we worked till lunch time, when all three of us were invited to the house of a senior engineer, who could not say exactly how may rooms they had. We were seated among about twenty relatives for the traditional turkey and pumpkin pie dinner and then the older of his six children showed us around their vast house. Perhaps the Hollywood version of America was not entirely correct.

Thinking of my recently completed project study for which I selected a Litton INS system, before leaving Weybridge I suggested making a side trip to Woodland Hills in California, where I could view the Litton platform, its test programme and results and the total operation. We would all feel more comfortable with my choice, if a first-hand inspection confirmed the credibility of Litton's claims. Henry Gardner agreed to this and after a week in Minneapolis, I took the Sunday evening flight to Los Angeles. Litton was to arrange a Hertz Rent-a-Car for my journey to Woodland Hills and for my use until I returned to Minneapolis on Tuesday. I had never driven an American car, nor any car with automatic transmission and the 17ft 'small Chevy' kangaroo hopped out of the parking lot, until I got used to keeping my left foot away from the pedals. Then it was only a matter of following some pencilled directions on a scrap of paper and the LA road map through the unfamiliar dazzling array of traffic lights and signs along roads with strange names like Sepulvada Boulevard then through the Santa Monica Mountains before getting back on the I-405 Ventura Freeway going West. All totally unreal, especially in the dark. Somehow, I navigated the 25-mile maze without getting lost or hitting anybody, reaping admiring exclamations by the Litton folk waiting at my motel. As in Minneapolis, straight out – this time for dinner at The Smokehouse and after a large steak, to bed and another exploration to find 'The Plant' next morning.

In a couple of days of whirlwind laboratory and clean room tours, presentations around their hardware and in response to my intensive questioning, explanation of their flight test and operational results with the systems in the F104 Starfighter, I had also seen a working LN-9 platform such as I had proposed for the Vickers NATO/VSTOL project – and was thoroughly impressed. Before leaving for the LA International Airport on Tuesday afternoon, I telexed my confirmation of the Litton platform choice back to Weybridge and was being shown back towards my Hertz car. Bob Marcille was my guide and before making my goodbyes, I told him that if the project moves ahead, somebody else would be handling the project because I was shortly expecting to leave Vickers.

A hand descended on my shoulder and another took my elbow, as I was propelled into the general manager's office. Somewhat resembling Orson Wells, Bill Jacobi took a couple of minutes to offer me a job. I could choose between three options – come to California and join the team there (on an American sized salary), go to Litton's company in Hamburg at Plath GmBH – or set up a new London Office, to market Litton navigation systems to the British Government and establish relationships with British Industry. If I took a job in Europe, I would report to Litton's director of marketing (Europe) – one Bob Kirk (years later to be a director of BAe) located in Zurich. I would be able to make my office at Bush House in London, where another Litton company was established. Despite the attractions of sunny California, the challenge of setting up one-man operation to represent this great company in the UK looked by far the best, particularly in view of our recently acquired first own mortgage on a semi-detached in Surbiton – and with that fifth baby about to arrive.

We finished the proposal on time in Minneapolis, where I was able to track down a first cousin in Chicago whom I had never met. She promptly invited me to bring Les Vine for a weekend – and to meet her family of seven children. Mary still showed no sign of going into labour and becoming both confident and ambitious to see something of Washington and New York I made plans to delay my return by a few more days. That is, 'till I made (for those days) a rare telephone call to her from Pittsburgh. The precious 3 minutes was mostly taken up with her tearful description of keeping her legs crossed – since pains had begun. In a great panic, I took the first available plane back to London and as I walked into the house, she was waiting – 'take me to the hospital NOW'. Fourteen hours later, another daughter had arrived.

Although Howard Surtees, Dab, Frank Bond, Dennis Harris, John Goodwin, Jim Cole and others were going to start up EASAMS and the temptation to join these long established colleagues, I decided to take the job with Litton. However, while higher than my other three, Bob Kirk's offer did not reflect my expectations from an American company. It was, unfortunately, clear, that in Europe, Litton would not pay an American salary (except to American 'ex-pats'), so I turned down £2,150p.a. Nothing like this had evidently ever happened to the burgeoning Litton and after some delay, Bob increased the offer to £2,250p.a., a good £600 or 35 per cent more than my salary at Vickers. Before I left the company, I went to see Henry Gardner, who had first recruited me into Guided Weapons nearly ten years earlier. He shook me warmly by the hand and said that I would always be welcome to a job if I wanted to come back. However, as I heard later, he had suggested that I engineered the Litton Specification and the visit to them, in order to get a job there! Such a false accusation was my last expectation and had to be sorely resented.

When I told him Bob Kirk I had arrived home 14 hours before our baby's birth, his immediate repost was, 'Well – you had time for at least three more meetings'. I started my new life and flew to Zurich in the New Year, followed by many visits to the US – and much later to live there for over twenty years. So much for 'perhaps you may never get the chance to go to America again'.

Twenty-six years later in 1988, the Vickers operation at what had (between 1907 and 1939) been the famous Brooklands Motor Racing Track closed down altogether and most of the vast factory and office buildings complex was demolished. On one of our regular trips home from our current life in Atlanta, sagging structures with wires and conduit forming drooping spaghetti-like vines viewed through my taxi window en-route from Gatwick Airport was surely one of my saddest experiences. Fortunately, Spud Boorer and others saved the barely budding Brooklands Museum buildings – particularly the Brooklands Club House, which had for years served as Barnes Wallis's 'R&D Department' headquarters. Much of the banked racing track remained, but most of the large site was redeveloped, to house business parks, 'superstores' and some residential housing. With much lobbying and hard work, Spud and the others saved the Club House and enough of the original hangars and motor racing sheds from the developers' wrecking ball. With hard won funding from sponsors – and, later, the National Lottery, an enthusiastic team assisted by many volunteers developed the existing fine Brooklands Museum.

When I retired back to Weybridge from Atlanta in 2002, Spud had already given me a conducted tour of the many aircraft, aero engines, racing cars and other exhibits and when I went along to see if I could do anything useful as one of the many museum volunteers, it suddenly struck me that there was not a single sign of the Guided Weapons work that had occupied so many of us between 1950 and 1962. On asking about this, I was met with a blank stare – clearly, nobody realised what had taken place. My dismay at this was quickly met with a simple invitation: 'can you create a Guided Weapons exhibit?'. This became much of my life thereafter, although there appeared to be nothing of anything one could exhibit. No 1,000lb or 5,000lb Blue Boars, no Red Rapiers, no Red Dean, no Vigilant anti-tank missiles nor simulators – no mention of TSR2 Navigation Attack Systems – zilch! It took many visits to other museums around the country, searches in the National Archives, Vickers Archives and unearthing many thankfully saved archives within Brooklands, before I could locate examples of each of our missiles – hopefully for transfer into a GW exhibit at Brooklands. I also 'unearthed' many helpful ex-colleagues. Writing up the history became my next obsession and this book is the result.

REFERENCES

1   Sqdn. Ldr. K. S. Lockie, MBE, Bsc., ACGI, AMIMechE, (Technical Advisor on Air Armaments, Naval Gunnery and Naval Guided Weapons), 23.11.1960. From the Vickers Archives, Cambridge University.

2   Brooklands Museum Vickers archives, also Eric B. Morgan, July/August and September/October 1997 issues of Air Enthusiast; 'Red Rapier, Britain's Flying-Bomb'.

3   Public Records Office records of Ministry of Supply correspondence, 1952. Reference, SB.64744. Report on Visit to Vickers (Weybridge) on 8 August 1952.

4   Vickers GW archive and Public Records Office, Kew.

5   Vickers GW archive and Public Records Office, Kew.

6   Air Staff Requirement No. DR1059 – Control of Bombs Ref.C30349/46.

7   RAE Technician Note No. GW8 November 1947.

8   RAE Tech Note GW 35 by S/Ldr. S.H. Bonser and K.D. Thomson.

9   Imperial War Museum Film Archive.

10 Public Records Office, Kew.

11 Vickers Report V.GW 35.

12 Rocket Sled trials at P&EE, Shoeburyness from Brooklands Archive photographs.

13 Barry Jones photo archive, Warwick.

14 RAE Tech Note No. GW 86, in Vickers Archives at Brooklands Museum, 'on Simulator Trials of Proposed Stabilisation Head Control System for Blue Boar'.

15 RAE Tech Note No. 195, by F.G. Tarrant, First Report on Trials of the Blue Boar by night. From Vickers Archives at Brooklands Museum.

16 EMI Engineering Development Ltd. Blue Boar Final Report Volume 5, Part 2.

17 Joint Naval/Air Staff Requirement for an air-to-air active radar homing weapon for fighter aircraft.

18 From Vickers Wind Tunnel Report No. WT 2138.

19 Tech Note VGW/13, Red Dean Development Programme August 1953.

20 VA Report ref. VGW/39. (From VGW/13)

21 VA Report ref. VGW/31. (From VGW/13)

22 Tech note VGW.RD.20, Aerodynamic Characteristics of Red Dean by J.E. Daboo, 19.2.1954.

23 Air driven gyroscope retrieved from a rocket-launched firing. Owned by the author.

24 Red Dean Design Compendium, Section 3.

25 VGW/TP/R57, The Effects of Aerodynamic Forces on the Structural Stability of Red Dean. R.W. Levinge & others.

26 Red Dean exhibit at RAF Cosford Museum.

27 Red Dean Design Compendium Part 1, Volume 1, Section 3, Chapter 5.

28 Solid Fuel Rocket Propulsion, by J.E. Daboo (Temple Press).

29 Public Records Office files of MOS correspondence from ACAS (OR).

30 Red Dean Design Compendium Part 1, Volume 1, Section 9, Chapter 2 Brooklands Archives.

31 RAE letter to MOS 7.9 1951 – Altitude Range for Red Dean – Public Records Office.

32 HQ Fighter Command letter – Height Bands – Guided Missiles 25.2.1952.

33 Photo owned by Vickers test pilot P. Murphy.

34 Photo Brooklands Archives.

35 Red Dean Design Compendium.

36 Red Dean Design Compendium Volume 1, Part 2, Section 5, Chapter 2 (Smiths Aircraft Instruments)

37 Author's cockpit records take on Red Dean Canberra flight trials, on loan to Brooklands Museum.

38 Red Dean Design Compendium Volume 1, Part 2, Section 5, Chapter 4 in Brooklands Archives.

39 Red Dean Design Compendium Volume 1, Part 2, Section 6, Chapter 1 & Appendix A in Brooklands Archives.

40 VGW/31 Design Study for Red Dean, E. Smyth & J.E. Daboo, February 1952.

41 GEC Report No. SL.021 by J.G.W. Munns, October 1952.

42 Red Dean Design Compendium Volume 1, Part 1, Section 4.

43 GEC Report No. SL.139 by G. Gordon, November 1955.

44 Red Dean Design Compendium Part 1, Volume 1, Section 4, Chapter 1.

45 Red Dean Design Compendium Part 1, Volume 1, Section 4, Chapter 3.

46 Author's cockpit record log on loan to Brooklands Museum.

47 Red Dean Design Compendium Part 1, Volume 1, Section 3, Chapter 7.

48 Red Dean Design Compendium Volume 2, Section 8, Chapter 2.

49 Red Dean Design Compendium Part 1, Volume 1, Section 3, Chapter 1.

50 Red Dean Design Compendium Part 2, Volume 1, Section 8, Chapter 3.

51 VGW/TD/787, The ability of Red Dean to see Targets before launch when carried on F153D.

52 VGW/RD/49 Preliminary Assessment, use of Red Dean on the CF-105, J.E. Daboo.

53 Red Dean Design Compendium, Part 2, Volume 1, Section 10, Chapter 3.

54 Photo from John Stroud, Vickers Environmental Test Department 1950s-1960s.

55 English Electric Brochure No.33, 5/3/1956 for Canberra P.12.

56 LRWE Planning Specification No. 24, April 1954.

57 VGW/RD/42. A production study of the guided missile Red Dean. Tanner and Wastling.

58 Special Project S.P.2. Report REF 99235 (superseding Ref. 96844).

59 Test Vehicle Specification Red Rapier Type 725.

60 VGW/RR/6 of March 1953.

61 V.G.W. 24. Technical Note No. 6 of 19 January, 1952.

62 Public Records Office, Ministry of Supply report of Cluster Bomb and dispersion ejector mechanism test.

63 V.G.W./RR/5 16 Apr. 1953 Policy Meeting at MOS.

64 Advisory Conference on the Specification, at MOS 16 April 1953. Brooklands Museum Vickers
    Archives.

65 VGW24 Tech Note No. 64 in Brooklands Museum Vickers Archives. Magnetostrictive Delay Lines.

66 V.G.W.43 Report on Vickers internal meeting of 27 June 1952.

67 UK MOS office letter from Melbourne to London of 25 February 1954, ref SM2026.

68 Memo to Dep. Sec. (C) at MOS by G.W. Clark P.S./Secretary June 1959 per PRO Archives.

69 Vigilant firing depicted in Peter Mobsby's artist's impression. Brooklands Museum Vickers
    Archives.

70 Illustrations from Vigilant Instructors Handbook. Brooklands Museum Vickers Archives.

71 Photo from Brooklands Museum Vickers Archives.

72 W.H. Nicolson, project officer at Summerfield Research Station.

73 Vigilant Type 897 draft manual by Jerry Hitch, Brooklands Museum Vickers Archives.

74 Vigilant 2nd Progress Report, 6 months to September 1957. Brooklands Museum Archives.

75 Vigilant 3rd Progress Report, 6 months to March 1958. Brooklands Museum Archives.

76 Vigilant 3rd Progress Report, 6 months to September 1959. Brooklands Museum Archives.

77 Vigilant 3rd Progress Report, 6 months to March 1959. Brooklands Museum Archives.

78 BAC Vigilant Handbook, Section 2 Chapter 5. Brooklands Museum Archives.

79 Original Vickers Technical Publications Draft Handbook by Jerry Hitch. Brooklands Museum
    Archives.

80 Vickers Type 891 2nd Progress Report to September 1957. Brooklands Museum Archives.

81 Vickers Vigilant progress reports to March 1960 and recollections of engineer A.C. (Chuck) Fry.

82 BAC Vigilant Handbook, Section 3, Chapter 5. Brooklands Museum Archives.

83 BAC Vigilant Handbook, Section 3, Chapter 7. Brooklands Museum Archives.

84 Vigilant in the Royal Army Museum, Chelsea.

85 BAC Vigilant Handbook, Section 3, Chapter 1. Brooklands Museum Archives.

86 Photo from Brooklands Museum Archives.

87 BAC Vigilant Handbook, Section 3, Chapter 3. Brooklands Museum Archives.

88 Vigilant 7th Progress Report, 6 months to March 1960. Brooklands Museum Archives.

89 Vigilant 4th Progress Report, 6 months to September 1958. Brooklands Museum Archives.

90 Vigilant 5th Progress Report, 6 months to March 1959. Brooklands Museum Archives.

91 Public Records Office archives of War Office documents.

92 Recollections of system designer Harry Fryer.

93 Vigilant in India, BAC video in Brooklands archives.

94 MOA comparative assessment of Vigilant & Foreign anti-tank missiles 14.9.1961, Public Records
    Office, Kew.

95 Author's photo from Brooklands archives, with permission of the Army Tank Museum at
    Bovington.

96 Brooklands Museum, Photo Archives.

97 British Aircraft Corporation, A History by Charles Gardner published by Batsford

98 British Defence Manufacturers Association.

99 ARDE Internal Memo 'Impact Tests of Vigilant Nose Switch', J.S McVeagh, April 1962.

100 British Aircraft Corporation. A history 'by Charles Gardner, Batsford.

101 Author's handwritten notes in anticipation of the actual meeting.

102 'Fire Across the Desert', Peter Morton, Australian Dep. of Defence.

103 Author's photo archive.

104 Tank Museum Archives.

Copyrights:

MINISTRY PERSONALITITES

History of GW at Vickers – Personalised at govt ministries, from PRO documents

Government	Treasury	Ministry of Aviation	War Office	MOD
				Wheeler
				Locke
				Kendrick
			Lt. Gen. Sir John Cowley	
			Master Gen of Ordnance	
			George Leitch, A.U.S.(A)	
			Maj. Gen. A.F.W. Craddock	
			DMO	
			Maj. Gen. C.T.D. Lindsay	
			D.G. of Artillery	
			Dr. Caward, Ch. Scientist	
			W.T. Horsley AS/ES1	
			J.F. Ezechiel, ES1(a)	
			Maj. Ottey	
			Fogarty	
		H. Hardman, Perm. Secretary	H.L. Lawrence-Wilson	
		G.W. Clark, P.S. to Secretary	L.J. Sabatini	
		C.L. Silver, Dep. Sec. (C)	N. Craig	
		after LGW1(d)	Ellis-Rees	
		D.G.W.L. Haviland, Dep. Sec. (C)	J.M. Parkin	
		G.P. Chamberlain, D.C.L	A.J. Wiggin	
		R. Burne, U.S., (L.G.W.)		
		W.G. Downey, (L.G.W.) later		
		George T. Rogers, A.S./L.G.W		
		Sir Steuart Mitchell, C.G.W.L		
		J.E. Serby, D.G./G.W, then DCW		
		R.E. Sainsbury, D.G. (Production)		
		Lt. Col. D.G. Proudman,		
		D.G.W. (M) 1		
	D. McKean, (top?)	Brig. C.W. Denison, D/GW (M)		
	D.L. Skidmore	W.H. Stephens, DG/BM		
	A.D. Peck.	W.E. D. Bruton, LGW1(a)		
		J.C. Steen, LGW1(d)		
	J.A. Marshall	D.G. Purnell, L.G.W.4(b)		
	D.J.S. Hancock	Latter? Mr. Platt L.G.W.4(b)		
	A.M. Bailey	Patrick Jeffries, A.S. LGW4		
	P. Mountfield	A.C. Russell, LGW1(d)		
	P.D. Parmella	(after Silver)		
Harold Watkinson, Minister of Defence		C.E. Barnes, DDC(E)		
		H.J. Blanks, DW1(d) (in 1965)		
John Profumo, Minister for War		T.M. Wilson, AD/LGW 1		
Christopher Soames, Sec. State for War		Col. A.T. Abaté, DGW(M)		
Geoffrey Rippon Parliamentary Sec. Minister of Aviation				
T.J. Bligh 10 Downing St.				
Benjamin A.P.S. to Minister of Aviation				
George Brown Sec. of State, Economic Affairs				
Denis Healy Sec. of State, Defence				
Roy Jenkins, Sec. of State, Aviation				
Harold Wilson, Prime Minister				

INDEX

If you are interested in purchasing other books published by Tempus,
or in case you have difficulty finding any Tempus books in your local bookshop,
you can also place orders directly through our website

www.tempus-publishing.com